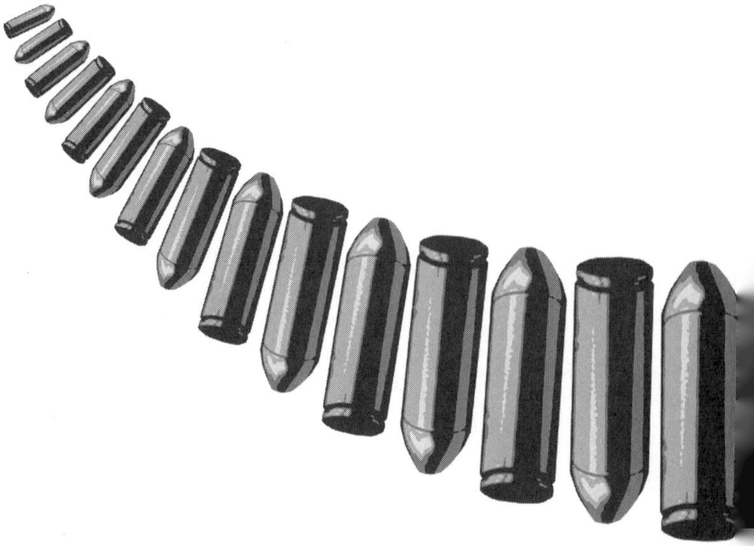

CREATING A MOVEMENT WITH TEETH

A Documentary History of the
George Jackson Brigade

edited by Daniel Burton-Rose

PM

Creating A Movement With Teeth:
A Documentary History Of The George Jackson Brigade
Edited by Daniel Burton-Rose
This edition © PM Press 2010

ISBN: 978-1-60486-223-2
Library of Congress Control Number: 2010927765

Cover design by Josh MacPhee/Justseeds.org
Interior design by Josh MacPhee/Justseeds.org

10987654321

PM Press
PO Box 23912
Oakland, CA 94623
www.pmpress.org

Printed in the USA on recycled paper.

Contents

Permissions

Acknowledgements

Thanks are due first of all to Jamie of Abraham Guillen Press in Quebec, whose reprinting of the Brigade's Political Statement and *communiqués* precipitated this expanded collection. Dan Berger prompted fuller editorial comment with his pointed queries on the manuscript, as did André Moncourt, who also read through, corrected, and commented on the manuscript. Moncourt and J. Smith's monumental documentary history of the Red Army Faction also inspired fuller annotation.

I am grateful to Alyssa, Ava, Lauren, Sha, and Trinh for keying in the *communiqués*, articles, and editorial commentary. I realize it's a blast from the sexist past to thank a number of women for typing services, but as an e-gimp with a persistent repetitive strain injury, hiring assistants was better than suffocating silently.

Josh MacPhee provided the engaging cover, and more than a decade ago played a catalytic role in putting me on the path of encountering former Brigade members. Thanks as well to Ramsey Kanaan and Craig O'Hara, who enthusiastically greeted this project. I am also indebted to Ward Churchill for his preface. Despite the slander campaign directed against him after his essay "Some People Push Back" attracted the attention of Fox News et al., he remains one of the most careful and knowledgeable scholars of 1970s social movements and the repressive forces arrayed against them.

Preface

ReVisioning a Movement with Teeth
Ward Churchill

> The government of the U.S.A. and all that it stands for, all that
> it represents, must be destroyed. This is the starting point, and the
> end. We have the means to this end; the problem is to develop ac-
> ceptance of their use.
> —George Jackson, *Blood in My Eye*

There was a time, not so long ago, when an appreciable segment of those professing opposition to the policies pursued by U.S. élites proved capable of transcending the banality of liberal analysis, arriving at a genuinely radical understanding both of what they were up against and what would be required to transform it. Thus were the obtund constraints of "responsible" protest discarded in favor of armed struggle undertaken not only by such iconic organizations as the Black Panther Party and the Weather Underground Organization (WUO), but also a host of other groups around the country, many of them tiny, highly localized, and now all but forgotten.

Considered in light of Santayana's famously irrefragable observation that those unknowing of their history are doomed to repeat it, the "forgotten" dimension(s) of the armed struggle waged against the domestic status quo during the late 1960s and early '70s represents a problem of genuine significance. If we may agree that to draw reasonable conclusions from or about *any* phenomenon, historical or otherwise, it is essential to have as complete and accurate an apprehension of it as possible, the nature of the deficiency should be clear. Its ramifications are no less apparent in the discourse of the few who might presently assert that armed struggle constitutes *the* signifier of revolutionary purity and the *sole* means through which fundamental change can be precipitated as it is in the anodyne catechism mouthed by the multitudes who smugly dismiss recourse to arms as being both "unrealistic" and "self-defeating."[1]

While much good work, and no shortage of bad, has been done in documenting and assessing the strengths, weaknesses, and potentials of the Panthers and Weather Underground over the years,[2] nothing of the sort can be said regarding the welter of autonomous entities that followed more or less comparable trajectories during same period.

Indeed, it is arguable that the degree of attention afforded the former has to some extent *precluded* anything resembling a proper analytical emphasis being placed on the latter. The result has been, and remains, a decided skew in how the interplay of sociopolitical elements in the struggle has been perceived by those seeking, often urgently, to discern its meaning. They have in a sense been placed in the position of the proverbial three blind men attempting to determine and describe the physical characteristics of an elephant.

The magnitude of the imbalance is indicated, though by no means defined, by the facts that during the fall of 1968, there were at least 41 political bombings on U.S. campuses alone—an undetermined number of others occurred off-campus—and that this nearly doubles the number carried out by the Weather Underground during the entire seven years of its operational existence. The spring of 1969 saw a further 84 on-campus bombings, making a total of 125 for the school year. During academic year 1969–1970, the tally of bombings on U.S. campuses rose to 174.[3] At least seventy off-campus corporate facilities were also bombed in 1969, as well as several military facilities; on November 11 that year, a small, non-Weather-affiliated collective in New York—having already bombed the Whitehall Military Induction Center, the Federal Building, the offices of United Fruit, and a Midland Marine Bank earlier in the fall—hit the corporate offices of Chase Manhattan, Standard Oil, and General Motors, all on a single day.[4]

From 1970–1975, while the number of political bombings attributable to "the Left" underwent a noticeable decline, there was an equally-noticeable rise in proficiency, both technically and in terms of target selection. Such efforts were, moreover, sustained at relatively high levels through the end of the decade. Since the WUO carried out only a miniscule fraction of these actions—estimated as having added up to well over a thousand by 1980—a question obviously arises as to who carried out the rest? Part of the answer, of course, is that the clandestine *Fuerzas Armadas de Liberación Nacional* (FALN), a highly disciplined and efficient component of Puerto Rico's national liberation movement, can be credited with more than 120 of them.[5]

That acknowledged, however, aggregating *all* the bombings claimed by centrally-directed cadre organizations like the Panthers, Weather Underground, FALN, the Black Liberation Army (BLA), and including even such problematic entities as the Symbionese Liberation Army (SLA),[6] produces a total amounting to no more than a quarter of the whole. Throwing in the known and probable contributions of FBI/police *agents provocateurs* like Tommy Tongyai ("Tommy the Traveler") and Darthard Perry ("Othello") still leaves less than a third of the bombings accounted for.[7]

There is, of course, far more to armed struggle than bombings. Many groups emblematic of the posture during the 1960s and '70s placed little, if any, weight at all on such actions. These included the Panthers, as well as such nationally-prominent organizations as the Republic of New Afrika (RNA) and the Revolutionary Action Movement (RAM), all of which concentrated primarily on developing their respective capacities to engage in armed self-defense.[8] In this, they were joined by a plethora of localized organizations like Robert Williams's "renegade" NAACP chapter in North Carolina,[9] the Deacons for Self-Defense and its various spinoffs,[10] the Lowndes County Freedom Organization (the "Original Black Panthers," established in 1965 by Stokely Carmichael and others in one of Alabama's most Klan-ridden areas).[11] Substantially different postures were assumed by entities like the BLA[12] and the Puerto Rican Macheteros.[13]

Nonetheless, the question plainly dangles: Who carried out the great bulk of all politically-motivated bombings between 1968 and 1980? Others follow: What motivated them to do so? What fate befell them? Can such questions be answered? If so, how completely? If not, in what sense can it be said that genuine understanding of the phenomenon of armed struggle in the United States during the critical period been attained, or that such is even possible? And, to reiterate, if something approaching an accurate picture of the phenomenon is lacking, on what basis can it be assessed in terms of its potential viability—or lack of it—in whatever altered form either now or in the future?

Fortunately, a few of the blanks have already been filled in to some extent. It has long been known, for example, that the earlier-mentioned string of bombings culminating on November 11, 1969, was carried out by an autonomous four (or six)-member collective nominally headed by Sam Melville, that the collective was infiltrated by a police agent, that three bona fide members of the collective were captured and two imprisoned while one jumped bail and went underground, that Melville was one of the forty-three prisoners slaughtered by the New York state police during the assault with which they quelled the 1971 Attica prison insurrection,[14] and that his former lover—and collective member—Jane Alpert later redeemed herself in the eyes of the status quo not only by apologizing for her actions and repudiating the whole notion of armed struggle, but by traducing Melville in the most personal possible terms.[15]

True, much of the story is far from inspiring, but the issues at hand are whether it adds to the knowledge-base necessary to constructing a comprehensive view of armed struggle, and whether there are important lessons to be gleaned from it. The answer is obviously affirmative on both counts. The same pertains to a handful other autonomous entities—Madison, Wisconsin's so-called Vanguards of the Revolution (or "New Year's Gang," as it was popularly known),[16] for instance, as well as the Sam Melville/Jonathan Jackson Unit *cum* United Freedom Front (UFF, or "Ohio 7," as the latter is often and simplistically referred to),[17] the Revolutionary Armed Task Force (RATF),[18] and the Armed Resistance Unit/Red Guerrilla Resistance[19]—the reasoning and attendant actions of which have been to some extent recorded. Much more needs to be known about each of these groups, but at least there's a start.

On the other hand, almost nothing is known, other than to participants, about the New World Liberation Front (NWLF), a Bay Area entity which announced itself in September 1974 with the bombing of a San Francisco stock brokerage and, over the next three years, carried out nearly fifty additional bombings of such targets as power stations, banks, corporate offices, and the South African embassy, all without causing a single injury to anyone, and without a single underground member being caught.[20] The same applies to the Luis Cabanas Unit, the Nat Turner/John Brown Unit, the Sam Melville/Jonathan Jackson Unit, and other autonomous groups aligned and/or functioning in solidarity with the NWLF,[21] while a still greater void is evident with respect to New England's Red Star Brigade, the so-called Radar Gang in downstate Illinois, and scores—perhaps hundreds—of others.

In truth, a paucity of information exists with respect to a number of entities associated in one way or another with armed struggle and exhibiting a relatively high degree of name recognition; Yippie! and New York's Up Against the Wall Motherfucker spring readily to mind in this regard,[22] as do Chicago's Young Lords Organization (YLO), Young Patriots, and Rising Up Angry collective,[23] the Detroit-originated White Panther Party,[24] and the South Bay's Venceremos Organization.[25] The most conspicuous omission of all, perhaps, is that of "Soledad Brother" turned Panther field marshal George Jackson's People's Army,[26] an entity distinct from the BLA and known to have been in formation by 1970, but about which a thundering silence has been maintained for the past three decades.[27]

All things considered, then, there is ample cause for a sense of relief bordering on jubilation at the release of Daniel Burton-Rose's *Creating a Movement with Teeth*. Subtitled *A Documentary History of the George Jackson Brigade*, the volume is a fine compilation of the statements, communiqués, and other such material wherein one small, autonomous, grassroots insurgent formation explained its thinking—plainly inspired by that of Jackson—during the period of its operational existence. While the book is perfectly capable of standing on its own, moreover, it is intended both as a complement to and as a reinforcement/amplification of its editor's separately published *Guerrilla USA: The George Jackson Brigade and the Anticapitalist Underground of the 1970s*, an in-depth narrative history of the Seattle-based Brigade and its context.[28]

Taken together, the sheer comprehensiveness with which the subject group is examined—and empowered to speak in their own voices, both then and now, individually and collectively—in the two volumes is not simply unparalleled, it is unprecedented. A unique window has thus been opened on a corner of what might rightly be described as the "hidden dimension" of armed struggle in the United States. This is *exactly* the sort of work that is necessary, and Burton-Rose is to be commended for having undertaken it. His breakthrough achieved, it is to be hoped not only that he himself will continue to pursue such efforts but that others will be inspired to follow his lead.

Only through excavations of many comparable sites can the real history of what was unquestionably the most coruscating revolutionary moment in recent American history be revealed, its meaning(s) honestly/accurately evaluated, its theoretical/tactical defects identified and corrected, its utility recalibrated for more effective present/future application(s). The process is self-evidently important in Santayana's sense, still more so in terms of Marx's oft-recited dictum that the point of all such endeavors is not merely to understand the world but "to *change* it."[29] As George Jackson observed in the passage epigrammatically quoted above, we have long possessed "the means to this end; the problem is to develop acceptance of their use."[30] This remains the task at hand.

Introduction

Daniel Burton-Rose

> The enemy can never be driven out by words alone, no matter
> how sound the argument. Nor can the enemy be driven out by force
> alone. But words of truth and justice, fully backed by armed power,
> will certainly drive the enemy out. When right and might are on the
> same side, what enemy can hold out?
> —Ngugi Wa Thiong'o, *Matigari* (1987)

Writing from his cell in Soledad Prison in 1970, George Jackson delivered a threat to his captors: "The monster they've engendered in me will return to torment its maker, from the grave, the pit, the profoundest pit. Hurl me into the next existence, the descent into hell won't turn me. I'll crawl back to dog his trail forever."[1] In the event of his death, Jackson desired "something to remain, to torment his ass, to haunt him . . ."[2] On August 21, 1971, he was gunned down by a correctional officer during an escape attempt from San Quentin's Adjustment Center. Four years later, in the Pacific Northwest, an ex-convict and his grad school dropout partner decided it was past time to fulfill the wishes of Comrade George.[3]

Ed Mead was politicized in the McNeil Island federal penitentiary in the late 1960s, where he was serving time for a pharmacy burglary (guilty) and an escape attempt from jail (innocent).[4] He eagerly followed the developments of the U.S. antiwar movement, as its demands crescendoed in tandem with the increasing destruction being inflicted on North Vietnam. When he came out of prison, he gravitated to those who advocated revolution at home to disable imperialism abroad; in particular, the politics of Weather Underground supporters exerted a strong pull. In this circle, it was considered that the corporations and state agencies culpable in perpetuating global inequality were so well known as to require no further discussion. The relevant question was what militants would do with this knowledge.

As Mead read the situation, the path forward was clear: the Left needed to deliver on its angry rhetoric.[5] Bombings by members of the New Left had become common by the late 1960s, but by the mid-'70s campus radicals' bombing collectives had largely ceded to a second, deadlier generation of armed militants with their roots in the prison movement.[6] In 1974, Mead visited San Francisco to try to join up with one of these later organizations, the Symbionese Liberation Army.[7] Instead he found the New World Liberation Front (NWLF); they taught him how to make pipe bombs.[8]

Upon returning to Seattle, Mead consulted with his good friend Bruce Seidel, a former graduate student in economics at the University of Illinois, Urbana-Champaign, who was also doing prison work in Seattle. They resolved to enact their politics of confrontation. As a declaration of intent they called themselves "The George Jackson Brigade"; they would deliver on the promise of the hyper-militant Black Panther Lieutenant, now deceased. Fittingly for their immersion in prison activism and, in Mead's case, experience as an incarcerated activist,[9] the first bombing they committed was of the Washington Department of Corrections in Olympia.

The second was of the Safeway on Capitol Hill in Seattle. It was spectacularly careless and widely denounced. Mead placed a pipe bomb in a fifty-pound bag of dog food and set it to go off during store hours. He phoned in a warning which he insists was dismissed as a prank; the Seattle press reported that the call was to the wrong store. A number of customers were physically and emotionally wounded. In their accompanying communiqué, the Brigade wrote darkly: "as the contradictions heighten it becomes harder and harder to be a passive and innocent bystander in a war zone."[10] Even those sympathetic to "armed struggle," in the prevailing Lefty lingo of the time, were unable to discern any positive support for the epic struggle of the United Farm Workers, the ostensible reason for targeting Safeway.[11] Nor did it promote sympathy for Ralph "Po" Ford, a member of a nascent cell of the NWLF (no ties to the San Francisco chapter) who died at the same Safeway three days earlier when the poorly constructed bomb he was planting behind the store detonated in his hands.[12]

One of Mead and Seidel's first steps in expanding their organization was to recruit women. Seidel solicited the membership of Rita Brown, a working class ex-convict from southern Oregon active in the Seattle prisoner support community. Therese Coupez, a college-educated local and Brown's girlfriend, would also join. The two women were cofounders of Women Out Now, which facilitated community involvement in the new state of the art women's prison in Purdy. Brown made her membership conditional on the Brigade apologizing for the Safeway action. She joined the Brigade and it did apologize—"This action was wrong because we brought violence and terror into a poor neighborhood"[13]— in the course of bombing Safeway regional headquarters in a diligently safety-conscious manner. The apology earned the Brigade the distinction of being the first and only group of non-state-armed actors in the United States to publicly concede that an action was mistaken while insisting on the overall legitimacy of their tactics.[14]

For our current generation, inundated as it is with images of terrorists blithely unconcerned with human life, who actively target people rather than institutions,[15] the ethical dimension of the strategic debates the Brigade laid out in its writings and in interviews by captured members will likely seem discordant. Indeed, even Brigade cofounder Mead acknowledged in an early interview that when starting out he was not indisposed towards the terrorist label, imagining himself a dispenser of "counterterror" to those most responsible for society's ills.[16] Yet in their third claimed action, only three and a half months after the Safeway disaster, the expanded organization stated clearly: "We are not terrorists." They also wrote, unequivocally, "We have no qualms about bringing discriminate violence to the rich."[17]

As the reader will see, debate and polemic over just what constituted "terrorism" and "armed struggle" occupied a prominent role in discussion of the Brigade in the progressive community.[18] At issue was the legitimacy of the organization's endeavor: could they be dismissed as enemies of the Left—either deliberately or by virtue of their drastic wrong-headedness—or were even those who resented the consequences of Brigade members' decisions compelled to grudgingly acknowledge that the Brigade was on the same side politically, regardless of tactical differences over how to achieve shared goals?

Around the time Brown joined up, two other ex-convict prison activists were also drawn into the circle: John Sherman, a former cellmate of Ed Mead's on McNeil Island Penitentiary and a fellow Washington State Prisoners Union member, and Mark Cook, organizer of the annual CONvention conference of prison activists.

Mead and Sherman had first met in McNeil Island Penitentiary, then again on the outside at the Steilacoom Prisoners Support House. Afterwards, Sherman got a job doing research and development on missiles at the Boeing plant in South Seattle. A member of the Revolutionary Union by this time, a giddy Party leadership assigned Sherman to clandestinely-organized workers in his new "shop floor." At the time individuals who joined the RU (later Revolutionary Communist Party) were issued a rifle; when it became clear that other members didn't intend to use theirs, John grew impatient with the organization and quit in a huff.

While imprisoned at the Washington State Penitentiary in Walla Walla, Cook had founded a chapter of the Black Panther Party and collaborated on an underground prisoner-produced newsletter, *The Bomb*, which agitated for expanding prisoners' civil rights.[19] With others he pushed for and won a (relatively) democratic self-governing body for prisoners, the Residents Governance Counsel. After his release he began organizing CONvention. He supported the Brigade out of a commitment to the legacy of George Jackson and the conviction that aboveground and underground work were equally important.

In the winter of 1975, Mead, Seidel, and Sherman robbed a liquor store to obtain money for Brigade activities. They netted a bag of coins—a fair amount of work and risk for little reward. In response, they determined to secure a chunk of money that would give them some breathing room to plan actions and to travel, orienting themselves in a national landscape of urban guerrilla organizations. They planned a bank robbery of not just the teller drawers but of the vault. Their effort, on January 23, 1976, in the small South Seattle suburb of Tukwila, resulted in the death of Seidel, the wounding of Sherman, and the arrest of both Mead and Sherman. The police came in shooting, which Brigade members had not anticipated. Seidel's death added a new weight of responsibility for at large Brigade members and fostered an unwillingness to let go of the project because of the dramatic cost one of their own had already paid.

At that point, everything began to accelerate. John's repeated visits to Harborview Hospital to have his face surgically reconstituted presented an opportunity to free him. March 10, 1976, Cook jammed a pistol in the back of Sherman's police escort and informed him: "I'm taking your prisoner." The officer reached for his keys to comply, but the keys were next to his gun. Cook misinterpreted his movements and shot him in the stomach. Sherman was whisked away as planned, but police picked up Cook a few days later. He spent the next two and a half decades in prison. Before this event, the Brigade was more or less on the offensive; for the next year they were on the defensive, retreating to Oregon and committing small but consistent bank robberies to support themselves.

Brown, now known by some of her intimates as "Bo," dressed in drag when she acted as the triggerperson. Her girlfriend Janine Bertram, with whom Brown had gotten together after she and Coupez split and Sherman and Coupez became a couple, joined the small group underground and became the designated getaway driver.

By the fall of 1977, the Brigade felt sufficiently powerful to head back to the Seattle area. They bombed the Capitol Complex in Olympia in support of striking prisoners at Walla Walla, committed several bombings in an attempt to bolster the auto machinists' union, and set off another pipe bomb at a Mercedes-Benz dealership in retaliation for the deaths of three Red Army Faction members in Stammheim prison in West Germany.[20]

Their frenetic pace was interrupted on November 3, 1977, when Brown was captured while casing a bank in North Seattle. On March 21, 1978, Bertram, Sherman, and Coupez were arrested at a Tacoma hamburger chain just before executing another robbery. The flyer printed as the last communiqué in this pamphlet on Easter Sunday of 1978 and signed by "the rest of us" was bluster.[21] There were no "rest of us," just some support people who wished to perpetuate the paranoia and confusion of law enforcement. Bertram and Coupez went on to serve six years in prison; Brown eight; Sherman a decade and a half, punctuated by two escapes; Mead sixteen years; Cook twenty-three. Cook was released just before the protests against the World Trade Organization flooded Seattle in 1999 and brought a new global cycle of anticapitalist activism into public view.

The Brigade was both a product of its times and exceptional. In a period when the movement (anti-imperialist, prisoners' rights, feminist and queer liberation) was dividing along political, racial and gender lines, the George Jackson Brigade was striking for its diversity. Out of seven members five were queer or bisexual (according to Mead, Seidel was moving in the direction of the latter before death interrupted). Four were ex-convicts (and soon to be convicts again). Three members were women, one member black. College-educated intellectuals worked equally with underclass theoreticians. As Brown and Bertram put it in a poem published in the International Women's Day communiqué "dykes niggers cons . . . a collection of oppressed people turning inside out with action."[22]

Armed opposition to the policies of the U.S. government in the late 1960s and early 1970s is generally presented by media and police as coming from two organizations: Weatherman (later the Weather Underground Organization) if the practitioners were white, and the Black Panther Party (followed by the Black Liberation Army) if they were black. The media is comfortable with this categorization because it is simple and, because clear, less threatening; in a related contemporary analogue, as the 2004 BBC documentary trilogy *The Power of Nightmares: The Rise of the Politics of Fear* argued, the ostensible coherency of al-Qaeda was largely summoned into existence by Cold War leftovers nostalgic for an enemy that reflected their own organizational proclivities. Conversely, the PATRIOT Act and other "counterterrorism" measures are premised on the potential omnipresence of diffuse enemies.[23]

As far as the 1960s and 1970s were concerned, there was a groundswell of armed protest against the U.S. government from 1965 into the early 1970s.[24] These actions briefly spiked again in the mid-1970s, then slowed to a trickle throughout the 1980s. Among the groups active in the 1980s were the United Freedom Front, Armed Resistance Unit, and Revolutionary Fighting Group Red Guerrilla Resistance. Targets were chosen based on opposition to U.S. military involvement in Central America, to South African apartheid, the Israeli occupation of Palestine, and oppressive domestic policing.[25]

The organizing principle of the Brigade was the imperative to create "a movement with teeth," as they stated in the "International Women's Day" communiqué and again in "The Power of the People is the Force of Life" (both while speaking of Seidel's vision). The Brigade saw armed struggle as an integral component of an effective mass movement. In the oft-quoted words of George Jackson: "Any serious organizing of people must carry with it from the start a potential threat of revolutionary violence."[26] It was an element they deemed too often absent, and they aimed to correct the imbalance. In doing so they were in line with the Weather Underground Organization, the Black Liberation Army, and other like-minded organizations prior to and contemporaneous with the Brigade. Their own expansive sense of their peers is evident in the long list of shout-outs to other armed groups throughout the world contained in their political statement.

Though they committed propaganda of the deed and physical attacks against infrastructure, many of the activities in which they exhorted people to engage are calmingly doable. In the Capitol Hill Safeway Bombing communiqué they presented their vision of what it would take "to force Safeway out of the Capitol Hill Community":

> All that is required is the will to do so. Using a coordination of both peaceful and violent tactics, people educate and build toward a winning strategy. Progressive forces would have to reach out beyond themselves; talking to people at bus stops, going door to door

asking people about their daily lives and their problems. A program should be developed and implemented around their grievances.

In "Bust the Bosses" their pleas got rowdier but remain on the continuum that today is called "diversity of tactics":

1. Don't cross a picket line for any reason! . . .
2. Tie up the dealers' phones! Call in as a concerned person and complain, or call from a phone booth and leave the line hanging.
3. Put sugar in the gas tanks of dealers' new cars, or potatoes in the tailpipes! . . .
4. Break the dealers' windows! Use bricks, slingshots, small arms, etc. Slash their tires too!
5. Lock the bosses out! Put super glue in any and all locks of buildings or cars. (This is easy and it works great!)

Similarly in their "Open Letter to Jailers Spellman and Waldt" they asked people to make phone calls to local prisoncrats urging the improvement of conditions of confinement at King County Jail. They include a tacit personal threat to Spellman and Waldt by providing their addresses and asking people to "stop by their homes and discuss these demands with them." Too impatient to maintain the questionable subtlety of this suggestion, no. 3, no. 6 is "Sabotage Spellman and Waldt's offices, homes, cars, etc." No. 8, for good measure, reads "Sabotage (Superglue for example) any and all ruling class institutions (banks, supermarkets, insurance companies, etc.) and their capital equipment until these demands are met."

The document concludes: "If [these measures] are taken up by enough of us, they would mean a hundred times more than any bomb." If one is to have bombers active in one's own city, it seems desirable that they at least be ambivalent and self-denigrating, as Brigade members were in these moments.

This collection is intended as a companion volume to *Guerrilla USA: The George Jackson Brigade and the Anticapitalist Underground of the 1970s*. It provides the original documents upon which that work is in part based so that interested readers may access the writings of the Brigade and their interlocutors relatively unmediated. My goal in collecting these documents is not apologia: reproducing the communiqués implies no more an endorsement of their contents than reprinting the accompanying poems implies aesthetic appreciation. Likewise, the choice of title speaks to the self-conception of the Brigade, and is not to be taken as an assertion that I, or any former Brigade members, consider bombing and bank robberies to be the only, or primary, elements of powerful oppositional social movements. Rather, I am attempting to supplement an anemic record of the radical social movements of the 1970s, and to preserve and pass down a collective engagement with the ever-vexing problem of community self-defense and revolution in the United States.

None of the Brigade members had *the answers*, but by discounting a hegemonic program and acknowledging their own limitations, uncertainty, and fears, they did have *an answer*. They would have agreed wholeheartedly with the assertion in "The Urban Guerrilla Concept," the foundational statement of the Red Army Faction released in April of 1971, that: "Whether it is right to organize armed resistance now depends on whether it is possible, and whether it is possible can only be determined in practice."[27] By their own criteria, the Brigade achieved its goal of feeling for cracks in the system. Their discovery that the fissures were not as great as they had hoped was still a contribution to revolutionary praxis.

The Brigade arose from the prison movement and its members were themselves soon incarcerated; in the cases of Brown, Cook, Mead, and Sherman, for a second, third, or fourth time. The centrality of the experience of incarceration is a key to understanding this organization and its matter of fact willingness to employ violence against law enforcement when in a pinch. Brigade members did not see themselves as initiating a cycle of violence; the violence had already begun, and had dictated the circumstances of their lives to an extreme extent. They considered themselves to be taking decisive steps to interrupt the cycle. And as long as the United States persists in its indefinite policy of caging millions, the frustration and rage engendered will have to be faced not only by the state, but by social movements which seek to transform or dissolve it.

Conventions

I have based the communiqués reproduced here on the originals. These documents were preserved in former Brigade members' personal papers and a file kept by the now-defunct Toronto-based political prisoner support collective Arm the Spirit. I note if they were published along with date and place of publication. The primary venues were: *Dragon*, a Berkeley-based newsletter that specialized in covering domestic armed struggle; *Orca*, the publication of a Seattle collective which focused on distributing information on the GJB;[58] and *The Sunfighter*, a publication of the Washington State Prisoners' Union. Many also appeared in the FBI's file on the Brigade (#105-295956) and all in that of the Seattle Police Department Intelligence Division.

I have sought to reproduce documents as they were, but opted against the dunning pedantry of inserting *sic* after every misspelled word or inadvertently duplicated preposition. Instead, I have silently amended errors unless they are significant, such as misspellings of the names of individuals or organizations. In these cases, I provide the correct spelling in the body of the text and a note with the original spelling. I have maintained a few quirks, primarily differences like "Left" or "left" and "guerilla" or "guerrilla," some of which change within a single article. I have also kept alternate conventions that are clearly deliberate, as in Brown's use of lower cases and spellings like "womyn." None of the original texts wrote "communiqué" with the accent. I have preserved this practice but used the accent in my own interventions. Punctuation has also been standardized.

I have sought to provide introductory information on individuals and organizations that may not be immediately familiar to readers. The most detailed information appears upon the first occurrence of the name in this collection. For those who do not read this collection straight through and come upon a person or organization on which they would like further clarification, the first page given under the relevant entry in the index should provide it.

Brackets indicate insertions for clarity, while parentheses represent insertions reproduced from the original. Ellipses are also produced from the original, except for one case given in brackets, in which that which is omitted is indicated. In order to provide a broader sense of the debate sparked by this material, in both Parts I and II, I periodically include public commentary in the form of letters to the editor in various publications responding to the documents being reproduced. All URLs were checked just prior to the publication date.

Former Brigade member Therese Coupez has expressed a wish not to be associated with this project. As a result, I have chosen not to include two *Northwest Passage* articles which were particularly personal in nature, Michelle Celarier's "Mothers, Daughters, and the GJB" in the April 10–May 2, 1978 issue, and Coupez's reply, which appeared as "The Daughter Responds," May 1–22, 1978, 2–3. I have also excised her photograph from the "Our Losses Are Heavy . . ." flyer reproduced in Part II. I have not, however, deleted quotations from her in Bill Patz's jailhouse interview, "Captured Members Explain Their Politics," reproduced in Part III, as I consider this an indispensible aspect of the public face Brigade members presented at the time.

Part I

PROFILES OF THE GEORGE JACKSON BRIGADE

This section is divided into three ways in which the Brigade was seen and made visible: i) the clipped and error-prone reports of law enforcement on the group as a whole; ii) press coverage from major print media corporations; and iii) accounts in the countercultural press focusing on statements published by supporters. The latter two are intertwined to a certain extent in that the corporate press did at times give significant space to interviews with Brigade members in custody and even printed communiqués.

The first section, "Law Enforcement Perspectives," begins with a chronology of Brigade actions, prepared by Intelligence Division of the Seattle Police Department. It is undated but can be no earlier than late December 1977: i.e., three months before the arrest of the last remaining Brigade member. It is a small fragment of a file weighing in at approximately 750 pages.

The following report, by an anonymous agent of the Seattle offices of the Federal Bureau of Investigation (regional headquarters for the Pacific Northwest), provides an overview of the George Jackson Brigade that is conceptual as well as chronological. It dates to the days before the final arrest when the ideology and the membership of the organization had become gradually clearer but members were still at large and presented an immediate threat. The report is rife with inaccuracies: George Jackson was killed August 21, not 11, 1971; CONvention, not "Convention Movement"; "The Family" at the Washington State Prison in Walla Walla began in 1973. Yet for all these faults, the author(s) of this document also understood something of the distinctiveness of the George Jackson Brigade—that it grew out of the prison movement, and, as the report states, did "not envision itself as an 'elite' faction for an ultimate revolutionary government."[1]

The proverbial "Agent Smith," or group of agents, completely missed other elements. For example, he (there were no female agents in the office) referred to "the writer for the GJB," though the Brigade's political statement, which was released two months before this report was completed, was so clearly a collective project that it contained separate statements of two distinct ideological perspectives: antiauthoritarian and socialist. The assertion that "The communiques and notations written by the GJB indicate a strict dedication to the precepts and disciplines included in the writings of KARL MARX" would make an orthodox Marxist cringe, though the agent is correct in observing that the Brigade's Marxism-Leninism had been processed through South American revolutionaries (the Brazilian theorist-practitioner Carlos Marighella more so than Che Guevara, while Asian and African theorist-practitioners influenced them as well). Note, as well, that the author finds the Brigade's activities so reprehensible that he does not even permit them ideals, only "imagined ideals."

The Bureau apparently still remembers the Brigade as a major case, and has chosen to post their entire file on the Brigade on their website.[2] The author of the introduction to the Brigade, however, seems to have read the file too literally, claiming for example that the Brigade carried out an attack against a "custom house," when the object of their attention was the adjacent FBI offices.

The next section, "Difficult to Digest: The Corporate Media on the George Jackson Brigade," contains mainstream press profiles of Ed Mead, Bruce Seidel, Janine Bertram, and John Sherman, all of whom were in custody—or in Seidel's case, deceased—at the time. The stories are framed as explorations of the "two-faced" character of revolutionaries: the journalists struggle to reconcile friends' and family members' testimonies to the warmth and humanity of the Brigade members with prosecutors' and law enforcement officers' condemnation of the violence inherent in their chosen path.

The tone of the coverage varies by the class background of the Brigade member under scrutiny. Bertram and Seidel came from middle class backgrounds. Appropriate to the demographic of daily newspaper readers, their profiles reveal a discernable undercurrent of parental introspection: 'What did we do wrong?' Ed Mead came from a working class background, and is placed at a further remove from the reader; he is more of an ominous curiosity than a prodigal son. Sherman hovers in between: his golden tongue clearly won a degree of sympathy from the reporter.

The last section "Invisible People: A Working Class Black Man and a White Dyke," deals with the members of the Brigade the corporate press could not perceive as multidimensional people. The mainstream press paid significant attention to Mark Cook, but he also remained a mystery to them for reasons they could not have overcome. Unlike Mead, who claimed responsibility for Brigade actions and declared his politics to anyone who would listen, Cook kept his own counsel, and consistently denied membership in the Brigade. Cook exhibited an equal respect for, and commitment to, aboveground and underground work. This was not schizophrenia, as implied in the press profiles in the second section, but a focus on a purpose which—in the perception of Cook and his peers—demanded to be realized by the distinct, but complementary, means too often categorized simplistically as "reformist" and "revolutionary."

The irony of Cook's case is that, though guilty as charged, he was also framed. He was pulled in by police because he was on a watch list of African-American radicals known informally as the "crazy nigger list." He was then released and rearrested several days later after being fingered by a former friend from his days in the Washington State Penitentiary in Walla Walla, Autrey "Scatman" Sturgis. Cook states that he never disclosed his involvement in the Brigade to Sturgis, and speculates that Sturgis, also in custody and in forced withdrawal from heroin, followed the leads of investigators in asserting that Cook had confessed to him. Because he maintained his innocence, a full portrait of Cook was thus not possible until 1999, the year he acknowledged his past involvement in the Brigade and was released from prison.[3] Michelle Celarier's article included here gives a thorough overview of the prosecutorial dirty tricks in the case, and reflects the understandable uncertainty of the aboveground Left as to the degree of Cook's involvement in the Tukwila robbery attempt.

Rita "Bo" Brown, a butch lesbian as well as a proletarian, was even more difficult for the press to digest than was Cook. According to Brown, law enforcement officials, concerned by the press coverage that had been received by Mead and Sherman, obstructed press access after her arrest. Facing trial in Portland, Oregon, she was also far from her base in Seattle. As a result, no corporate profiles exist comparable to those on her fellow Brigade members. I have chosen to include an autobiographical sketch Brown wrote for her defense committee in order to compensate for her elision from the public eye.

i.

Law Enforcement Perspectives

Domestic Insecurity: A page from the FBI files of the George Jackson Brigade obtained through the Freedom of Information Act.

GEORGE JACKSON BRIGADE
Seattle Police Department Intelligence Division

This is the first of three chronological lists of Brigade actions in this collection, the other two being the one by the FBI in the following document and the Brigade's own tally in its political statement.[4]

Saturday	May 31, 1975	WASHINGTON STATE CORRECTIONS OFFICE Olympia, Washington
Wednesday	June 11, 1975	UNIVERSITY OF WASHINGTON Administration Building[5]
Tuesday	Sept. 5, 1975	F. B. I. OFFICES–TACOMA, WASHINGTON
Wednesday	Sept. 6, 1975	BUREAU OF INDIAN AFFAIRS OFFICE Everett, Washington
Saturday	Sept. 13, 1975	FEDERAL OFFICE BUILDING Seattle, Washington
Monday	Sept. 15, 1975	SAFEWAY STORE (Death) Seattle, Washington[6]
Thursday	Sept. 18, 1975	SAFEWAY STORE Seattle, Washington
Saturday	Dec. 31, 1975	SAFEWAY OFFICE BUILDING Bellevue, Washington
Saturday	Dec. 31, 1975	CITY LIGHT SUBSTATION Seattle, Washington
Thursday	May 12, 1977	RAINIER NATIONAL BANK Redmond, Washington

Thursday	May 12, 1977	RAINIER NATIONAL BANK (Attempt) Bellevue, Washington
Monday	July 3, 1977	PUGET POWER SUBSTATION (Attempt) Olympia, Washington
Thursday	October 6, 1977	WESTLUND BUICK (Attempt) Seattle, Washington
Thursday	October 13, 1977	S. L. SAVIDGE DODGE Seattle, Washington
Saturday	October 16, 1977	B.B.C. DODGE Burien, Washington
Tuesday	November 1, 1977	PHIL SMART MERCEDES Bellevue, Washington
Wednesday	November 2, 1977	DIEBOLD, INC. Seattle, Washington[7]
Friday	November 4, 1977	GEORGE JACKSON BRIGADE Residence–ARREST AND SEARCH[8]
Friday	December 23, 1977	POWER SUBSTATION Renton, Washington
Saturday	December 24, 1977	NEW VEHICLE ON RAILROAD CAR Kent, Washington

ROBBERIES

Friday	January 23, 1976	PACIFIC NATIONAL BANK Attempt Robbery, Shootout Tukwila, Washington
Wednesday	March 10, 1976	KING COUNTY DEPUTY SHOT During escape of JOHN SHERMAN

Tuesday	June 8, 1976	WESTERN BANK Coos Bay, Oregon
Thursday	July 8, 1976	MARK COOK arrested for Tukwila Bank and Shooting King County Deputy
Tuesday	July 13, 1976	CARTER NATIONAL BANK Ashland, Oregon
Monday	August 1, 1976	THE OREGON BANK Medford, Oregon
Thursday	October 28, 1976	FIRST STATE BANK OF OREGON Portland, Oregon
Tuesday	January 4, 1977	U. S. NATIONAL BANK OF OREGON Portland, Oregon
Monday	February 7, 1977	U. S. NATIONAL BANK OF OREGON Wilsonville, Oregon
Saturday	May 21, 1977	WASHINGTON STATE LIQUOR STORE Bellevue, Washington
Monday	June 20, 1977	RAINIER NATIONAL BANK Bellevue, Washington
Thursday	September 8, 1977	OLD NATIONAL BANK Kirkland, Washington
Monday	September 19, 1977	PEOPLES NATIONAL BANK Skyway Branch Seattle, Washington

RE: George Jackson Brigade
Federal Bureau of Investigations, Seattle Office

The base of the first page bears the warning: "This document contains neither recommendations nor conclusions of the FBI. It is the property of the FBI and is loaned to your agency; it and its contents are not to be distributed outside your agency." It is included in the FBI's file on the Brigade.

UNITED STATES DEPARTMENT OF JUSTICE
FEDERAL BUREAU OF INVESTIGATION
Seattle, Washington
January 4, 1978

RE: GEORGE JACKSON BRIGADE

GEORGE JACKSON, a member of a group of dissident prisoners termed the "Soledad Brothers" at Soledad State Prison, California, in 1970, was a prolific writer, who stated that the U.S. Government is "fascist" and should be resisted by "people's urban-guerrilla activity." JACKSON was incarcerated at San Quentin Prison, California, when during a violent riot and attempted prison break, he ran into the prison yard and was shot and killed by a guard, on August 11, 1971.

Development of the George Jackson Brigade (GJB)
In October, 1972, an organization was formed at Washington Sate Reformatory (WSR), Monroe, Washington, as an outgrowth of Adult Basic Education, Seattle Opportunities Center, Seattle, and Work Release Programs at the WSR. The organization, called "Awareness Project" published a newspaper called "Sunfighter." The staff of that newspaper included various persons, including JOHN SHERMAN, EDWARD ALLEN MEAD and BRUCE SEIDEL. Two references were listed as RITA BROWN and THERESE COUPEZ. COUPEZ was also listed as an "outside sponsor."
During 1973, certain volunteers from the Awareness Project, led by JOHN WILLIAM SHERMAN of the Washington State Prisoner's Labor Union Support Committee, Seattle, Washington, attempted to form a prisoner's union within the WSR at Monroe, Washington. Denied this by prison authorities, the group of volunteers then attempted to promote a sitdown program and encouraged prisoners to commit acts of sabotage within the prison, but without success. EDWARD ALLEN MEAD was

also a member of that group. Proved ineffective, and growing radical, the Awareness Project volunteer lost support and began to fade out about 1974. The "Sunfighter" newspaper continued as a radical prisoner-protest publication, whose staff in 1974, included MARK EDWIN COOK.

RE: GEORGE JACKSON BRIGADE

During 1974, an organization called "Convention Movement" headed by MARK EDWIN COOK, a prisoner on work release from the Washington State Penitentiary at Walla Walla, Washington, emerged in Seattle. This group formed to protest treatment of prisoners in Washington, and promoted a prisoner's union, offering the "Convention Movement" members as mediators between the state government and state prisoners, in disputes over demand for prison reform. On various occasions, COOK led loud and disorderly protest groups into the offices of the Washington State Adult Corrections Authority at Olympia, to make demands related to the "Convention Movement" program. COOK was also a leader in the highly militant "Black Panther" chapter formed inside the walls of the WSP at Walla Walla.

About Summer of 1974, MARK COOK became an active volunteer with a program known as "The Family Group," an organization formed by a former inmate at WSP to provide a program of self-help to increase wages for prisoners at the WSP. This program lasted about seven months and was dissolved.

The "Sunfighter" newspaper continued publication through 1974 and into 1975.

About the latter part of 1975, an underground group emerged from the above semi-legitimate prison reform groups, calling itself the "George Jackson Brigade." The group, founded on a communist philosophy, was apparently dedicated to the commission of acts of urban guerilla warfare, including acts of violence to further the realization of the imagined ideals of the organization.

Members of the George Jackson Brigade

From information resulting from members who have been arrested, or from records discovered in a search of a house previously occupied by members of the GJB, the following persons were determined to be members of the George Jackson Brigade:

JOHN WILLIAM SHERMAN, aka Karl Joseph Newland, Barry Albert Grimes, Jay R. Newmarch, Paul Davis, William Harris, George

Lindsay: white, male, American, born August 28, 1942, 5'10"-11," 170 pounds, brown hair, hazel eyes, medium build (Fugitive).

THERESE ANN COUPEZ, aka Carol Alice Newland, Katherine E. Wilson: white, female, American, born November 30, 1952, 5'6," 120 pounds, blue eyes, brown hair, usually wears glasses, slender build (Fugitive).

RITA DARLENE BROWN, aka Anna Joyce Blakely, Carole Alice Newland, Nikki Marie Simpson: white, female, American, born October 14, 1947, at Klamath Falls, Oregon, 5'6," 150 pounds, hazel eyes, brown hair, stocky build, _____[9] (Captured, awaiting trial).

BRUCE RICHARD SIEDEL, white, male, American, born April 17, 1949, at Chicago, Illinois, 5'6," 150 pounds, hazel eyes, brown hair, medium build (Deceased—Died of wounds from police bullets received at bank robbery January 23, 1976).

MARK EDWIN COOK, Male, Negro, American, born October 26, 1936, at Seattle, Washington, 5'10," 170 pounds, brown eyes, black hair, medium build, _____[10] (Captured and convicted of bank robbery and assaulting an officer).

EDWARD ALLEN MEAD, male, white, American, born November 6, 1941, at Compton, California, 6', 160 pounds, blue eyes, blond hair, slender build (Captured and convicted of bank robbery).

Since the capture of RITA DARLENE BROWN, the only known active members of the GJB are JOHN WILLIAM SHERMAN and THERESE ANN COUPEZ. One other female is referred to in notes kept by the GJB, as apparently residing with Sherman, Coupez and Brown within the past year. Her identity is not known and it is not known whether that person has engaged in any criminal activities or criminal conspiracies with the GJB.[11]

Several writings found as a result of a search of a house previously occupied by GJB members indicate that certain "meetings" were held between members of the GJB and apparent "above ground" support persons in August, 1977. The identities of the persons are unknown, and it is unknown whether those persons engaged in any criminal activities or conspiracies with the GJB.[12]

PHILOSOPHY OF THE GJB

In their "communiques" the members of the GJB justify their various acts of violence by stating they are done to further the ends of a revolution of the "masses" to overthrow the present governmental and international business structures and establish a system of communism. Robberies of banks and liquor stores, they explain, are merely "expropriations" of money from "the ruling class" to finance the "revolutionary activities" of the GJB.

The communiques and notations written by the GJB indicate a strict dedication to the precepts and disciplines included in the writings of KARL MARX. The writer for the GJB claims adherence to Marxist-Leninism, and to the example of South American communist guerilla leader Che Guevara. According to the GJB communiques and writings, the GJB sees the international business monopolies of the world, holding the world's masses, particularly those in the "third world" (including Africans, Asians, Latinos, and in a large sense, women in general) in a vice of oppression. The GJB, by committing violent acts and publishing communiques, apparently envisions itself as a kind of fulcrum upon which a great communist inspired uprising can be successfully mounted, as promised in the writings of KARL MARX, and the masses will thereby be freed to live in peace, without want.

Unlike other recent student-revolutionary groups, the GJB does not envision itself as an "elite" faction that will provide a leadership faction for an ultimate revolutionary government, and criticizes those groups who would place themselves in such a role. Rather, the GJB sees itself more as a catalyst to make the masses aware of their oppressed state, and inspire them to create their own general uprising to overthrow their "oppressors."

ACTIVITIES OF THE GJB: A CHRONOLOGY

All of the following events were claimed by and/or have been directly attributed to the GJB:

May 31, 1975, a bomb exploded in the offices of the Adult Corrections Department, Capitol Center Building, Fourth and Sylvester Streets, Olympia, Washington.

August 5, 1975, a bomb exploded in a men's washroom adjacent to the resident agency offices of the FBI in the U.S. Post Office, Customs House and Court House, 1102-A Street, Tacoma, Washington.

September 15, 1975, a bomb exploded inside a Safeway Grocery Store, 1410 East John Street, Seattle, Washington. (This explosion, which injured several customers of the store, was reportedly in support of a young self-styled communist, RALPH PATRICK FORD, who blew himself up three days previously, while attempting to place a bomb at the same location.)[13]

December 31, 1975, a bomb exploded at an electrical power substation of Seattle City Light, Northeast 41st and 45th Northeast Avenue, Seattle, Washington.

December 31, 1975, a bomb exploded at the Safeway grocery stores Distribution Center, Bellevue, Washington.

January 23, 1976, an armed robbery of the Pacific National Bank of Washington, Tukwila Branch, 13451 Interurban Avenue South, Seattle, Washington, occurred. The robbers were thwarted in their attempt by the prompt response of Tukwila Police. The robbers refused to surrender and began to shoot at the police officers with handguns. One of the robbers, BRUCE RICHARD SEIDEL, was killed by police bullets. Two more, JOHN WILLIAM SHERMAN and EDWARD ALLEN MEAD, were captured by the police. Another suspect, seated in the getaway car across the street from the bank, fired several shots at the police, missed, and struck JOHN WILLIAM SHERMAN in the jaw with one of his bullets. The suspect drove away from the bank, and escaped. He was later identified as MARK EDWIN COOK.

March 10, 1976, while awaiting trial, JOHN WILLIAM SHERMAN was being escorted to the Harborview Hospital at Seattle, by an armed Sheriff's Officer, for treatment of SHERMAN's bullet wound, when a man stepped up and shot the officer down, enabling JOHN WILLIAM SHERMAN to escape. The man was later identified as MARK EDWIN COOK. COOK was subsequently arrested and was convicted of bank robbery and shooting a police officer.

July 13, 1976, the Crater National Bank, South Ashland Bank, South Ashland Office, 1632 Ashland, Ashland, Oregon, was robbed by a lone gunman, later identified as RITA DARLENE BROWN.

August 2, 1976, the Oregon Bank, Rogue River Valley Branch, 1025 Cort Street, Medford, Oregon, was robbed by a lone gunman, later identified as RITA DARLENE BROWN.

October 28, 1976, the First State Bank of Oregon, Sunset Office, 805 NW Murry Road, Portland, Oregon, was robbed by two armed persons, later identified as RITA DARLENE BROWN and JOHN WILLIAM SHERMAN.

January 4, 1977, the U.S. National Bank of Oregon, Raleigh Hills Branch, 4870 SW 76th Avenue, Portland, Oregon, was robbed by a lone gunman, later identified as RITA DARLENE BROWN.

February 7, 1977, the U.S. National Bank of Oregon, Wilsonville Branch, 30120 SW Boone's Ferry Road, Wilsonville, Oregon, was robbed by a lone gunman, later identified as RITA DARLENE BROWN.

May 12, 1977, a bomb exploded in a safe deposit box, inside the Rainier National Bank, 2245 NE Bellevue-Redmond Road, Redmond, Washington.

May 12, 1977, an attempt was made to bomb the Rainier National Bank, 815 – 116th Avenue NE, Bellevue, Washington.

May 21, 1977, the Washington State Liquor Store, 5608 119th SE, Bellevue, Washington, was robbed by a lone gunman.

June 20, 1977, the Rainier National Bank, Factoria Branch, 3724 – 128th SE, Bellevue, Washington, was robbed.

July 4, 1977, an unexploded bomb was discovered at a substation of Puget Power and Light Company, 16th and Cherry Streets, Olympia, Washington, and was rendered inactive by a police bomb disposal squad.

September 8, 1977, the Old National Bank, Juanita Branch, 13233 – 100th NE, Kirkland, Washington, was robbed.

September 19, 1977, the Peoples National Bank, Skyway Branch, 12610 – 76th South, Seattle, Washington, was robbed.

October 6, 1977, there was an attempt made to bomb the Westlund Buick Company, 9600 First NE, Seattle, Washington.

October 13, 1977, a bomb exploded at the S.L. Savidge Auto Dealership, 825 Lenora, Seattle, Washington.

October 15, 1977, a bomb exploded at the B.B.C. Dodge Company, 14650 First Avenue South, Burien, Washington.

November 1, 1977, a bomb exploded at the Phil Smart Mercedes automobile dealership, 10515 Main Street, Bellevue, Washington.

November 2, 1977, there was an attempt to bomb the offices of Diebold Company, 1520 Fourth South, Seattle, Washington.[14]

November 4, 1977, acting on information of a suspicious person seen in several north Seattle banks, the FBI arrested RITA DARLENE BROWN in Seattle, Washington. She was traced to a residence being used by the GJB members at 13746 Roosevelt Way North, Seattle, Washington, and that house was searched the following day. The search revealed a short wave radio which members of GJB had used to monitor and keep logs concerning police calls, and a large quantity of equipment and written material.

December 23, 1977, a bomb exploded in an electrical transformer in South Center, Tukwila, Washington.

December 24, 1977, a bomb exploded inside a railroad freight car containing new automobiles, in a railroad yard, Kent, Washington.

Current Status

JOHN WILLIAM SHERMAN and THERESE ANN COUPEZ have both been declared fugitives, and are presently being sought by the FBI.

ii.

Difficult to Digest:
The Corporate Media on the George Jackson Brigade

ED MEAD: TWO FACES OF A DANGEROUS MAN
Walter Wright
Post-Intelligencer, April 11, 1976[15]

Ed Mead.

Is he "self-anointed deliverer of life and death," a dangerous fanatic "not possessed of an orderly, logical and reasonable mind" whose "perverted sense of right and wrong" gives him "an absolute, total callous lack of concern" for others?

Or is he child of a broken home, a man who has "never hurt anyone in my life," product of poverty and prison oppression, whose experience fits a Marxist view of reality and places him, as a member of the George Jackson Brigade, in the vanguard of the revolution?

Or is he part of both?

The two pictures of Mead emerged when he took the stand Thursday in his own unsuccessful defense on charges he tried to kill two Tukwila police officers responding to a bank robbery alarm.

One picture was painted by King County deputy prosecutor Phil Killien, the other by Mead himself, who now faces sentences of 20 years to life on each of two counts of first degree assault.

Both men agreed on one point: Mead is dangerous.

"The state sees me as a dangerous person. I am—to the state," Mead, 34, told the nine-woman, three-man jury as he attempted to explain the life and politics which brought him, gun in hand, to a Tukwila bank Jan. 23.

No, Killien argued, Mead is not simply dangerous to the state, but to anyone who happens to get in his way, from a policeman trying to stop a bank robbery to a child who might be killed by a blast from a bomb planted by Mead's paramilitary George Jackson Brigade.

Mead's comrade across the street, Killien said, was "shooting Officer Mathews in the back."

No, Mead corrected, he was "resisting the excessive use of force by police."[16]

Mead described another comrade, one-time economic student Bruce Seidel, as "gentle and loving." Killien said "peaceful, loving gentle Mr. Seidel, the economist, went into the bank with his belt of ammunition on and carrying his long-barreled gun."

And Mead expressed his "desire for social change" by carrying in a 9 mm. pistol with three clips of ammunition, Killien said.

Mead's defense, Killien said, was that "it's all right to rob banks, and if police show up they don't have the right to take action."

Who did Mead think he was when he talked about holding the bank manager hostage to "negotiate" a surrender? Killien demanded. Did he think he was Henry Kissinger?

Or did he think he was some political messiah, this man "with a fanatical obsession with violence, hurting others, death," this classic adherent to Marxist thought, leading the "vanguard" toward "the dictatorship of the proletariat" on the grounds that "we know what's best for them, and we make the rules, [because for] some reason we are better than others.

"He accepts the right to bomb rich neighborhoods,[17] on the grounds that shrapnel and glass are less (dangerous) to rich three-year-olds than to poor three-year-olds," Killien argued.

Killien said he wasn't arguing about Mead's politics. "He can believe anything he wants as long as he leaves other people alone . . .

"I don't care how revolutionary he wants to be, but his idea he can shoot people on his own choosing isn't politics—it's intent to kill."

Killien didn't understand, for instance, Mead's view that crime is bred of poverty and the solution to crime is not police repression which defends ruling class property and diverts crime toward working class victims. The solution, in Mead's view, is revolution.

He had not always thought so.

As a child growing up with his mother in Alaska, Mead said, he had been taught "that it's all right sometimes, if someone has more than you do, to equalize the wealth."

And everyone had more than Ed Mead did, he felt. His parents had separated when he was seven, and his mother had later taken him from California to Alaska for the "big money" she thought she could earn there.

The big money wasn't there, and Mead's mother, trained as a welder, worked as a B-girl in clubs, he said. When she got a chance to homestead some land outside Fairbanks, they moved out there, "carrying a chest of drawers on our backs." The first summer they lived in a tent, the second in an abandoned bus, building a cabin.

"We were hungry a lot of the time; I remember eating tapioca pudding right out of the box because we had no milk, and once we were on a straight diet of potatoes for a while."

Mead said he quit school in the 9th grade partly because he got tired of hitchhiking 14 miles to school in subzero weather from the unheated shed where he lived and worked in a gasoline station.

At 13, he burned down a government airplane hangar and did $120,000 damage. He was sent to Utah State Industrial School for six months, then released to his father in California, where he stole a car and was shipped back to Alaska. He was arrested several more times as a juvenile.

In 1961, at 19, Mead was charged with theft of a U.S. government property after he broke into an armory, apparently for weapons. Paroled in 1965, he was out for less than a year when he was convicted of a burglary of a pharmacy.

His conviction was later reversed because he was denied time to prepare for trial, he said, but the reversal had little actual impact. His federal parole had been revoked and an attempted escape resulted in another five-year federal sentence in 1969. He came to the U.S. Penitentiary at McNeil Island.

Mead says he had no politics then. His view on the Vietnam war then was "bomb the dirty gooks and get it over with." He was content to work in the law library, writing writs for himself and others, a genuine jailhouse lawyer.

Convinced of the injustice of his own plight, Mead decided to resist what he considered ruling class attempts to use the prison to make him conform to a sick society.

He had suddenly 'discovered,' he says, that the problems were society's problems, not his own. It was society that was out of step, not Ed Mead.

He read Marx, Lenin and Mao, writings which the conviction of anti-war radicals had helped bring to the prisons.

One day, it dawned on him "that I was not a criminal anymore. I saw that I was a radical." He had, he says, "stepped over a line."

He turned from filing suits against the warden to helping to organize "non-violent" prisoner strikes. "They came down on me, and I came back at them."

He was later transferred to Leavenworth in an attempt by authorities to break up the nucleus of convict activists. His politics hardened in an isolation cell at Leavenworth where he says he was placed when guards found him writing a prisoners' activist handbook.

He began to feel that nonviolence didn't work, that nonviolent prisoners lost. He began to feel sympathy for those who talked of riots.

When he was paroled in 1972, Mead went to Steilacoom House, a hostel near McNeil for prisoners' families and visitors.

He had met John Sherman, now also identified as a member of the George Jackson Brigade, in McNeil, and now he and Sherman and others worked in a prisoner-help organization called 'Inside Out.'

Mead, with Sherman and Seidel and another ex-convict named Mark Cook, tried unsuccessfully to organize a Washington State Prisoners Union beginning at Monroe.[18]

Cook is now Mead's codefendant on bank robbery charges, indicted as the man who shot at police from across the street and then fled.[19]

Precisely what happened to Mead's thoughts of the possibilities of prison reform after the prisoners union failed is not known.

What is known is that on May 31, 1975, a pipe bomb tore out a wall of a State Department of Corrections office in Olympia, and the bombing was claimed by a group no one had ever heard of before, called the George Jackson Brigade.

PAGES IN THE LIFE OF BRUCE SEIDEL:
TWO SIDES OF A REVOLUTIONARY
Walter Wright
Post-Intelligencer, April 22, 1976

"There will be a special page in the book of life for the men (women) who have crawled back from the grave. This page will tell of utter defeat, ruin, passivity, and subjection in one breath; and in the next overwhelming victory and fulfillment. So take care of yourself and hold on."[20]

The words belong to George Jackson, prisoner, writer, revolutionary.

They were chosen by Bruce Seidel as an introduction to his own last political testament, written days before he died of gunshot wounds suffered in a bank robbery shootout with police.

The testament, portions of which were published by *The Post-Intelligencer* yesterday [see "Communiqué Fragment" in Part II], declares the writer to have been a member of the revolutionary George Jackson Brigade and implicates him in at least three bombings.

But it does not tell what should be written in the book of life of Bruce Richard Seidel, 26, variously described as would-be cop killer, gentle scholar, radical fanatic and lost soul.

The state prosecutor has portrayed Seidel as a man who cold-bloodedly entered a Tukwila bank Jan. 23 with a belt of ammunition draped around his waist and a .38 caliber long-nose revolver in his hand.

When police arrived, juries have agreed, Seidel stepped from the bank and tried to kill one policeman with his gun and later tried to kill another after being hit by a bullet himself.

But one of Seidel's comrades in the brigade, Ed Mead, describes Seidel as a murdered, martyred, revolutionary folk hero bandit who tried to surrender and then died with a blazing gun in one hand and a sack of money in the other.

Another, John Sherman, described him as "a revolutionary who had a lot of convictions, a lot of courage," and was "into struggle more than a lot of people were."

Many friends and relatives in the small Illinois city where Seidel grew up know little if anything of this side of Seidel.

They have been told by his distraught family that Seidel died not in a bank robbery but in a traffic accident on his motorcycle.

Seidel's parents refuse to talk with reporters about him.

"He came from a very religious Jewish family, an upper middle-class background, very achievement-oriented, and he had cut his ties with all that," a friend in Seattle says of Seidel.

Perhaps the ties were cut. But Mead remembers Seidel kept with him always an 8-by-10 glossy photo "of his dad and mom and a whole bunch of relatives standing in a doorway."

"He knew there was a possibility we wouldn't survive," Mead said, "and immediately after this appropriation Bruce was going to go back and see his family."

The family included an aging grandmother who sent Bruce $5 every week, and probably wouldn't understand why this promising scholar had left school just short of his master's degree.

Seidel attended the University of Illinois at Urbana from 1966 to 1971, majoring in economics.

Sources there say he became active in anti-war activities there. He told friends he was beaten by police during a demonstration in Chicago, and others say he was beaten by police after smashing a police car window in Washington, D.C., during the May Day "Stop the Government" demonstrations in 1971.

Arriving in Seattle from Illinois, Seidel immediately became active in anti-war activities, organizing on the University of Washington campus, joining demonstrators camping on the federal courthouse lawn in 1972, taking up signs in peace marches.

Seidel's streak of impatience was not limited to the political status quo. Acquaintances say the small man (5'3", 125 pounds) often refused to hear others out, was contemptuous, sarcastic, antagonistic, a strutting "tough guy."

Mead envied Seidel's ability to relate to others. But one person who met Seidel in 1972 described him as "a lost soul type, the kind of person who did better relating to communist theory than relating to other people. He made points instead of making friends."

But others say Seidel was basically unselfish, loving, committed to helping others.

By early 1972, Seidel had moved out of campus organizing and into the "workplace," learning a trade as a welder at Seattle Opportunities Industrialization Center. This economics student, friends say, wanted to "proletarianize the proletariat" and felt he had to work with them to do so.

At the same time, Seidel had become intensely involved in prison reform and prisoner-aid project, the cause that succeeded the Vietnam War for many on the left.

He showed up at Monroe State Reformatory to help with a "consciousness raising" program for white prisoners,[21] and soon helped launch a prisoner newspaper called "Sunfighter."

His prison experiences, he said once, "had a really great impact on my life. I have truly learned a great deal . . ."

He was clearly impressed with Mead and Sherman, both fresh from federal penitentiaries and bent on organizing state prisoners into a labor union, when he met them in Seattle in 1972.

And Mead, a ninth-grade drop-out, was clearly impressed with Seidel as a scholar and "revolutionary teacher."

But yet another friend called Seidel "kind of strange—not crazy but very intense, devoted to radical causes but not necessarily with a consistent ideology."

No, counters another, "his consistent political ideology was one of being unselfish."

Seidel was barred as a Monroe volunteer because of "rumors" about narcotics being smuggled to inmates.

Seidel helped to organize CONvention, an annual gathering of ex-prisoners, and was active in prison reform efforts while a student at Seattle Central Community College in 1974.

His work on *Sunfighter* and in CONvention brought him in contact with another SCCC student, ex-convict Mark Cook, a CONvention founder who now is charged in federal court as one of Seidel's suspected accomplices in the Jan. 23 Tukwila bank robbery.

Many of Seidel's former friends—afraid to identify themselves for fear of being subpoenaed by a federal grand jury now investigating the bank robbery and several bombings—condemn both the bank job and the bombings.

"The results of the political line put forth by the George Jackson Brigade," one said, "are that Bruce is dead, Mead is headed for prison, and Sherman has escaped only to be forced underground for the rest of his life."

"And the grand jury is investigating a lot of people on the left who had nothing to do with the Brigade, but who will go to jail before they say anything to authorities."

But the George Jackson Brigade says it doesn't end there. Their "rage" over Bruce's death won't end, the Brigade has threatened, "until his killers and the class they serve are destroyed."

JANINE AND JORI:
THE TWO FACES OF A JACKSON BRIGADE SUSPECT
Neil Modie
Post-Intelligencer, March 30, 1978

Jori Uhuru is thin, severe-looking, with dark hair chopped short and baggy, turtleneck sweater and slacks—a visual stereotype of the radical, bomb-planting, bank robbing revolutionary the government has charged her with being.

Janine Bertram was a frail-looking, soft-spoken, neatly dressed young woman with shoulder-length hair, a compassionate and religious woman with a strong but not radical social conscience, too independent-minded to be given to extremism and dogma.

Jori Uhuru is accused of being a member of the George Jackson Brigade, a violent band of radicals the FBI says it has finally broken.

Janine Bertram evolved from a church-going Lutheran to a civil rights worker to a teacher of African villagers to an occasional prostitute to a founder of a local chapter of COYOTE, a prostitutes' civil rights organization—always with an individualistic, adventuresome spirit, a relish for experiencing something new.

Jori Uhuru used to be Janine Bertram. How she changed from one to the other is baffling to those who knew her.

"I'm very surprised because Janine was basically not that kind of personality," Dr. Jennifer James commented yesterday after learning that Bertram, 27, was arrested last week with purported George Jackson Brigade members John W. Sherman and Therese Ann Coupez.

James, a University of Washington psychiatrist and a national authority on prostitution, worked with Bertram four years ago when the latter founded a Seattle branch of COYOTE, which offers legal protection and refuge to prostitutes.

"I found her sensible," James said. "I always found her to be a good person . . . She was a very decent person."

"I simply don't understand it," her mother, Vina Bertram of Tacoma, said yesterday, two days after finding out for the first time in a year and a half where her daughter was.

But the young woman's mother added—and others agreed—that Janine Bertram wasn't one to accept established views passively, and she was motivated more by a deep compassion for others than by the way the rest of society saw things.

"She would always help people who were in trouble. She would have put herself in danger to protect the others," James said.

"She was very receptive to new ideas and always wanted to think a thing through for herself," said the Rev. Kent Spaulding, a Lutheran minister in Seattle who formerly was the Bertram family's pastor in Tacoma.

A federal grand jury Tuesday indicted the young woman, along with Sherman and Coupez, for conspiracy, robbing four Tacoma banks since last December and manufacturing three pipe bombs last October on dates when three local auto dealerships were bombed.

On March 21, FBI agents in Tacoma surrounded a car in which Sherman, Coupez and Bertram were parked at a drive-in restaurant. After arresting the three, the agents found three handguns in the car.

When booked into the King County jail, where she now is being held under $100,000 bail, Bertram gave her name as Jori Uhuru. "Uhuru" is the Swahili word for freedom.

When Janine formed the Seattle branch of COYOTE in 1974, her mother recalled, "I was a little taken aback by it . . . But after some long talks with her about it, I felt she had some right to stand up for what she believed in, because that's the way we tried to raise our kids, to stand up for what they believed in."

Jennifer James said Bertram was "never a very dedicated or hard-line" prostitute.

James felt Bertram became interested in COYOTE through "a combination of social conscience and an interesting thing to do"—factors which also may have been a reason for the latter's civil rights concerns in high school and a period spent teaching in a remote African village in Kenya after she attended Fairhaven College in Bellingham.

Mrs. Bertram, a widow, said her daughter disappeared abruptly on October 9, 1976, when the two of them were visiting a relative in Vancouver, Wash., and a man and a woman who gave their names as "Bill" and "Rachel" showed up there to see Janine.[22]

"She left the house with these people, then she called the house and left a message saying she was leaving for California with these people," Mrs. Bertram said.

She has never seen Janine since then although she received two letters from her—but with no forwarding address. The young woman has talked with her mother by phone from jail twice since Monday.

Jennifer James was surprised that Janine been an apparent associate of the George Jackson Brigade members.

The psychiatrist-sociologist was acquainted with Therese Coupez as well as Rita Brown, another brigade member and a self-styled lesbian feminist revolutionary who now is serving a prison sentence for bank robbery.

"There was no comparison between that pair and Janine. Terry (Coupez) and Rita were very rough characters," James said.

She last saw Bertram about three years ago when the young woman said she wanted out of COYOTE, and James took that to mean Bertram was "settling down." But apparently she didn't.

"With someone like Janine," Pastor Spaulding observed, "You know there's a great potential there for something. But you never know quite what."

Community Response
AN OPEN LETTER TO DR. JENNIFER JAMES,
U. OF W. AND THE COMMUNITY

The reproduction below is based on the original, signed copy of this letter. It appeared as "Objections to Bertram Interview" in Northwest Passage, *April 10–May 2, 1978. I have omitted the address in the header.*

April 1, 1978

Dear Dr. James,

We are writing to protest the recent interview you gave in the Seattle *P-I* concerning Janine Bertram. It gave a distorted history of Coyote and several women's involvement in it, including Janine Bertram, Therese Coupez, and Rita Brown.

We object to your statement that "Janine was never a very dedicated or hard-line prostitute." Besides implying that nice girls aren't prostitutes, it also implies that Janine never took the risks or dealt with the oppression that is part of a prostitute's life. This is simply not true. Janine's commitment to the real lives of prostitutes was evidenced by her fight to keep the Coyote office in the Urban League building on 14th and Yesler, though she lost to your efforts to move it to the 17th floor of University Hospital. This same commitment was shown by her appearance on Coyote's behalf at Purdy women's prison, while you declined in favor of a cocktail party.

We also object to your reckless and misleading comments about "that pair" Therese Coupez and Rita Brown. As two of the founding members of Coyote, Therese and Rita deserve more respect. If you were going to do a character analysis of Therese, "Jenny," you could at least use her correct name. As to your statement that "Terry and Rita were very rough characters," maybe what you mean to say is that they were very open lesbians. It was unfair to bring your own prejudices into a public interview.

The whole interview makes Janine appear passive, a dupe, the stereotyped good girl gone bad. If you were as close a friend of Janine's as you want to believe you are, you would not be making such statements.

We would like to know why you did the interview. We get the impression that you did it to cover yourself and to draw attention to your status as a "national authority on prostitution." Your careless attitude discounts the significance of the work that Janine and others have dedicated themselves to.

in love and struggle,
[signed]
Chris Beahler
Janine Carpenter
Shelle Finch
Jane Hope

cc: Janine Bertram, Therese Coupez, Rita Brown, Margo St. James (San Francisco),[23] Flo Kennedy (New York)[24]
media
community

SHERMAN—'READY WHEN THE TIME COMES'
John Arthur Wilson
Seattle Times, April 5, 1978

In soft-spoken tones, John Sherman speaks of revolution in America, of taking up arms to fight the ruling class and of destroying capitalism bit by bit.

"I don't think that we're going to run around with guns and over-throw capitalism," the George Jackson Brigade member told *The Times* in a jail interview. "But I did come to the decision that when the time comes, the guns and the skills are not going to fall from the sky."

Sherman said the only way "to learn how to do it was doin' it, and here I am, still doin' it."

For the past three years, Sherman has been one of the central figures in a small revolutionary band, the George Jackson Brigade.

Named after the late California prisoner and author, the brigade has claimed responsibility for numerous bombings and bank robberies here and in Oregon since it first surfaced in 1975.

For Sherman's part, there are numerous charges pending against him with a staggering amount of possible prison time.

He faces federal charges for a January, 1976, Tukwila bank robbery, in which he was wounded, potential state charges for his daring March 10, 1976, escape, more federal bank-robbery charges, a conspiracy indictment and charges in connections with three area bombings last October.

The road to his revolution conversion began 35 years ago, a continent away from where he sits in jail today.

Born in New Jersey during World War II, John William Sherman was an only child. His father was a machinist and his mother a secretary.

Sherman remembers leading a "relatively normal childhood," and eventually moving to California in the early 1950s. He dropped out of school in 10th grade and enlisted in the Army at 16 because "there was nothing better to do."

"I spent a lot of time drinking, carrying on like everyone else," he recalled of his military stint. "I didn't mind it too much."

Following the service, he returned to New Jersey and worked in the Camden shipyards as an apprentice machinist. In 1969, he was arrested on an interstate, auto-theft charge. Other criminal charges caught up with Sherman, who says he was "'criming,' checks and stuff like that" during that period.

The federal charge finally sent him to McNeil Island federal penitentiary for three years.

It was at McNeil where Sherman became politicized by readings of Karl Marx and Mao Tse-Tung. "I started to gain a determination to fight back, and not to just complacently sit there and let what happened happen," Sherman said.

While there, Sherman met a man who would figure into the brigade, Edward Allen Mead. Mead, an avowed member, is serving lengthy prison terms for the Tukwila bank robbery.

Both Sherman and Mead became involved in a 1971 prisoner strike. About this time, the controversial shootings at Attica State Prison in New York happened.

"Attica really angered us," Sherman said. While Sherman and other inmates discussed the weaknesses of the previous strike, prison officials moved swiftly to snuff any future trouble.

A handful of strike leaders, including Mead, were transferred to other prisons. Sherman, with only months left in his sentence, was placed in segregation.

Sherman wasn't out of jail long before he was involved with prisons again, this time organizing inmates at the Monroe state reformatory. Working with Mead and Bruce Seidel, a brigade member killed during the Tukwila robbery, Sherman helped inmates stage a work slowdown.

But the administration cut off their access to the inmates, effectively killing the prisoners' union.

To support himself, Sherman worked as a machinist in Pacific Car & Foundry's Renton plant and in Boeing's research-and-development facility.

About this time, Sherman, who had been a member of the Revolutionary Union, was entering another phase of his political metamorphosis.

"I was getting more dissatisfied with my political practice," he recalled. After recontacting Mead, the two discussed with others the necessity of "armed work" and ultimately decided "to do it."

In May 1975, a bomb exploded in Department of Social and Health Services corrections offices in Olympia. For the first time, a group calling itself the George Jackson Brigade took responsibility. They said it was in support of state-prison inmates' demands.

Their "armed struggle" led to other bombings, including the September, 1975, Capitol Hill Safeway bombing in which several persons received minor injuries.

The bombing, in response to Patty Hearst's arrest and the death of another young man attempting to plant a bomb at the store, drew sharp criticism from Seattle's above-ground left.

It also drew self-criticism from the brigade, which later apologized for bringing "terror to a poor neighborhood."

With that, momentum was building toward the fateful month of January, 1976.

A few minutes after midnight on New Year's Day, two bombs were detonated. One knocked out a City Light power substation in Laurelhurst. The other damaged Safeway distribution facilities in Bellevue.

"Laurelhurst was the big turning point," said Sherman, who had been critical of the grocery-store bombing.

"I think it was at this point that we really articulated the fact that we weren't terrorists. We didn't see ourselves as saviors of the people."

Sherman considered the Laurelhurst bombing a success. "It had to be clearly directed against a class enemy," he said.

The brigade bomb did $250,000 damage to the substation, knocking out power in the well-to-do neighborhood, no one was physically injured and the group felt it had struck the ruling class.

The substation bombing was to be the first step in increased brigade actions, a possible prelude to a Bicentennial push by the revolutionary group.

If Laurelhurst was a success, the aborted Tukwila bank robbery three weeks later was a near-fatal blow to the brigade.

When the gunfire quieted, Seidel lay fatally wounded, Sherman had been wounded and captured along with Mead. They had gone to the bank to "expropriate" money for weapons and explosives, a communique later said.

In March 1976, Sherman escaped, spending two years on the run, refining his political philosophy, before being recaptured in Tacoma last month.

As Sherman spoke this week, he expressed his continued dedication to waging war against the American ruling class and the economic system it upholds.

"I want to do away with the rich and the right to be rich," Sherman said. Capitalism, with so much money and power concentrated in the hands of a few, is the "roof of oppression" against poor people and women, Sherman added.

Until that changes, Sherman says in a soft, often disarmingly relaxed voice, there will be a need for groups like the George Jackson

Brigade. And eventually, Sherman says, history will vindicate him.

"They're going to give John Sherman a bucket full of (prison) time," he said looking ahead to charges pending. "But John Sherman is going to keep on fighting."

"I'm still disgusted by capitalism and I'm still determined to do whatever I can do to help sweep it away."

Invisible People:
A Working Class Black Man and a White Dyke

Does the State Conspire?
The Conviction of Mark Cook
Michelle Celarier
Northwest Passage

> Usually there's a crime and an investigation to see who commit-
> ted it. In this case there was a crime and a suspect and an investiga-
> tion to prove the guilt of the suspect.
> —John Henry Brown, Chief Attorney, Seattle-King County
>   Public Defender's Office

In the case of Mark Cook, convicted June 28 on three counts surrounding the George Jackson Brigade's attempted January 23 Tukwila
bank robbery, the line between being set up and not getting a fair trial
is hard to draw. During both the pre-trial investigation and the four-
day trial, political persuasions bounced off and reinforced each other,
raising the ever present question: Why Mark Cook?

"Mark Cook was the most dedicated, effective prison organizer in
the state; he's black, and he's not afraid of them" was Bernice Funk's
explanation. A member of his defense committee and a co-worker
with Cook on the American Friends Service Committee (AFSC) Justice
Committee studying paroles, she's known him for three years.

Both defense committee members and Mark Cook think he got
less than a fair trial. It's not hard to understand why: the main witness
against him was a heroin addict who received personal gain for his testimony, the key witness for the defense was not allowed to testify, two
officers were taken off the case after they were unsuccessful in proving
Cook's presence at the crimes, and eye witness identification was spu-
rious and contradictory.

It was only two days after John Sherman escaped from custody
March 10 at Harborview that Cook was picked up and charged as the
"get-away" man in the January robbery. Sherman was being treated
for a wound received while caught inside the bank with Ed Mead and
Bruce Seidel, who was killed there. Two months after being charged in
the robbery, Cook was also charged with aiding in Sherman's escape.
He goes to trial in September for that charge, although he has repeatedly denied involvement with the either the Brigade or the robbery.

Mead also denied that Cook was a member in his trial testimony,
calling Cook a "reformist who wants to work aboveground." Countering
Mead's charge, Cook wrote in a letter to the defense committee the day

after his conviction: "I will continue to work as hard, if not harder than ever, in changing 'prison.' Even in the face of having to live down Ed Mead's accusation of 'reformist.'"

Mark Cook's prison activism began while an inmate at Monroe State Reformatory, where he served on an inmate council. The 39-year-old Seattle native has spent 18 years of his life in confinement and knew of Sherman and Mead through his prison work. He had established CONvention, a yearly meeting of ex-cons, after he got out on parole three years ago and is most interested in securing voting rights for prisoners. It was through CONvention that he became involved with the Friends (AFSC).

Sherman and Mead, both ex-cons, worked on prisoners' unions and *Sunfighter*, a prison support newspaper. Produced as a court exhibit was a copy of that newspaper which listed Mark Cook as a "staff member"—the only established link between him and the Brigade members. Defense committee members, however, maintain that Cook's involvement with *Sunfighter* was minimal.

These political activities shed some light on the confusing chain of events which led to Cook's arrest on the bank charges and the two-month delay before being charged in the March 10 escape. In the letter Cook wrote June 29, he commented: "All of you may get the impressions that I don't believe I got a fair trial. I'll go a step further than that. I don't believe I was treated fairly as a suspect during both arrests."

The issue of fairness goes all the way back to the two government informants in the case, Suzanne LaBray and Autrey Sturgis. Sturgis, Cook's childhood friend and heroin addict, was the prosecution's main witness and testified that Cook had confided in him the details of the robbery.

It was revealed at the trial that shortly after Cook's arrest, Sturgis had visited public defender John Brown, who was then Cook's attorney. Brown testified that Sturgis told him that Cook was innocent and that he had heard there were two government informants, one of them his lover, LaBray, also a heroin addict. In court, Sturgis denied that he had proclaimed Cook's innocence in his meeting with Brown. He also denied becoming an informer until March 15, three days after Cook was arrested.

Whether or not Sturgis was, in fact, the second informant or whether he went to Brown with the fear that LaBray had turned against him is still uncertain. Defense counsel Bob Czeisler told the *NWP* that his conversations with LaBray led him to believe that her testimony would have cleared up these muddled facts. He says she would have testified that before Cook's arrest she'd been approached to be an informant and offered money if she could produce a conviction, that she too was a heroin addict.

Her testimony would eventually have shown "the improbability that the events were as Sturgis portrayed, i.e., that Cook would have spilled the beans to two known heroin addicts and two people known to be informants," says Czeisler. But Federal District Court Judge Donald s would not allow her as a defense witness because he said Czeisler would attack her credibility. Part of the defense's appeal will be based on the ruling regarding LaBray's testimony.

The case of the two police officers who were investigating the Harborview escape also corroborates Cook's beliefs about the pre-trial treatment. Officer Strunk testified that he and an Officer Whalen "thought we were" in charge of the case but were dismissed when they could not get eye witness identification of Cook. They had showed photos of Cook and another suspect to Police Officer Virgil Johnson, who was wounded in the escape. Johnson originally said the other suspect was definitely the man who shot him, not Cook. In May, however, the investigation of the other suspect was mysteriously dropped and Cook was identified by Johnson and charged in the escape. Strunk testified that he didn't think Cook was involved in the escape.

The situation of Officer Whalen is even more curious. He could not be located to testify, but Sturgis identified him as the government agent who approached him before the robbery, "indirectly" offering $20,000 for information which would lead to the conviction of persons involved in the bombings claimed by the Brigade, placing Sturgis' initial conversations with the government at an earlier date.

The trial itself raises many questions about the validity of some standard judicial and police procedures and how they can be manipulated for the verdict desired. Eye witness testimony, paid informants, government harassment and intimidation are all legal procedures which served to put Mark Cook back behind bars.

Four persons gave eye witness testimony, two regarding the robbery and two regarding the escape. Although Cook was not being tried for the escape, one of his charges was "conspiracy" to rob banks and evidence surrounding the escape was thus admissible.

The conflicting eye witness stories attest to the difficulties in remembering minute details during times of trauma and the possibilities of racism entering identifications.

The two robbery eye witnesses, Doug Flouiatte and Jack Stockham, contradicted each other on minor details—such as which side of the getaway car the driver was on while firing. In addition, Flouiatte never made a positive identification of Cook, and Stockham, a former policeman, changed his story repeatedly. Stockham was coincidentally never "available" for interrogation by defense counsel prior to the trial.

Furthermore, according to Janis Lien, AFSC and defense committee member who is studying irregularities in the trial, "The way they identified Mark was not a fair and impartial use of photos and lineups." It is another link in the chain of the pre-trial investigations which indicate that Cook was treated unfairly, to say the least.

She explained that the witnesses were given a series of seven photos, which included Cook's pictures, as is the usual procedure in making identification before line-ups. None could identify him. A few weeks later, they were given another series with Cook's the only picture duplicated. The process continued, which Lien called "an obvious way of biasing eye witnesses."

At least one of the witnesses, Ernestine Sanders, never identified him until she was given a single color photo of Cook by federal agents and asked if he was the man she saw. This picture was "lost" and couldn't be produced at the trial. Lien also commented that Sanders' testimony had many contradictions.

The black Harborview employee had said she noticed and she was attracted to the person aiding Sherman's escape because he posed as a black doctor, an oddity at Harborview. She also said that she was not attracted to men with beards and that this man did not have a beard.

In both the robbery and the escape, the suspect was said by eye witnesses to be clean shaven and without glasses. Cook wears glasses and has a full beard. An ophthalmologist testified that he could see only a short distance without his glasses.

What is further jarring about the eye witness testimony is what Funk called the "increasing certainty" of the witnesses. The prime illustration of this phenomenon was the wounded Officer Johnson, who only saw the man who shot him for 3 seconds yet changed his story to finger Cook.

Although the eye witnesses proved quite valuable to the prosecution, its mainstay was the testimony of Sturgis, also an ex-con who had participated with Cook in robberies before. He gave a lengthy account of the Tukwila bank robbery which he said Cook had described to him. However, the defense noted that the information which he revealed could just as easily have been obtained from a communiqué from the Brigade distributed through Left Bank Books shortly after the robbery. Czeisler believes that LaBray's testimony could further discredit Sturgis' story by possibly showing that he received this information from her.

The use of informants in itself is an ugly procedure; when they are heroin addicts, poor people, ex-cons or other vulnerable persons, it becomes even more despicable. But in this case, the court refused to rule on Sturgis as an informant.

"Here you have a case of a man doing in his best friend," said Funk. The reasons for Sturgis' behavior will never be known, for he is now in the government's "Witness Protection Program." Which means he's being given a new job, home, even a new name.

The use of government intimidation and harassment, both in and out of the courtroom, is yet another procedure commonly used against blacks and political activists of all kinds. Funk said Treasury agents visited her at her job at Monroe and added that the FBI visited Cook's lover, Sandra Hastings, 15 minutes before she was to testify in his defense, asking "Where is John Sherman?" Prosecuting attorney Jack Meyerson also visited the AFSC office, asking questions about Cook for which he later was forced to apologize in court, due to defense objections.

Another form of government harassment was the prosecution misconduct during the trial, on which grounds Czeisler repeatedly demanded a mistrial. "Meyerson deliberately asked questions which were improper after the court made rulings against them," said Czeisler. "He tried, through questioning, to inject that Cook tried to change his appearance. There was no evidence to support this."

Meyerson insinuated that Cook had taken a razor to his hair to remove a white patch which Sanders testified she saw, that he was wearing contact lenses. He went so far as to ask Cook's supervisor at Pivot, a training center for ex-cons, if it was true that Cook was fired for threatening him with a pair of scissors, which the supervisor flatly denied.

"Even though these things are stricken from the record," Funk said, "You can't strike them from the minds of the jurors."

And so, after four days of confusing, contradictory and circumstantial evidence, and four hours of debate, the all-white jury[25] returned a guilty verdict on Mark Cook. He was sent back to solitary confinement and is being held in the King County Jail in lieu of $200,000 bail. Cook now awaits sentencing July 23 for the charges of: attempted bank robbery, bank robbery conspiracy and aiding the escape of another suspect in the attempted Tukwila bank hold-up.

Aside from his dedication to the prison movement and his involvement in the AFSC, one learns little about Mark Cook from the newspaper articles or from the trial. His has not become the cause célèbre of the Left in Seattle; most of supporters thus far have remained those who worked closely with him, many of them members of the American Friends Service Committee, a pacifist organization.

Although the government case against him is shaky and the prejudice and discrimination he has received far outweigh all other considerations, proving he was the victim of a set-up is another matter. Because his prior record of bank robberies would have been revealed through cross examination, Mark Cook could not testify in his own behalf without further prejudicing the jury against him. So there was little way for either the jury or the general public to understand specifically how his politics differ from those of the Brigade. A news release from the Defense Committee contains a segment of a letter from Cook regarding his 12-year-old son which is perhaps the most insightful:

You know, I have tried to develop 'spiritual politics' in my son Marcus. We talked a lot about violence and guns, and he figured that wasn't the way people should live, even though he found he often couldn't avoid some fights at school. So our reasoning was—'guns aren't toys because guns are bad; then why should toys be guns?' He threw all his guns in the garbage two years ago and hasn't had one since, knowing that I won't prevent him from either buying one or prevent his playing with one. If he was an organizer I bet he would organize against the sale of toy guns = Bad Guns for Fun. It would probably be more successful than adults' weak attempts at gun control. Killing and hurting are the most perverse acts people can commit against each other, and toy weapons are a symbol of that perversity. We really teach our children young, huh?

a short autobiography

rita d. brown

This document was written at the request of the rita d. brown defense committee, which formed to support Brown while she was jailed in Oregon in the winter and spring of 1977–1978.[26]

I turned 30 on October 14th and have discovered my first grey hairs in recent weeks. I grew up in Klamath Falls, a redneck Weyerhaeuser town in rural Oregon; my parents fled the poverty of the South a couple of years before I was born. I have one sibling who lives in that same town, raises a family and works for that same mill. My mom was a passive, nagging, battered wife and my dad an uneducated, insecure alcoholic most of my life. They have both made huge changes in their lives in more recent years. I started working outside the home about age 14; my first encounter with the police was age 16 about a stolen car. Luckily, the owner dropped the charges—his daughter (my lover) was also joy riding. As far as I knew we were the only queers in the world and I had never heard of a clitoris. My parents took out a small loan and sent me to a small local business college. They did this because I was good in school and it was all they could do. I transferred to the Salem branch where I graduated with accounting and IBM skills. Almost got kicked out of the dorm for a hot romance with a wonderful womyn; we never made it to bed and she had to stay there so I called them a bunch of liars and squeaked by.

I moved to Seattle in '68 where a lifetime/school/neighborhood male friend lived. He helped me learn the city and eat—no strings attached and certainly no sex. Got a job in a bank balancing the savings department to a computer, that lasted nine months and then i got hired by the Post Office. I discovered the gay bars and went through changes with my bi-sexual lover (the same one from high school) until she finally split, then I became a working class bar butch dyke. I drank a lot, got even tougher and went to work every day for over a year.

Eventually there was another lover; we lived closer to the hippie-dopers and tripped out frequently. I "came out" verbally at the job. There were other queers there and we were pretty strong and took care of one another even though we never organized as such. All through this period I had several more encounters with the police, mostly around traffic violations and once for shoplifting. I'd always hear stories in the bars and see bruises on the people who'd been in various police hassles—mostly because they were queer. The police were still kicking in and tearing up gay bars on a fairly regular basis. In '71 I got busted for stealing from my boss who was still the U.S.P.O. Did 7 months of a one year and one day sentence in Terminal Island Federal Penitentiary, Calif. Learned a whole lot about racism, queer hating, mean police, junkies and other such facts of life; I learned a lot from sisters there, like that self-hate, disgust and feelings of helplessness experienced throughout my youth could have easily led me (if I'd been raised in a city where it was readily available) to dope and getting strung out. George Jackson was murdered—shot in the back—and the Attica massacre happened while I was locked up.

Came back to Seattle to find no lover, no home, only a couple of friends and no job. So I went through a couple of government programs and a few lovers and finally learned from another dyke that "womyn are not chicks." The first womyn's event I went to was at the U[niversity] of W[ashington]—an I[nternational] W[omen's] D[ay] conference. There was a prison workshop going on, run by some social workers who had all their experience on the outside of the bars. Well I told them they didn't know what they were talking about and I became a public speaker and the token ex-con that very day.

Shortly after this, I was at S[eattle] C[entral] C[ommunity] C[ollege] where they paid (work study jobs) people to do prison work. After a bullshit trip with an egomaniacal man there, a womyn's prison project was formed with a fine strong sister/lover. I was part of the politico lesbian community. I worked on lots of different projects with children, womyn, men and 3rd World peoples but prison work was always the most important in my life. In a couple of years, I heard a lot of folks in a lot of places talk about the revolution, but nobody did anything except talk. The BLA and Assata were working their asses off but nobody in Seattle did a thing. Then the SLA stormed over the ruling class's toes and met a fiery death; still nobody did anything. Then the GJB started happening right under our very noses—it made sense to me that you just can't talk rockefeller et al. into giving up what they have stolen from the people. I knew it was time for me to put my words into action.

—rdb

Part II

Communiqués

Olympia Bombing

This communiqué was released in the early morning of May 31, 1975, posted to a telephone booth near the intersection of First Avenue and Cherry in downtown Seattle.[1] It appeared in the periodical of the Washington Prisoners Labor Union, which Mead and Seidel edited themselves: "Olympia Bombing," Sunfighter 3, no. 2 (July-August 1975). It was also printed in Dragon *(Berkeley, CA), no. 3 (October 1975): 28, with the same title.*

> Settle your quarrels, come together, understand the reality of our situation, understand that fascism is already here, that people are already dying who could be saved, that generations more will die or live poor butchered half-lives if you fail to act. Do what must be done, discover your humanity and your love in revolution. Pass on the torch. Join us, give up your life for the people.
> —George Jackson

There has been an ongoing debate recently over national and local law enforcement policies. On the issue of the criminal sentencing process, for example, there appears to be a conflict of opinion between conservative law and order advocate [Christopher] Bayley (the recently promoted county prosecutor) and liberal [King County Superior Court] judge [Donald] Horowitz. Bayley adopts a get tough attitude toward crime, the old lock 'em up syndrome which has proven so ineffective in the past. Horowitz, on the other hand, says warehousing criminals is not only ineffective, it is cruel, and suggests "treatment" of the offender. Neither Bayley or Horowitz deals with the type of hypocrisy that allows Nixon and gang to escape justice while the poor and confused are made example of by the courts.

Crime is not some sort of a disease that suddenly possesses an individual and causes them to act criminally, and which requires treatment in order for the offender to be rehabilitated. Nor is crime a problem resolvable by increasing the sentences of the offender. Every day prisoners are released from prison. Give them longer sentences and people would still be leaving the prisons every day; the only difference would be in the degree of anger felt by the released prisoner. The anger gets taken out on the community. The problem has not been solved, simply prolonged and aggravated, like the way [President Gerald] Ford deals with the economy.

Crime is the natural response for those caught between poverty and the Amerikan culture of greed, aggression, sexism, and racism.

The increasing level of crime is a measure of the sickness of our society; treating or punishing individuals will have little effect on the rate of crime. Sexual aggression against women, for example, has its roots in the sexist attitudes of men. Rape is the logical extension of the sickness of viewing women as objects to be used or abused like any other possession.

What is going to stop crime is when people get together and drive our criminal ruling class and its fascist government up against the wall. Crime will be eliminated when people create a society based on human need rather than greed; a society in which our children are taught that the object in life is something other than making a buck or being sexy. The Amerikan people support the most notorious criminals in existence: U.S. imperialism. Our high standard of living comes from the outright plunder of the "free" world, especially Third World countries. We share the loot stolen from the mouths of hungry children in Africa, Korea, and even here in Amerika, and then wonder why our society is so violent. If people want a better society, they can start by becoming active feminists, anti-racists, and anti-imperialists. The ruling class is white, male and imperialist.

Notwithstanding the rhetoric of the great debaters, the state's actual response to crime is to respond with terrorism. Just as the recapture of the Mayaguez was an international act of terrorism,[2] so too is the shooting of unarmed blacks such as Joe Herbert. The national and state governments are so unstable that the only way in which they can maintain "order" is through the selective use of terrorism. Those who maintain rule through the use of terror are fascists. Revolutionary counter-terror is the appropriate response to fascist lawlessness.

Maintaining order is not only a problem of the urban and rural governments, it is a growing problem inside the nation's prisons as well. In an attempt to maintain order within the nation's prisons the government has implemented the practice of behavior modification techniques on prisoners who resist the command to be silent in the face of slavery and mind torture. The effect of behavior modification is to grant freedom to those who are dishonest and deceitful enough to mouth the master's line, and to punish with long term confinement those who are politically or legally active in trying to create a better society.

The "treatment concept" is a euphemism for psychofascism. It consists of electro-shock, psychosurgery, massive druggings, averse conditioning, sensory deprivation, and more. Such practices have found their way into the nation's schools, especially in high poverty areas. In fact, it was to stop such abuses that the Symbionese Liberation Army executed school superintendent Marcus Foster.[3]

In order to effectively apply the treatment concept, the Adult Corrections Division needs the power to move prisoners from prison to prison (or hospital). The prisoners at Walla Walla realize this fact, and in an attempt to transfer prisoners, they made the following demands central to their struggle: Demand IV (k) "That no member of the population shall ever be transferred to another mental or psychiatric facility out of state unless personally requested by the prisoner in writing." Demand IV (l) goes on to say "That no member of the population shall ever be transferred to another penal facility in any location unless personally requested by the prisoner in writing." These demands were so important to the prisoners that they followed them up with the only threat of violence in the entire list of demands. VI (m) "That if the foregoing insistence indicated in items (k) and (l) are not honored, the Resident Government Council[4] shall see to the destruction of the Washington State Penitentiary." Prisoners also demanded the removal of the chief doctor, the head nurse, and the associate superintendent of custody. When negotiations failed, prisoners seized 8 wing and the hospital and used hostages in an attempt to push their demands forward.

Today is exactly six months from the final deadline prisoners set for the implementation of their demands. Not a single demand has been met. Today's bombing of the offices of the Washington State Department of Corrections is a measure of our determination to see the implementation of the just demands of the Walla Walla prisoners. We of the George Jackson Brigade hereby demand: (A) That the state give prisoners the power to decide for themselves whether or not they want to be transferred; (B) Stop the use and threatened use of psychofascist techniques on the minds of prisoners and school children; (C) The removal of three administrators: Dr. August Hovnanian, hospital surgeon, James Harvey, associate superintendent for custody, and Mrs. Eva Nelson, chief nurse. And (D) That the prison administration follow the Resident Government Council's constitution and otherwise follow the law (the R.G.C. must be permitted to exist).

Capitol Hill Safeway

The following communiqué appeared as "Communique from the George Jackson Brigade," Dragon, no. 3, October 1975, 9. It was Mead and Seidel's immediate response to an attack gone terribly awry: the store was not evacuated as intended, and a number of customers were injured. Both the attack and this communiqué were perceived as callous by Seattle's progressive community, while non-leftists simply denounced its authors as insane. The Brigade apologized for this action in its "New Year" communiqué.

Thursday, September 18, 1975

At 9:15 this evening we placed a call to the Safeway store at 15th and E. John and clearly told the employee who answered that "high explosives were planted in the store and would go off in 15 minutes—Evacuate the store!" Simultaneously we called the newsrooms of KING-TV and articulated the same message.

At 9:30 P.M. the bomb exploded inside Safeway. There had been no effort to heed our warning and no evacuation even in process. Our warning procedure was based on our own experiences and similar experiences of guerillas in other parts of the country where injuries have also occurred. We clearly realize that our attacks must be discriminate and both serve and educate the everyday person. We also realize that as the contradictions heighten it becomes harder and harder to be a passive and innocent bystander in a war zone.

Our attack on the Capitol Hill Safeway had two purposes: First and foremost it was an act of love and solidarity toward the courageous comrade who risked his life in the furtherance of his political convictions.[5] Second, the bombing was in retaliation for the capture of four members of the Symbionese Liberation Army.[6]

We will not belabor the ways in which Safeway criminally exploits farmworkers and its clerks, rips off the public through price fixing, and sells food poisoned by preservatives. Safeway is not only an agribusiness, but its tentacles reach out through the entire world and suck the spirit and blood of poor and oppressed peoples. These crimes are all well documented and have been the subject of numerous educationals, marches, demonstrations, boycotts, strikes, and even anti-trust suits.

Four days ago Po died while arming a bomb he had just planted behind this same Safeway. He died because his oppression, today not just someday, was so real that he found it necessary to risk his death in order to free himself.

We grieve over the murder of this comrade; just as we grieved over the murders and capture of George and Jonathan Jackson, the SLA, three dead Weatherpeople,[7] and countless fallen warriors. But grief is not enough. We must transform grief into righteous anger and our anger into directed action.

It is clearly within the power of the left to force Safeway out of the Capitol Hill Community. All that is required is the will to do so. Using a coordination of both peaceful and violent tactics, people educate and build toward a winning strategy. Progressive forces would have to reach out beyond themselves; talking to people at bus stops, going door to door asking people about their daily lives and their problems. A program should be developed and implemented around their grievances. People should be educated about Safeway and the need for selected violence.

It is time that people start thinking in terms of gaining control over their communities. A victorious struggle against Safeway—even if it takes reducing those two stores to burned-out ruins—would be a major step in the direction toward people's power.

Safeway Off Capitol Hill!
The George Jackson Brigade

We Cry and We Fight

We have a right to cry for our dead,
for every life is unnamably precious
and the death of even one woman or one man
who loved the human race
is an intolerable loss.

Only the frozen robot rulers of Amerikkka
have no tears for human suffering.
Only the fascists watch gleefully when people die.

For us, the life of each comrade is everything,
and is always remembered.

Someone somewhere thinks today of every fallen comrades
of each of the thousands killed in 1927 at Shanghai,

of the vanguard at Moncada,
of the Vietnamese sapper blown up inside Bien Hoa.

Someone somewhere cries today for every fallen comrade:
for Che and Tania
for Malcolm, George and Jonathan,
Fred Hampton, Sam Melville,
Diana, Ted and Terry
Sandra Pratt,[8] Zayd Shakur,[9] Twyman Meyers.[10]

The memory of our immortal sisters and brothers
helps us to find our tears and rage.
Today our weeping and our anger are for Fahiza, Cinque, Mizmoon,
Camilla, Willie and Gelina,[11] gone into History with the others.

Our grief is real, and it makes us stronger and more human.
Our rage is real and it makes us righteous and powerful.
We cry, but keep on moving, building, loving!
We cry in the night and go see Ruchell [Magee] in the morning![12]
We cry one day and defy the grand jury the next!
In the dark of the night we put our arms around our friends to
    comfort them,
and in the dark of night we spraypaint with them!
We turn our grief for the dead into love for the living
and write a letter to Assata! (346 W. 20th St. N.Y.)
We cry for our comrades, and we step into their places!

WE CRY AND WE FIGHT!

Community Response
LEFT BANK STATEMENT
Left Bank Collective

The following appeared as "Left Bank Statement," Northwest Passage, September 29–October 13, 1975, 11.

We of the Left Bank Collective were close friends of Po (Ralph Ford), who was killed attacking the Safeway store last Sunday. We know, from our friendship with Po, that his first concern at all times was the safety and security of people with whom and for whom he struggled. The action last Sunday (Sept. 14)[13] most certainly was in outrage against the giant Safeway corporation which exploits and rips off the people, particularly poor people.

If the Sept. 18 action by the George Jackson Brigade, in its choice of location, was intended to be an act of solidarity with Po, as well as with the SLA, then its gross disregard for the safety of the people was in total contradiction of everything Po stood for.

Po's bomb was placed so that only mechanical equipment could be damaged. It was done at night, so that the safety of passerby would be assured. The Sept. 18 action failed to take even minimal precautions, and injured seven people. As Po's friends, we know he would have strongly disagreed with such lack of responsible concern. There can be no connection between the hasty actions of people whose callousness injures others, and Po, whose concern for others was so great that concern for himself became secondary.

"The true revolutionary is guided by great feelings of love."
—Che Guevara

New Year 1976

*The following communiqué appeared as "George Jackson Brigade" in
Dragon, no. 6, January 1976, 21. In contrast to the impatience of the
"Capitol Hill Safeway" communiqué, this document explains the reason for
targeting the chain. It includes an unqualified rejection of the Brigade's attack of several months earlier, and carries an explicit rejection of the "terrorist" label.*

At 12 midnight December 31, 1975, we exploded two bombs
at Safeway's main office for the Seattle area in Bellevue, Wa.
Simultaneously, in support of the City Light workers and their long
and courageous strike,[14] we bombed the main transformer supplying
power to the very rich Laurelhurst Neighborhood.

City Light, Laurelhurst

We of the George Jackson Brigade are *not* City Light workers, but
we do live and work in Seattle and City Light is our enemy too. For the
past two years we have watched City Light workers stand up and fight
for their rights. This has been in the face of a massive campaign by the
ruling class to force poor and working people to shoulder the burden of
this economic crisis. So we have chosen to bring in the New Year with
respect and solidarity for the brave example the City Light workers
have set by sabotaging the power source for Laurelhurst.

We urge the City Light workers to rely on the people; to tap, expand and direct the widespread support you have as a means to win
your strike and to further the complex process of revolution and liberation for all oppressed people. And we urge all workers, poor, oppressed and progressive people in Seattle [to] openly and materially
demonstrate their support for City Light workers.

Safeway Offices and Depot, Bellevue

> They call us bandits, yet every time most Black (and poor and
> working)[15] people pick up our paychecks we are being robbed. Every
> time we walk into a store in our neighborhood we are being held up.
> And every time we pay our rent, the landlord sticks a gun in our ribs.
> —Assata Shakur,[16] Black Liberation Army Sister

Safeway is one of the largest corporations in the world. It is the
world's largest food chain and a powerful agribusiness and imperialist.

Safeway has effectively monopolized all facets of the food processing, distribution, and retailing industry on the west coast. As a large international landowner, it is the recipient of large federal subsidies and [has] actively forced the small farmer from his land and livelihood. As a large grower, Safeway has consistently and violently oppressed the farmworkers and fought their struggle for a union. Safeway makes its superprofits by charging poor and working people outrageously inflated prices for nutritionally deficient and chemically poisoned food.

So it is not surprising that Safeway has been the target of massive resistance by the people including pickets, boycotts, educationals, demonstrations and anti-trust suits. And it is not surprising that Safeway has been the target of bombings and armed actions up and down the west coast throughout 1975.

Early this summer, at the 15th and John Safeway in Seattle a plainclothes mercenary shot an "alleged" shoplifter. In September our comrade Po in an independent action, died while arming a bomb behind that store. A few days later, and only a few hours after the capture of the SLA, we exploded a bomb inside that store in an attempt to complete the job Po began. Safeway disregarded our warning, and people inside the store shopping were injured.

This action was wrong because we brought violence and terror into a poor neighborhood; a neighborhood already racked with the violence of hunger and the terror of the police.

We have tried to make this New Year's attack a reflection of the lessons we learned this past year. We are not terrorists. Safeway and City Lights are our own class enemies and the class enemies of all who have felt hunger in their bellies or who have been cold in the winter because they couldn't pay their electric bill. We have no qualms about bringing discriminate violence to the rich.

> For us there is always armed struggle. There are two kinds of armed struggle; the armed struggle in which the people fight empty handed, unarmed, while the imperialists or colonialists are armed and kill our people; and the armed struggle in which we prove we are not crazy by taking up arms to fight back against the criminal arms of the imperialists.
> —Amilcar Cabral,[17] Guinea

LOVE AND STRUGGLE
HAPPY NEW YEAR!
THE GEORGE JACKSON BRIGADE

On the Weather Underground, Class Struggle and Armed Struggle
Unfinished draft . . . January 1976

The following is a draft statement on behalf of the nascent George Jackson Brigade, which Bruce Seidel had been working on at the time he was killed. Turned over to the press after his death, it directly implicated him in the Capitol Hill Safeway bombing and the New Year's Eve attacks. Though the Brigade claimed all of these, they had remained unsolved.

The document is in response to a 1975 statement by the Weather Underground stressing the need for "politics in command." The Weather Underground first made this turn, though without employing this particular phrase, in their "New Day, Changing Weather" communiqué, in which they blamed the mindset which allowed the townhouse disaster to occur on military considerations being in command. This debate came to the United States via Régis Debray's Revolution in the Revolution? Armed Struggle and Political Struggle in Latin America. *Translated into English in 1967, this popular text distilled the contributions of the Cuban Revolution and related them to non-conventional anti-imperialist warfare throughout Latin America. Debray insisted that the military apparatus—the "foco"— be in control of political considerations. The text reproduced below is contained in Walter Wright, "Slain Man's Document: Self-implication in Three Bombings,"* Post-Intelligencer, *April 21, 1976.*

> "There will be a special page in the book of life for the men (women) who have crawled back from the grave. This page will tell of utter defeat, ruin, passivity, and subjection in one breath; and in the next overwhelming victory and fulfillment. So take care of yourself and hold on."[18]

For many years, thru both our words and deeds, we have consciously supported and respected the example set by the Weather Underground Organization. After collectively reading and discussing Weather's last two articles, "Politics in Command" and "Armed Struggle and the SLA,"[19] we found points which we wholeheartedly agree, points which we disagree, and we have many questions and contradictions that we wish to address.

To begin, we certainly agree that "the only path to the final defeat of imperialism and the building of socialism is revolutionary war." And we wholeheartedly agree that revolutionary war is a class war which is "complex and ongoing" and, as Martin Sostre[20] wrote, that it includes mass struggle and clandestine struggle, peaceful and violent, political, economic, cultural, and military, where all forms are developed "harmoniously around the axis of armed struggle."

We ourselves are a product of this complex and ongoing struggle. We are a product of various cultures, neighborhoods, 'fronts' and forms of struggle. We have learned and directed the issues, grievances and rage that eat away ourselves and all oppressed peoples. Like most, our practice has varied from leafleting, boycotting, participating in strikes, bombing and coordinated guerrilla attacks . . . whatever the situation called for.

From all this we have learned what the Weather Underground has re-affirmed, the important lesson of Ho Chi Minh: "A military without politics is like a tree without roots—useless and dangerous." This is Marx, Engels, Lenin and Mao Tse Tung. It is the lesson of Cabral, who very consciously distinguished between militarists and armed militants. And it is the lesson of George Jackson, who taught his fellow prisoners that it is not enough to be fearless warriors; rather, we must become organizers, educators and revolutionaries. And, of course, putting politics in command is the opposite dictum the U.S. military and police forces teach their soldiers and recruits.

For us in the George Jackson Brigade, we understand politics in command to mean something different than just paying lip service to struggles of oppressed peoples, writing radical and/or Marxist essays, or even placing pipebombs in a shit-house adjoining the local FBI office. For us, Politics in Command means understanding that continual struggle and contradictions exist on three fronts: internal, among friends, and against the enemy. And, being revolutionary means critically and self-critically analyzing these contradictions, resolving them and transforming the resolution into unity and strength. In essence, it means honesty or purpose, change and growth.

Internally and collectively sexism, impatience, and individualism remain our prime contradictions. Our contradictions among our friends primarily stem from our not achieving self-reliance sooner. Consequently, we have bickered and quarreled with friends over resources and support. Unlike stated in "Armed Struggle and the SLA," we do not and have not in the past, "evaluated other forces primarily by their support for armed struggle." And it has *not* been our practice to "ridicule the process of developing political analysis and organization . . ." We do, however, evaluate "other forces"; specifically the local Prairie Fire group, the now defunct Seattle Liberation Coalition and their false leaders ____, ____, ____,[21] from their commitment to servicing the people and their pronouncements on supporting armed struggle. Our judgments are based on honesty; on the gap or lack of gap between their words and deeds. In more than one situation, we were told or led to believe that we had support but when we arrived with a communique or resource needs for ourselves [none was to be found]; or last winter for Indian brothers on the run, we found many old doors locked tight.[22] While some new ones opened up, all in all we relearned to go directly to the people and to rely on the people.

Our key error in fighting the enemy—an age old error—has been in not clearly identifying and isolating the ruling class from behind the many classes of people, laws, and gimmicks where he hides. Last September we understood and wrote, "that our attacks must be discriminate and both serve and educate the every day person."[23] But, we wrongly planted a bomb inside Safeway located in a poor neighborhood. On New Years Eve we took two bombs to Safeway's main offices for the Seattle area in the very white suburbs of Bellevue; and simultaneously in solidarity with a long and progressive city workers strike, we destroyed the main power source for Seattle's very rich Laurelhurst neighborhood. On New Year's Eve our attack was "specific, comprehensible . . . and humane"; to quote the local media, "it was well planned and bloodless."[24]

In 1848, with all of Europe in turmoil and on the verge of revolution, Marx and Engels published the *Communist Manifesto* not as a theoretical treatise, but as a working paper. It reflects organization, a program, and a solution. And, as we all know, Lenin spent his entire life teaching the need for an organization "which spans periods of great activity and uprising, draws lessons and corrects errors . . . which recruits organizers and deepens their ties with the people . . ." And, Lenin successfully built and sustained a party of "professional revolutionaries . . . capable of leading the whole fight of the people." During the same time, Lenin was in Europe, an old woman traveled from strike to strike, from mining camps to mills to sweat shops all thru the cities and countryside of Amerika. Mother Jones exemplified what Le Duan[25] must have said many times: "organize, organize, organize."

So we wholeheartedly agree with the Weather Underground on the need for organization and the future goal of building a party to lead, direct, learn and be accountable to working people and all oppressed peoples. And we too, "would disagree with those who would have armed struggle wait for the creation of a leading proletariat party." For as Cabral said and Attica, McAlester[26] and San Quentin[27] taught us: "there is always armed struggle."

> ". . . any serious organization of people must carry with it, from the start, a potential threat of revolutionary violence—after all the 'stakes are high.'"
> —George Jackson

LOVE & STRUGGLE
Bruce

International Women's Day

The full text of the following communiqué was printed as "Text of Brigade Communique" in the Post-Intelligencer, *March 31, 1976, and in* Dragon, *no. 8 (April 1976): 7–9.*

On March 10th, members of the George Jackson Brigade rescued our comrade John W. Sherman from police custody. John had been captured during our unsuccessful attempt to expropriate $43,000.00 from the Tukwila branch of the Pacific National Bank of Washington. A brutal attack by Tukwila police and King County sheriffs left our comrade Bruce Seidel dead, Sherman shot in the jaw, and Sherman and comrade Ed Mead in custody. All other participating units of the Brigade escaped after firing on police from the rear in an attempt to assist our three comrades trapped in the bank.[28]

There can be no revolution without money—for weapons, explosives, survival, organizing, printing, etc. The people are poor. We will make the ruling class pay for its own destruction by expropriating our funds from them and their banks.

We have so far identified the following tactical criticisms of the Tukwila action: 1) We were unprepared for the level of violence that the pigs were willing to bring down on us and the innocent people in the bank. We should have had better combat training. 2) We waited too long to open fire on the pigs. We should have fired without hesitation on the first pig to arrive. Failure to do this allowed the police to murder our comrade while he was trying to surrender, and endangered everyone in the bank. 3) A silent alarm was tripped when we removed all of the money from a teller's drawer. When the phone began to ring to authenticate the alarm, our comrades should have split immediately with whatever they had in their hands. Instead, they stayed to clean out the safe. 4) Our comrades across the street should have had more firepower than they did. We had an enormous tactical advantage which we were unable to exploit because it took so long to bring the superior firepower that we did have into action. 5) Our getaway route was excellent. Comrades[29] were able to remain in the area, firing on the pigs until the three comrades inside the bank were taken into custody, and still get away clean. Over all, this action failed because we were not prepared to meet police terrorism with a sufficient level of revolutionary violence.

In the course of the escape raid it became necessary to shoot the police officer guarding Sherman. We did not shoot officer Johnson in retaliation for Bruce's murder. In fact, it was our intention to avoid shooting him. He was shot because he failed to cooperate as fully as possible with the comrade who was assigned to him. One of the many lessons we learned from Tukwila is that we cannot afford to give the police any slack when confronting them. While we don't particularly want to shoot police, we don't particularly care either. We will shoot without hesitation any police officer who endangers us. Also, we fully intend to get justice for Bruce's murder, but we prefer to retaliate against the murder[er]s themselves: officers [Joseph L.] Abbott and [Robert W.] Matthews.

Bruce saw himself as an inevitable product of the mass movement. Years of struggle for progressive change taught him that poor and working people will not listen to communists who are unwilling and unprepared to back their demands with revolutionary violence. Bruce understood the need for a movement with real (not symbolic) teeth, and he set about changing this understanding into a reality. His contribution to this process is beyond measure. Had he survived beyond his mid-twenties, he would have changed far more than the shape of Northwest politics.

Bruce recognized and implemented the need to expropriate banks as a means of furthering specific political goals. He also understood the possible risk of capture or death involved in such an undertaking. Unlike so many of his racist counterparts, Bruce did not believe the lives of U.S. communists to be somehow more precious than those of comrades throughout the world who are fighting and dying in the international class war against imperialism.

The death of our comrade weighs like a mountain on our shoulders. We loved Bruce in life and we love him in death. His passing leaves us with more than grief and sorrow; it has kindled a rage that will not be abated until his killers and the class they serve are destroyed along with the misery and suffering they bring to all humanity.

We are learning to avoid the self-appointed "left"; to go directly to the people and to rely on them for our strength. The people in our community have made enormous sacrifices and have given us shelter and sustenance and safety from the pigs. Because of this, the escape raid is a complete success. The victory belongs to the people.

We're also learning to rely on ourselves. Using urban guerrilla ingenuity, members of the George Jackson Brigade removed the torsion arch bars from comrade Sherman's mouth.

Our comrade is free, the pigs have been badly beaten and they're throwing a temper tantrum. They are using their Grand Jury to try to terrorize the people by issuing subpoenas to numerous progressive people and hauling them before their star chamber. Now they have started taking hostages from among progressive above ground fighters. But they will soon learn that the people don't terrorize so easily. And they would do well to remember that what goes around—comes around.

We send our greetings and love to our comrade Ed Mead still in custody and to all freedom fighters above ground, underground and locked down. Take heart Ed, we miss you and we will continue fighting. Later.

We urge all progressive people in Seattle to organize and fight the Grand Jury. Struggle for correct politics. Don't talk to the FBI. Don't testify. Don't collaborate. Support the hostages.

CELEBRATE INTERNATIONAL WOMEN'S DAY
CELEBRATE THE ROLE OF WOMEN IN STRUGGLE

> Love and Struggle,
> GEORGE JACKSON BRIGADE
> March, 1976

In order to authenticate this communique, we are sending a bullet recently fired from a gun used across the street from the bank to the *Post-Intelligencer* (Seattle). We are also sending one of the torsion arch bars from comrade Sherman's mouth to KZAM, a Bellevue radio station.

> We're not all white and we're not all men
> said a white male member
> of our collective
> to a liberal masked media man
>
> Why struggle with
> arms, tools, commie Q's?
> dykes niggers cons
> when you could slip away with
> left support action
> or vague mass movement construction
>
> I can love
> I can slip into class, bitch privilege

love don't mean unity with another
privilege doesn't change alienation
both mean slipping into darkness
alienation is masses of couples buying
coca cola and grapes at safeway
and owning own stereos t.v.'s and cribs

Just like slumlords pimps I.T.T.
organized us
We will dis organize
learn struggle and skills
move ment action new ways

Not the vague vanguard
We are a collection
of oppressed people turning
inside out with action
this united few breaks
barriers of
race class sex
workers and lumpen
all going together
combating dull sameness
corporations, government
and the established rule of
straight white cocks

I cannot be one
acting alone with my
little toe outside the line
its both feet
whole body
ain't no turning back now
no more mass meetings stale mating action

Loving learning laboring
with a few comrades
oh won't you harbor me?
joining you sistah brother
in freedom, Sue,[30] Assata[31]

George,[32] Jill,[33] Martin[34]
new family being sane
small, not like charlie's
leader ship[35]

We are cozy cuddly
armed and dangerous
and we will
raze the fucking prisons
to the ground

[signed by hand] Love and Struggle, GJB

Community Response
A LETTER TO THE GEORGE JACKSON BRIGADE
snapdragon

This letter, dated April 21, 1976, was printed in Dragon *no. 9. Ed Mead penned a detailed reply in the following issue: "A Note to Snapdragon,"* Dragon, *no. 10, September 1976, 38–43.*

Sisters and Brothers of the *Dragon*:

My love to you. I have some criticisms of actions that have taken place recently: this is to the George Jackson Brigade (Seattle).

First I have some heavy criticisms of the rest of us that did not participate in these actions. We failed to support, communicate doubts or encouragement, and for the most part we completely avoided any responsibility for actions that took place. I would say we did not really believe in the reality of what was happening until we were forced to, by fear of our own individual safety.

At this time there are more people who take responsibility, and a clearer conception of reality.

Criticisms of the GJB:

1. I think there is prevailing confusion between aboveground support and underground action. It is irresponsible for any individual or group to provide both aboveground and underground action at the same time. A guerrilla does not need to prove her/himself by public words. She may appear harmless, liberal, spaced out, ineffectual. He should be overlooked. The ruling class and their police dogs will wake up to your courage and brilliance in the night—let them sleep and befuddle themselves during the day.

Don't expect the *Dragon* to provide safe shelter. Don't ask an underground fighter to make a speech at a demonstration.

It is inevitable that many of us will move through a period of aboveground support of armed struggle before deciding to act. This is dangerous. (Recognize this danger, brothers and sisters, and deal with it.)

Also: aboveground support is just as dangerous. We all know what's coming. People, don't guilt-trip yourselves into choosing danger because it's dangerous. There is enough danger to go around already. Make decisions on other grounds than to prove to yourself you have courage.

2. People supporting you should know only as much as they need to know. They need to know: How much danger they are in. What risks

are you taking with their lives? They need to know: What to do if/when something goes wrong. Plan for arrest. Plan for death. Take care of business. People must not be left lost and ignorant as to how to protect you (and themselves).

Watch out for vulnerable people and maneuver them to safe places. When a house is potentially unsafe to live in, don't invite children, parolees, aliens or fugitives to live there.

Watch out for careless, frivolous people. Don't let them get too close to you.

3. Why are you doing this? We are not satisfied with your reasons. Expropriation is not enough: Robin Hood was wrong. Robbing from the rich to give to the poor will not work, because the rich are far more efficient at robbing than we are. They own the guns and the laws.

4. Don't give information to the press that you would not give to the police![36] Don't say how many people were involved in an action if they don't know—don't give away details of how you did it and who you are. You are the people. That's enough. You don't have to specify that you are Chinks and Faggots. This tends to make vulnerable sub-communities of the people betrayed and endangered, and certainly exposes specific people to harassment they do not need. Remember, remember, remember—you are the underground. Let them guess who you are. And why leave *out* some of us? You are all of us—or not, as your actions prove.

The early stages of armed struggle seem to be as destructive and alienating as an urban riot. We are losing people, and faith in each other, and they lose, TEMPORARILY, a few dollars. Which they get back, from us.

"Are they *stupid*," someone asked [referring to the Brigade], and she needed to know, "or are they not with us?"

I know you are with us, and I know we can learn from our mistakes, no matter how costly they have been, because we have each other. Venceremos.

I love you,
snapdragon

May Day

The following communiqué was printed in Orca, *no. 1, Fall 1977, 10–12. It also survives as a teletype dated May 13, 1977, from the Seattle offices of the FBI to headquarters in Washington, DC. Former Brigade members consider this one of their most successful communiqués; the demand that the* Seattle Times *interview prisoners about the on-going strike at the Washington State Penitentiary was eventually met, though not immediately and the* Times *did not acknowledge pressure from the Brigade as a reason for doing so.*

In reporting on the contents of the "May Day" communiqué, Seattle Times *reporter[37] John Arthur Wilson explained the* Times's *failure to interview prisoners by stating: "Prisoners were in lockup and unavailable for interviews when a* Times *reporter went to Walla Walla last week."[38] Wilson was referring to Paul Henderson, who on May 5 began reporting on what had by then become "the longest running lockup in the prison's history."[39]*

The first reference to the inmates' perspective on the strike in the Times *did not come until May 23, and it still was not a quote and did not indicate direct contact with anyone incarcerated. The penultimate paragraph in an article by Wilson stated: "Inmates say they have been on strike to protest shakedowns in the segregation unit and harassment of prisoners by officials."[40]*

On May 24, the slated reopening of the institution was thwarted by a walkout of approximately forty percent of the guards on the morning shift.[41] That day for the first time in their coverage of the strike the Times *printed words from a prisoner. Though signed by "the Walla Walla Brothers," an activist group of inmates confined in the institution's Intensive Security Unit, the twenty-three page letter to the* Times *was authored by captured GJB member Ed Mead.[42] It acknowledged that, "We have all been convicted of crimes and understand that the state is lawfully entitled to its pound of flesh," but complained: "they are taking far more than their rightful pound." The letter demanded the abolition of a contract between prisoners and the administration which stated that an inmate could be held in segregation for the remainder of his minimum term if found guilty of violating institutional codes. Regarding placement in the isolation wing, the letter asserted: "The point we are trying to make . . . is that there are no standards for release beyond the subjective judgment of the administration. If this judgment were anywhere near fair, we would not complain."*

Other demands included:

Release of all prisoners who have spent more than ten consecutive days in isolation.

Visitation rights for prisoners in maximum-security blocks, as is given the rest of the population.

Full use of the maximum-security yard and "adequate recreational equipment" and exercise periods.

Access to personal property, such as tape recorders, televisions, books and hobby supplies, and complete commissary privileges.

Direct access to the prison law library so inmates can do legal research on pending litigation.

In closing, Mead wrote that he and his comrades in the isolation unit needed "breathing space" and wished for the administration to "treat us as human beings and [to] relate to us in an honest and lawful manner."[43]

The first direct interview with a prisoner came only after the strike ended on May 25. Henderson spoke with Wayne Steeves, a Canadian-born professional thief on his eighth incarceration. In contrast to the "Walla Walla Brothers" quoted by Wilson, Steeves was, in Henderson's estimation, a "non-assertive inmate."[44] Steeves shared his experience of forced inactivity: "I found it very rough. You've got to try and keep busy somehow in there, otherwise you'll start to flip out. You can only sleep so many hours a day and your mind starts playing tricks on you when you're not asleep. The silence gets to you and so does the noise."

The Times *by no means became an organ for prisoners' voices, but in the constant conflicts that wracked the state penitentiary through 1979 they did occasionally convey perspectives of prisoners, including Mead, and outside advocates such as the United Friends and Families of Prisoners at Walla Walla. In the immediate wake of the 1977 lockdown, the latter helped secure a commitment for a legislative subcommittee and a citizens' review panel to investigate charges of harassment and brutality of prisoners by staff.[45]*

Today the George Jackson Brigade bombed two Bellevue branches of Rainier[46] National Bank in support of the prisoners' struggle at Walla Walla state prison. We chose Rainier National Bank as a target because of its links to the *Seattle Times*, a bourgeois daily newspaper. The *Seattle Times* has led the propaganda campaign in Seattle against the prisoners.

Walla Walla

The past year had seen the strengthening of prisoner struggles throughout the state of Washington. There have been hunger strikes, work strikes, demonstrations and uprisings at Purdy, McNeil Island,

and Walla Walla. For more than six months the prisoners at Walla Walla have been in the forefront of these struggles.

In October and in December, 1976, prisoners in the segregation units (the Hole), staged a hunger strike to protest guards tampering with their food and the overall brutality of the hole. In January, the Walla Walla brothers issued demands from the hole which included: shutting down the infamous behavior modification programs; firing three brutal employees of the mental health unit (Psychiatric torture unit); collectivization of the therapy programs; and due process in the hole. Throughout this period the Resident Government Council (RGC) tried to negotiate with the prison administration around grievances. The prison administration and the state government steadfastly ignored these efforts.

And things continued to get worse in the hole.

On April 5, a cigarette lighter bomb blew up in the hand of a particularly hated Walla Walla segregation guard. This happened while he was escorting a prisoner from the prison to Walla Walla county courthouse. (Although police there immediately claimed "good leads" and a "suspect" inside the prison, they haven't so far charged anybody. Perhaps they are waiting for the right scapegoat.)

Using this incident as an excuse, the prison administration, led by [Superintendent] B.J. Rhay, immediately launched an attack on all prisoner resistance and organization. Starting with the hole, they have systematically ransacked and looted all cells and meeting areas.

On April 10, while the administration was still busy with the hole, prisoners in the general population responded to this attack with a well planned and executed raid on the prison store. About 300 prisoners participated in this raid using fires as diversions.

Immediately following the raid, all maximum security prisoners went to their cells and locked up, starting a strike. A few days later, prisoner representatives issued a list of 14 "grievances" and a demand to meet with DSHS official and outside observers.[47] This list included protests against racial discrimination, the lack of meaningful work inside the prison, and poor medical treatment.

By April 27, a "Blue Ribbon Commission" appointed by Governor D.L. Ray had met twice with the RGC over these grievances. This commission was led by Harlan McNutt, a person the prisoners had specifically asked not to see. (His appointment was billed in the Seattle press as an "act of defiance" by the Governor.)

On May 7, as a result of these meetings, McNutt ordered the following "changes" at Walla Walla:

Transfer of "mental patients" to Eastern State Hospital
Accelerate work release opportunities
Improve dental care; hire a second dentist for 1,000 men
Regular sanitary inspections
Be easier on visitor searches (but allow orifice searches for "reasonable cause")
Transfer Associate Warden Paul Harvey (supposedly "coincidental"; at the same time, he denied the existence of racial discrimination.)

These "changes" are absurd. They actually consist of three attacks and four empty promises.

The involuntary transfer of "mental patients" to Eastern State is a fascist attack on prisoner resistance. Involuntary transfer of any kind allows the administration to ship out "troublemakers" and break up prisoner organization. In December, 1974, Walla Walla prisoners seized parts of the prison and took hostages after negotiations failed to resolve their demands against behavior modification and involuntary transfer. Twenty years ago, Eastern State Hospital was notorious as a torture factory used to break prisoner resistance. They shall not get away with it again.

Denying the existence of racial discrimination at Walla Walla authorizes the blatant racism that is the daily practice of the administration and guards there.

Harvey is being foisted off on Shelton where he can do his dirty work on younger, less experienced prisoners.[48]

As for sanitary inspections, better dental care, better visiting conditions, etc., we've heard it all before. We'll believe it when we see it.

The Seattle Times

The press plays a particularly important role in prisoner struggles. Prisoners are isolated from society and have no printing presses or money or outside organization to tell their story to the people. If people knew what really goes on in prison and understood what their true effects on society are they would shut them down tomorrow and send the parasites who run them to work. (Real work, useful work, hard labor, maybe?)

The role of the press is to keep us from knowing by telling us only what the rulers of the prisons want us to know. Period. When the level of struggle inside the prison forces them to admit that struggle is going on, they make it appear to be spontaneous, isolated incidents. Clearly, the present strike at Walla Walla is part of ongoing and progressive mass struggle there.

All of this is true of all of the bourgeois press in Seattle. The *Seattle Times* however, has led the propaganda campaign. The *Times* is not, as its bosses and editorial writers would have us believe, an independent and objective observer and reporter of fact. It is a weapon used by the ruling class to lie to us.

Throughout the struggle the *Times* has consistently printed and supported whatever the prison bosses had to say about what was going on. It had printed long diatribes by paranoid guards who are fearful of retaliation for their crimes. It has told us that prisoners have no real grievances; that the problem is really just "overcrowding"; and that prisoners are just animals anyway, duped into struggle by a few troublemakers. By not printing the RGC grievances, the *Times* has refused to even pretend to be objective.

The *Seattle Times* is tied with a thousand threads to the big capitalists who run this country. They are owned, like most bourgeois newspapers in this country, by one huge conglomerate; in this case Knight-Ridder Newspapers, Inc. William Pennington, President of the *Times*, is a director of Rainier National Bank (RNB) and other large corporations. Through these companies, he is tied to Sea-First, SafeCo, Boeing, Weyerhaeuser, Paccar, etc., etc. The owners and bosses of these companies are the real criminals—the real enemies of society. Capitalism and capitalists cause crime and prison. We attacked RNB because we are determined to seek out and attack this real enemy, behind all his fronts and flunkies.

We demand that the *Seattle Times* print the entire text of the RGC grievances and any RGC responses to the latest "changes." We demand that the *Seattle Times* print the text of this communique and any future communique the GJB issues. We also demand that the *Seattle Times* interview prisoners in struggle in the hole at Walla Walla and print those interviews.

We have no illusions that the *Times* will, because of this action, agree to any of these demands. But we will continue to attack the *Times* and its bosses until they do give in. However long that may take.

At the same time, we understand that, flunkies though they are, DSHS, the Department of Adult Corrections, the Governor, reactionary Warden B.J. Rhay, and the guards and staff at Walla Walla are the general staff and front line troops of the ruling class. They direct and carry out the bourgeoisie's attempts to crush prisoner resistance. They are responsible for their own actions and will someday meet the peoples' justice.

The Brigade

"There are two things to remember about revolution: we are going to get our asses kicked, and we are going to win."

So the GJB is back. We got our asses kicked real bad at Tukwila a year ago, and we've spent this last year licking our wounds and learning our trade. We've accumulated a lot of equipment and an enormous amount of experience. We've done 6 teller robberies in Oregon banks for more than $25,000. Without firing a shot. In the course of this, we've learned a lot about the police, the front line troops of capitalism.

Although we are armed and will defend ourselves if attacked, we are not crazy. We do not, as the FBI has claimed, "Believe in shooting it out with an army of police." We understand that we are vastly outgunned and out numbered and, if we are trapped, we will make a positive effort to surrender. But we have corrected the error that we criticized at Tukwila. We have a higher level of combat training and will never again be caught unprepared by the violence of an individual police officer. If captured, we will continue to fight wherever we end up.

Overall, we live pretty much like everybody else. We have landlord hassles, the car needs repair, the wiring in our home is bad. We are stunned (like everybody else) by the prices when we buy groceries.

For several months now we have been concentrating on political study and struggle to clarify what we think about revolution in this country. As individuals we have many disagreements. We will have more to say in the future about political struggle within the Brigade. We need criticism and analysis of our words and our actions.

We believe that capitalism is the source of all oppression at this time, and that revolution requires that it be overthrown by force of arms by the masses of poor and working people in this country. We believe that the struggle against racism, national oppression and sexism in all its forms are part of the struggle against capitalism. We are firmly united on these points.

> ". . . if people on the outside do not understand the necessity of defending them (prisoners) through force of arms, then it is because these people on the outside do not yet realize that they are in an immediate danger of being thrown into concentration camps themselves, tortured, or shot down in the streets for expressing their beliefs."
> —Communique 10, SLA

Remember the Compton Massacre! (May 17, 1974)

>In the Spirit of Mayday!
>Love and Struggle,
>the George Jackson Brigade
>May 12, 1977

Community Response
MESSAGE TO THE PROGRESSIVE COMMUNITY ON THE MEDIA AND THE
GEORGE JACKSON BRIGADE
The Walla Walla Brothers

This is excerpted from a longer statement written by incarcerated Brigade member Ed Mead in conjunction with other prisoners in the isolation wing in the Washington State Penitentiary in Walla Walla. The circumstances point to the risk of a closed-circuit feedback loop faced by urban guerrillas: their own members get captured, then write on behalf of prisoners generally, providing a constituency encouraging the continued actions of the outside group—actions that will inevitably send more members to prison. This cycle engulfed the Red Army Faction in West Germany. [49]

The reaction of ISU prisoners upon learning of the [May 12] bombing[s] was positive, enthusiastic and unanimous. The target was perfect and the timing ideal. [The George Jackson Brigade] showed themselves familiar with the essence of our struggle as well as the identity and nature of the enemy. We view the Brigade action as another level of the support we so urgently need. They were able to put the rulers on the spot for their criminal abuse of the power of the press, and they did so in a manner that could not have been as quickly and effectively accomplished by conventional means. We see the Brigade action as an example of armed propaganda at its best.

SUMMER SOLSTICE

The following communiqué was printed in Orca, *no. 1, Fall 1977, 12.*

Yesterday the George Jackson Brigade expropriated about $4,200 from the Factoria branch of the Rainier National Bank.

A month ago, May 21, 1977, we expropriated about $1,300 from the Newport Hills state liquor store.

Armed expropriation is a vital part of our work. Apart from the everyday cost of living (which is as a terrible burden for us as for everyone else); weapons, ammunition, explosives, medical supplies, vehicles, etc. cost an enormous amount of money. We will continue to take this money from the ruling class and its state. Most people understand that banks and the state are the real robbers of all society; and that the profit motive is the biggest robbery in history.

But we will under no circumstances steal so much as a penny from small businesses or from the working people. When we robbed the liquor store, for example, it was necessary to take the manager's entire purse because the liquor store money was in it. The day after the robbery we returned the manager's purse with all of her own personal money (about $45).

We are not prepared at this time to present a detailed analysis of the politics of armed robbery, but we feel it is necessary to claim these robberies to counter the attempt of the police to hide these actions from the people.

Both the King County Police and the FBI *know* that we did both these robberies. Exactly why they have chosen to hide this fact is a mystery to us, but we can see at least two possible advantages to them in their silence:

They would like very much to convince people that serious and successful revolutionary armed struggle is impossible and does not exist in this country, let alone in the Northwest.

One of the principal functions of the police is to repress progressive struggles and the left—sometimes openly, sometimes secretly by infiltration and harassment. Their strategy at this time is to do it secretly. If they tell people about our actions, they will also alert them to be more vigilant against these tactics.

Although any bank, ruling class corporation or state agency is fair game for revolutionary expropriation, we chose RNB this time because the *Seattle Times* (RNB's crime partner) still refuses to print any communication from the Walla Walla prisoners. In particular they have ignored the prisoners' strike that continued in the hole *after* the lock-up ended. The strike is part of the continuing struggle against the brutal conditions in the hole.

> EXPROPRIATE THE EXPROPRIATORS
> Love and Struggle
> George Jackson Brigade
> June 21, 1977

Capitalism Is Organized Crime

The following communiqué appeared in Orca, *no. 1, Fall 1977, 13-14.*

> . . . any serious organizing of people must carry with it, from the start, a potential threat of revolutionary violence—after all 'the stakes are high.'
> —George Jackson

Today we bombed the main substation for the state capitol complex in Olympia. The purpose of this action is to support the struggle of prisoners in the hole at the Walla Walla state prison. These men are still on strike as a focus of their militant fight against illegal confinement, barbarism and torture.

The ISU (Intensive Security Unit—the hole) prisoners have issued the following ten "Immediate demands." In solidarity with their strike, we demand the same changes—now!

1. Abolish the use of contracts and release all prisoners being held on contract violations.

2. Stop arbitrary punishments and conduct hearing committees in accordance to WAC rules.

3. Release all prisoners on Ad[ministrative] Seg[regation] status unless the warden can show a clear and present danger to prison security and order.

4. Remove all prisoners from "A" tier who have served more than 10 consecutive days on isolation status.

5. Give ISU prisoners the same visitation rights accorded the prisoners on the mainline.

6. Full use of ISU yard, not the cage, and provision of adequate recreational equipment on each tier. Exercise periods should be substantially longer than one hour.

7. Full access to personal property in the general population such as cassette recorders, TVs, packages from home, books, hobby materials, art supplies, etc.

8. Complete commissary rights for prisoners on Ad Seg status unless the warden makes a *written* finding that a specific item is an actual danger to order.

9. Direct access to the prison law library for prisoners in the ISU who have active litigation pending in the courts.

10. Clean up and paint the ISU; provide adequate clothing; and stop the constant harassment of prisoners.

These demands require no special "blue ribbon commissions"; no new legislation, and no budget increases. They demand only that the prison administration obey its own laws and adopt minimum standards of human decency. We will continue to provide armed support for this just struggle until all of these demands are fully met.

The main response of the prison bureaucrats and their guards to this struggle has been to deepen and intensify the repression and brutality; and to provoke the prisoners to violence with deliberate insults, constant harassment, and assaults. When these men rise up in self defense, the administrators are fully prepared to slaughter them as a final solution to resistance.

Public attention *must* be focused on Walla Walla; the actual conditions of torture and humiliation must be widely publicized. Armed work is only one of many forms of support necessary to the struggle of the Walla Walla prisoners. We urge people to seek out the truth about the Walla Walla struggle and to actively fight for the lives and safety of these prisoners. In particular, it is the absolute duty of progressive people on the left to join this fight.

Also, we give notice to the ruling class and its state that we hold them responsible as individuals for the safety of our comrade Ed Mead, and his comrades in ISU.

The struggle of *ALL* prisoners against their oppression in this country is a struggle for justice. It is a struggle that demands that society live up to its obligation to provide full productive life for *all* citizens— an obligation that capitalism *can not* meet.

Capitalism causes crime. Overwhelmingly, the victims of crime are poor and Third World people. Street crime is caused and perpetuated by joblessness and underemployment; by a ruling class that uses people for its own profit and discards them when it has no more profitable use for them. The capitalist prison and its bureaucracy is a loathsome parasite on society. Its sole purpose is to administer the warehousing and repression of human beings for whom capitalism has no use and no solution.

We congratulate the Walla Walla prisoners for winning their long struggle to get rid of bloody B. J. Rhay. But the new warden, Douglas Vinzant, is hardly an improvement. Although he is pretending to be a good guy, both he and his boss Harlan McNutt continue to ignore the hole and claim it isn't a problem. Be careful of these hoodlums comrades; no matter what they say, it is impossible to serve both the capitalists' prisons and the prisoners.

> There will be a special page in the book of
> life for the women and men who have
> crawled back from the grave.
> This page will tell of utter defeat,
> ruin, passivity and subjection
> in one breath; and in the next
> overwhelming victory and fulfillment
> So take care of yourself and hold on.
>   –George Jackson[50]

SUPPORT THE STRUGGLE OF THE ISU PRISONERS

> Love and Struggle,
> The George Jackson Brigade
> July 4, 1977

"Tell No Lies, Claim No Easy Victories"
—Amilcar Cabral, Guinea-Bissau

The following communiqué appeared as "Letters from the GJB—'Tell No Lies,'" Northwest Passage, *August 1–21, 1977, 3, and in* Orca, *no. 1, Fall 1977, 14–15.*

On July 4, 1977, we attempted to destroy the main substation supplying power to the state capitol complex in Olympia. Our reasons for this action are set forth in the communique attached to this letter. The bomb did not explode. Although there is always a chance for mechanical failure in any pipe bomb, we are virtually certain that this was not the case here. This was probably our most carefully built bomb. After the failure at Bellevue, we spent hours on this bomb checking and rechecking every piece of wire, every circuit, every connection, every possibility for failure. We are convinced that the police disarmed it before it was to detonate.

We had three main reasons for choosing this particular target:

1. We wanted to cause sufficient material damage to begin to make it unprofitable for the ruling class and its state to continue their barbarous treatment of the men in the hole at Walla Walla. Even though we obviously cost the police some sleep and labor time, the action was clearly a failure in this regard.

2. We wanted to breakthrough the bourgeois media blackout and reach the ordinary people in this state with the truth about what's going on at Walla Walla. It's too early to tell what effect, if any, this action will have on the blackout.

3. We wanted to localize the effects of this action to state owned and operated buildings only. So far as we can tell, this substation supplies power exclusively to the state complex. This is supported by the statements of three Seattle TV stations.

We made every effort to insure the safety of innocent people in the area of the target. The substation itself is located on the very edge of a residential district. The entire backside of it is deserted trees and brush. Across the street is the block long Washington State Patrol Capitol Security Offices which we determined to be empty at the time. There are two houses and one small apartment building in the immediate area. The nearest house is significantly farther from the target than the nearest house at Laurelhurst. The Laurelhurst explosion caused no damage to nearby dwellings other than window breakage from the concussion. Also, we took care to direct the explosion into the transformer and away from the houses. We gave the police detailed instructions on the location of the substation and exactly which houses needed to be evacuated and which streets should be blocked to insure everyone's utmost safety. All of this is as it should be. We also gave the police a full thirty minutes warning to be sure they had ample time to disarm the bomb. This represents one of the many contradictions in any bombing. One way to resolve this is to booby trap the bomb with mercury switches or trip wires or the like so that it will explode if tampered with. In the past, we have not booby trapped our bombs for fear that some crazy or "heroic" police officer would try to disarm it anyway and blow himself (we don't know of any women bomb squad members) up. We have instead used false booby trap warnings to keep them away. With the mechanical failure of one of our bombs in the Bellevue RNB however, they learned that it was not in fact equipped with a tamperproof switch as we had told them. We discussed this and decided that for this bomb we [would] continue to use a false booby trap warning on the assumption that no one would be crazy enough to try to disarm a bomb that could be booby trapped, even with the Bellevue experience. We were wrong. Now we are faced with the dilemma of either being willing to see some police officer killed trying to disarm a bomb that is truly booby trapped, or being willing to watch them disarm our bombs with impunity.

We welcome all constructive criticism and ideas about this and the other contradictions that surround bombing as a revolutionary tactic.

Love and Struggle,
The George Jackson Brigade
July 4, 1977

Community Response
In response to the George Jackson Brigade Communique of July 4, 1977
Vinegar Beard Collective

The Underground and the GJB

Many have the impression that underground political work and armed struggle are synonymous. This is not the case. Much underground work is performed by providing aid and comfort to fugitive politicals and harassed above-ground activists. Money, equipment and even political leafleting materials are often expropriated as underground work. The GJB has done much outside of armed struggle and in turn have received much support in maintaining their security. The very purpose of the political underground is to secure a functional political organization that opposes the state. To secure it from counter insurgent destruction. In this the GJB is succeeding with the aid of other underground as well as aboveground support. We, who oppose the oppressive economic and political state and ruling class, are assured by the very existence of the GJB and other underground activity that our political security has not been totally breached.

Armed Struggle & Bombing as a Revolutionary Tactic

The GJB in waging armed struggle in support of the politically vulnerable prisoners at the Washington State Penitentiary is exemplary action. Armed struggle waged against the state and the ruling class is a very clear and imperative political statement that the people will not tolerate the intolerable. In this vein bombing as a revolutionary tactic emphasizes to the oppressor that the limits of our resistance will be by any means necessary. The visibility of bombings, and even attempted bombings coupled with political statements ensure people in struggle that the people do control the force to neutralize an oppressive state and capitalistic progress.

"You'll get freedom by letting your enemy know that you'll do anything to get your freedom . . ." MALCOLM X SPEAKS

Booby-trapping Bombs

We oppose the booby-trapping of bombs because when a statement forewarns the people of the approximate time a bomb will detonate, it is a betrayal of the margin of safety to detonate it sooner. But we do feel that in the future the GJB might consider forewarning the people and the state that time to evacuate the area has been sub-stantially reduced because of past police interference with the timing devices. This also will compel the police to double their manpower (I don't believe the police have that much womanpower) and efforts in order to speed up the evacuation. Another alternative is to study the technology of "shaped charges" and thus not be concerned about deto-nating time as it is predictable which way the blast will go.

ALL POWER
TO THE PEOPLE:
The Vinegar Beard Collective

Community Response
A RESPONSE TO THE GEORGE JACKSON BRIGADE
Stagecoach Mary Collective

The following statement, dated August 10, 1977, circulated in the Seattle political community in mimeographed form. It was reprinted in Orca no. 1, 8–9. The membership of this collective has not been disclosed. It composed at least one other letter related to the GJB, a harsh criticism of the first issue of Orca, the periodical dedicated to documenting the exploits of—but not critically processing the impact of—the Brigade. The letter, dated December 5, 1977, appeared on page 32 of the second issue of Orca. A response from the Orca collective, dated December 16, 1977, followed on the next page, while a member of the Left Bank Collective weighed in that the Stagecoach Mary Collective's criticism had been uncomradely.

To date, there has been little principled discussion, coupled with an effective news blackout, on the subject of armed struggle, and in particular, the George Jackson Brigade.[51] The establishment news media has isolated the George Jackson Brigade (GJB) by defining and reporting on it simply as a "terrorist" group, completely ignoring the political principles by which it operates and the connections the Brigade sees between its actions and community organizing. We hope this article sparks continuing discussion.

In writing about the GJB, we feel it is necessary to analyze the role of armed struggle in the United States today. The media and the U.S government would like us to believe that those involved in armed actions against the State are the ones that are initiating the violence and terrorism. In actuality, the government of this country and the ruling class behind it ranks as the most powerfully destructive force in the world. In the interest of maintaining the huge profits of multi-national corporations it has taken control of the economies and sought to destroy the cultures of Third World countries through genocidal warfare (as in Viet Nam). Forced sterilization, drug experimentation, destruction of the land and natural resources and outright killings of whole populations are just a few of the ways the U.S. government has terrorized the world.

This same system has used these tactics on poor and Third World people here in the U.S. Children, women and men are killed daily on Indian reservations, in prisons and mental hospitals, and on the streets. Violence is institutionalized through the racist and sexist court, welfare, education and public health systems. This violence is a fact of life for poor and non white people. Our children are shot on the streets, workers are killed by unsafe conditions on the job, women die from back alley abortions because they can't support another child and can't afford a safe abortion. Third World and poor women are consistently sterilized without their knowledge or consent—for example: 40% of Native American women, 33% of Puerto Rican and 25% of Black women of childbearing age have been sterilized.

The other side of this violence inherent in these repressive conditions is a long history of resistance. Oppressed people have always had to fight to survive. It's time to broaden the struggle by giving up the benefits that come with white skin, being male and have economic privilege. Combating these privileges means joining the fight on the front lines and that takes many forms—organizing on the job, in prisons, around welfare; demanding adequate health care, housing and food for all people; defending ourselves and our children against attack; and taking up arms against the system that robs us daily of our basic human rights.

It is necessary to make connections between all of these struggles, and armed struggle has been especially isolated. It should be the shared responsibility of those involved in armed struggle and those involved in above ground organizing to make the links clear between our actions/work.

It is in this spirit that we give critical support to the George Jackson Brigade with the understanding that the Brigade is involved in an ongoing process. We have specific criticisms of the GJB's past actions. We feel they were closed to input and criticism from the communities they were claiming to represent. They made unclear and antagonistic criticisms of the Seattle Left community. They seemed to present armed actions as the most revolutionary means of struggle while giving little critical support to above ground organizing. This is a particularly dangerous attitude, because above ground work is vitally important to build mass support for revolutionary change, especially at this stage of the struggle. The Brigade's actions were not clearly connected to community or national issues, and the destruction of property sometimes seemed an end in itself.

We support the self criticisms of the GJB and the changes they have made. The most recent communiques have asked for community input and they have made good, clear connections between their latest actions and the strike at Walla Walla State pen. The Brigade has asked for specific feedback on the use of tamperproof switches on bombs which would result in the death of a policeman if he were to attempt to de-activate the bomb. The alternative is to bluff the police with a phony switch and possibly watch them de-activate another device. The GJB needs response, also, on the issue of bombing in a residential area where there is the possibility of death or injury to people who live there. We feel it's important to respond to these questions. However, after discussing them collectively, we have not yet arrived at consensus, and so will continue to struggle. We urge other community groups and individuals to consider these problems and respond in whatever way they can.

We cannot allow the government and the media to be successful in their attempts to portray armed struggle as "terrorist" events. We must help clarify the political motivations behind the George Jackson Brigade's actions, and all revolutionary armed struggle. We must create the means for an exchange of mutual principled criticism. WE STRONGLY URGE PROGRESSIVE GROUPS AND THE ALTERNATIVE MEDIA TO CONTINUE THIS DISCUSSION.

OPEN LETTER TO THE JOHN BROWN BOOK CLUB

The Prairie Fire Organizing Committee (PFOC) grew out of the Prairie Fire Distribution Committee, which formed to facilitate the aboveground circulation of the Weather Underground's Prairie Fire: The Revolutionary Politics of Anti-Imperialism (1974), *composed by members while they were underground. As a militant antiracist organization, PFOC would outlast Weather itself.[52] The John Brown Book Club (JBBC) was a PFOC project which reissued copies of the journal* Osawatomie, *"the voice of the Weather Underground Organization," in 1975 and 1976,[53] and produced the February 1977 pamphlet* The Split of the Weather Underground Organization: Struggling Against White and Male Supremacy. *This forty-five-page document pushes the line of the Clayton Van Lydegraf splinter of Weather the "Revolutionary Committee," as opposed to the "Central Committee" of Bernardine Dohrn and others.[54]*

While there was clearly bad blood between the JBBC and certain Brigade members, the Brigade members I interviewed could not recall further details. An article contained in The Split *provides a partial answer. Entitled "j.b.b.c. self-criticism," the relevant passage reads:*

> JBBC came into being, grew and developed, now ends its practice and sums up in a period that has been tumultuous here and elsewhere. Events in Seattle and the struggle surrounding them like the development of the George Jackson Brigade, its destruction by the state, the deaths of two revolutionary comrades, and a federal grand jury assault on the left all helped shape our politics. Physical injuries caused by misdirected revolutionary violence of the GJB sparked a reactionary response from us and much of the rest of the Seattle left. We participated in building a militant movement against the grand jury on the one hand, while on the other we attempted alliances with organizations of the left, which in the face of rising repression would not challenge the state. Our mistakes showed that we accepted, a piece at a time, the slow, sure sell-out of revolutionary armed struggle that the WUO made during the 1974-76 period.[55]

The theoretical cause of dispute between the JBBC and the Brigade was the appropriate time and place for domestic armed struggle. The practical ramifications for differences in interpretation, alluded to by the Brigade in the polemic below, were: the behavior of JBBC members in the anti-grand jury coalition; their presentation of the Brigade as already dead, when it had more than a year of life left in it; their newfound treatment of the Brigade dead, Seidel, as a "comrade"; and lack of concrete support for local indigenous militants.[56]

The following survives as a mimeograph dated September 1, 1977. It bears the words "Please post or distribute this letter."

(The use of "JBBC" throughout this letter refers to those of you who, during 1975, held the Weather/Prairie Fire political line, did distribution of Weather [Underground] literature, and participated in Prairie Fire study groups. You later helped form and are now involved in the Prairie Fire Organizing Committee and the John Brown Book Club.

(We're not publishing this letter yet because it is a direct criticism of you. We sincerely hope you will find time to publicly respond to it. Because we think the issues involved here are of vital concern, and therefore the business of the entire community, the letter will be released publicly in one month.)

The GJB is encouraged to read that JBBC has taken some responsibility for itself through the "initial sketch" as printed in "The Split." We are encouraged because we had been forced to give up all hope that such a change was possible. This loss of hope was based, as you may well know, on several shit experiences with JBBC people. We are encouraged but not dazzled. We understand clearer now some of the reasons for your "reactionary responses" to the GJB. Your actions falling so far behind your words was largely based on national orders. But, they were your words and actions; coming from your mouths. In having never publicly criticized yourselves until the "trusted leaders" did, [you provide] another subtle example of not taking responsibility for your politics. We strongly believe that your criticisms must go much deeper. We also feel that you should address some specifics in your future self-criticisms. These specifics are written vaguely for security reasons, but you know as well as we do that these events did occur, and that the true facts of them (if we could spell it out) are much worse than the vagueness written here implies.

1. You outright refused support and therefore failed to put your theory into practice in an extremely serious and real situation around Third World struggles in this country. In fact, you went so far as to destroy the equipment that was needed for this support.

2. You not only passively accepted the "slow sell-out of revolutionary armed struggle," you actively organized against the GJB, and along

with other reactionary groups, publicly "disassociated" yourselves.

3. You attempted to blackmail a progressive aboveground group by refusing to distribute their publications unless they ceased all coverage of the GJB. We also know of instances where you attempted bribery as a form of political struggle.

4. You played a leading role in expelling people from the 1976 Grand Jury Defense Committee by imposing a gag rule because some folks had publicly stated support for the GJB. This is not an isolated instance. It has been your practice for [some] time to bureaucratically purge dissenters in the name of political struggle from groups where you play a leadership role.

Any time a bureaucratic "style of work" is used it automatically alienates women, Third World people, prisoners, and other sufferers of special oppression. Historically, bureaucracy has been the weapon of male supremacy and class society. Red tape and volumes of high falutin' words help keep the oppressors in control. Organization from above will never succeed in producing freedom for anyone. By squeezing the validity out of Third World and women's liberation movements, you have played into the white male ruling class game by helping to create greater divisions and real lack of trust. In view of these repeated kinds of fuck-overs and sell-outs, your rectification cannot come overnight.

We find it not only disgusting but opportunist for you suddenly to embrace our dead[57] as your "revolutionary comrades." We don't know about Po because he was not a member of the GJB, but Bruce had many criticisms of you which you refused to acknowledge and thus never attempted to struggle with him about. In fact, you shined him on and even trashed him. You did nothing supportive or in any way positive that we know about at the time of either Bruce's or Po's death; except to attend a public memorial for Po. Your reaction was to close your mouths and turn your backs—the common reaction of sell-outs and/or cowards. The passage of time and the cloak of mysticism and romanticism should never be allowed to change dead freedom fighters into glorified martyrs as delayed announcement of these men as comrades implies. We righteously believe that much deeper and stronger, more sincere and honest self-criticisms are necessary before JBBC can call either fallen freedom fighter a real comrade. You have finally recognized the "development of the GJB"; but your assumption that we have been destroyed by the state is, at best, a sad example of unquestioning belief in the state's propaganda. When, in fact, it should have been very clear to you that all kinds of police were continually looking for us in Oregon. Also obvious is that our locked down brother, Ed Mead, has not been destroyed.

As you well know, Comrade Ed has many times been wrongly attacked personally and politically by you. Perhaps a move toward rectifying these attacks would be a show of real change in your practice around prison struggles. In the past year, there have been organized struggles in all Washington joints; the strongest at Walla Walla (primarily around behaviour modification torture and general conditions). Ed is one of the Walla Walla Brothers now actively engaged in struggle against an all out attack by the state. You could be helping to build active/public support for this life and death struggle.

We will soon issue a more lengthy political statement. The following is a draft of the section on the Weather Underground. We think you should consider these more general political criticisms of your ideology.

What followed is the "Weather Influence" section of "The Power of the People Is the Source of Life"—Part III of this collection—minus the closing quote from Cabral. I have omitted this "Weather Influence" section here, but reproduce the remainder of the "Open Letter" below.

We would also like to say something about the Brigade's role in this relationship between us and JBBC. It was by no means exemplary. Sometime before the January 1976 Laurelhurst action, the GJB ceased all attempts to relate to JBBC. Prior to this, individual Brigade members made numerous approaches to JBBC people. These approaches were always for the purpose of asking for support of one kind or another: resources, money, use of their equipment, contacts, advice, etc. When these requests were refused (as they always were), our consistent response was angry outbursts calculated to force/shame JBBC into acknowledging what we saw to be their revolutionary duty. We made little or no attempt to engage them in honest, principled political struggle; instead, our practice was characterized by the kind of liberalism and opportunism that grows from seeing immediate tactical needs as ends in themselves. We saw their refusals as proof of their deep-seated and unchanging opportunism and thought that forthright political struggle would be a waste of time. This kind of sectarian cynicism usually goes hand in hand with a "more revolutionary than thou" arrogance, and both are all too common in groups doing armed work. We continue to be determined to root out these errors in the Brigade; this letter should be seen in this light. Our criticisms have not been liberal, they have been harsh. Our words should not be interpreted as divisive; our intention is that your responses to these honest criticisms will move forward your rectification. We are encouraged because your statement is one step in material proof of real change. We are encouraged to see you begin this hard struggle. We are eager to hear more. We are also anxious to see a closer link between your words and your actions.

In The Spirit Of Struggle,
The George Jackson Brigade

BUST THE BOSSES

The following communiqué was printed as "Jackson Brigade Supports" in Northwest Passage, *October 24–November 7, 1977, 2, and appeared under the title "Dealer bombed" in* Seattle Sun *and* Orca, *no. 2, Winter 1977–1978, 10–11.*

Tonight we bombed the S.L. Savidge new car dealership in support of the four month long strike by the Automotive Machinists Union, Lodge 289. Sheet metal, Teamsters and Automotive Painters unions have also been on strike against the dealers for several months. We chose S.L. Savidge in particular because he was identified by striking workers as one of the leaders of the car dealers' attempts to break the union.

Also, on October 6, we attempted to test an incendiary bomb at Westlund Buick as punishment for Westlund's role as president of the 52 member King County Automobile Dealers' Association. The device failed to detonate. (To verify that we placed the device: the timer was a white plastic, 60 minute kitchen timer with red numbers; and the gallon bottle of gasoline and sulfuric acid was wrapped with cheesecloth containing a potassium chlorate solution.)

It is clear that the bosses only want more profit for themselves at the expense of their workers. In this particular strike, the bosses are clearly trying to break the union in an attempt to get more profit for themselves. The best strategy against this union busting attempt is to cost the bosses more than they gain by employing scabs.

We therefore encourage all people to support this workers' struggle. There are many ways to express support, some are more comfortable than others. Choose one of the following and act.

1. Don't cross a picket line for any reason! Take your business elsewhere or wait until the strike is settled.

2. Tie up the dealers' phones! Call in as a concerned person and complain, or call from a phone booth and leave the line hanging.

3. Put sugar in the gas tanks of dealers' new cars, or potatoes in the tailpipes! This will destroy the engine.

4. Break the dealers' windows! Use bricks, slingshots, small arms, etc. Slash their tires too!

5. Lock the bosses out! Put super glue in any and all locks of buildings or cars. (This is easy and it works great!)

We are not members of any of the striking unions, but we have talked (anonymously) with striking workers all over town. We are claiming these actions so that the workers will not be blamed for them.

AN ATTACK AGAINST ONE OF US
IS AN ATTACK AGAINST ALL OF US!

THE BOSSES NEED US,
BUT WE *DON'T* NEED THE BOSSES!

Love and Struggle,
The George Jackson Brigade
October 12, 1977

Letter to the Automotive Machinists Union Local 289

October 16, 1977
Automotive Machinists Union
Local 289
2701 1st
Seattle, Wa.

Friends:

We were responsible for the fire bombing last night at BBC Dodge in Burien. We were also responsible for the pipe bombing of S.L. Savidge earlier this week, and the attempted fire bombing at Westlund Buick on October 6.

In last night's action we used three gallon juice bottles containing a gasoline sulphuric acid solution. The bottles were wrapped with cheesecloth saturated with potassium chlorate and sugar as an igniter. A small pipe bomb was taped to the bottles to break them. Each of the bombs were detonated by a Westclox Travelalarm; two of the clocks were still in the red plastic cases they came in, one of them was taped in a piece of styrofoam. At least two of the timers were recovered by the King County Police.

We gained entry to the storage lot by cutting a chain link fence on the North side of the lot, about 20 feet east of a cluster of blackberry bushes. One bomb was placed on the hood of a sedan parked against the chain link fence; and the third was on the hood of a station wagon parked toward the center of the lot next to a large recreational vehicle.

We are certain that there is enough specific information in this letter to completely clear the union and its membership of any complicity in these actions. This letter itself is being typed on a typewriter used extensively by the Brigade, and the FBI has samples of this type, including bank robbery notes. To eliminate *all* question, we are including two copies of the right thumbprint of John Sherman, a known member of the Brigade. One thumbprint is at the bottom of this letter, and the other is on the enclosed xerox copy of this letter. You should give this letter to the police and keep the xerox for your own protection.

Also attached is a copy of our October 12 communique which sets forth our reasons for these actions.

We wish you complete success in your efforts to hold the line against ever increasing and ever sleazier attacks by the bosses.

Love and Struggle,
The George Jackson Brigade

Cc: BBC Dodge
John Reed, Special Agent in charge, FBI, Seattle
King County Automobile Dealers Association
KOMO TV News

[actual thumprint]
John W. Sherman's
right thumbprint

You Can Kill A Revolutionary, But You Can't Kill The Revolution!

On May 9, 1976, the prominent former journalist and Red Army Faction cofounder Ulrike Meinhof was discovered hanging in her prison cell. While the state called it suicide, her fellow prisoners cried murder. An International Commission eventually backed them up, presenting evidence that Meinhof had been raped and strangled before being hung up in her cell.[58] Meinhof's death came in the midst of a long-delayed trial and after years of dramatic activism by RAF prisoners and their outside supporters against the new isolation regimen implemented to neutralize political prisoners. Prominent radical intellectuals such as Jean-Paul Sartre and Simone de Beauvoir voiced their condemnation of the death in custody. A wave of firebombings hit West German governmental and corporate offices across Western Europe, militant mass demonstrations took to the street, and other prisoners launched hunger strikes in protest and mourning.[59]

On October 18, 1977, a government official announced the deaths of Andreas Baader and Gudrun Ensslin in Stammheim Prison, as well as the unsuccessful attempt on the part of fellow RAF prisoners Jan-Carl Raspe and Irmgard Möller to participate in a suicide pact. Raspe died of his wounds, while Möller lived to challenge the state's version of events. As with Meinhff's purported suicide, official accounts of the Stammheim deaths were deeply unconvincing.[60] Protests, kidnappings, and bombings rocked Europe.[61] The Brigade attack, explained below, seems to have been the only armed act of protest against the deaths in North America.

The following communiqué, dated November 1977, appeared in Orca, *no. 2, Winter 1977–1978, 12–13.*

On the night of November 1st, we bombed the Phil Smart Mercedes Benz dealer in Bellevue in retaliation for the murders of our German comrades of the Red Army Faction. This punitive action is in solidarity with the thousands of freedom fighters throughout Europe and around the world who have taken up the counter attack against the real terrorists: the international imperialist ruling class and all its instruments of terror.

This action is dedicated to:

Ulrike Meinhof, a political prisoner who was raped and strangled in her maximum security isolation cell in Stammheim, the special fortress prison in Stuttgart, Germany on May 9, 1976. The official coroner's verdict was suicide.

Andreas Baader and Jan Carl Raspe, political prisoners who were shot in the back of the neck in their separate isolation cells in the same prison on October 13, 1977. The official coroner's verdict was suicide.

Gudrun Ensslin, a political prisoner who was hanged from an electric extension cord in her isolation cell on the same day that Baader and Raspe were shot, in the same fortress prison. The official coroner's verdict was suicide.

We send a special message of support and revolutionary greetings to Irmgard Moller. She is a political prisoner at the same prison in Stuttgart, Germany. The state failed in its attempt to stab her to death with a bread knife. However her statement, made from her hospital bed that she did *not* try to kill herself, means that her life is still in danger. The ruling class freely uses murder and torture to silence people who expose their terrorism.

All four murdered freedom fighters, as well as Moller, were captured urban guerrillas, members of the Red Army Faction (referred to by the ruling class media as the "Baader-Meinhof gang"). They were tried and convicted under "exceptional" laws—laws designed to give the German ruling class a freer hand in crushing popular dissent. These people were subjected to increasing physical and mental torture, sensory deprivation and isolation from each other, their friends and their lawyers. The German government's excuse for the torture was the charge that these guerrillas were directing armed activity in Germany from inside the prison.

The German ruling class has a bloody history of disposing of their political enemies. In the early days of Hitler Germany, the Nazis began this murderous practice by herding their enemies into concentration camps, shooting them, and labeling it "an escape attempt." (Just like the murder of George Jackson at San Quentin.) Because the internationalist capitalist class wants us to forget its experiment with fascism, they now murder enemies through "suicides," instead of staged "escape attempts."

• • •

We chose Mercedes-Benz as a target because it is a German luxury car which is a favorite item of conspicuous consumption for ruling class bosses, and because of its association with Hanns-Martin Schleyer, late captain of German industry and unpunished Nazi war criminal.[62]

Schleyer was president of Daimler Benz, the manufacturers of Mercedes Benz. He was also head of the Union of German Employer's association (a combination national chamber of commerce and manufacturer's Association.). He was also an economic advisor and close personal crony of the boss of the West German government. During World War II, he was a high ranking Nazi SS officer in charge of war industries in Nazi occupied Czechoslovakia. He was the perfect representative of "democratic" German capitalism.

Schleyer was taken hostage by the Red Army Faction to win freedom for eleven of their captured comrades, including Ensslin, Baader and Raspe, who were murdered two weeks ago. Schleyer was executed in retaliation for those murders.

LOVE AND RAGE—FIRE AND SMOKE
REMEMBER THE STAMMHEIM MASSACRE

Love and Struggle,
The George Jackson Brigade
November, 1977

An Open Letter To Bo (Rita D. Brown)
From the rest of the Brigade

The following letter was printed in Orca, *no. 2, Winter 1977–1978, 16–19.*

> It could have been me, but instead it was you.
> So I'll keep doing the work you were doing as if I were two.
> I'll be a student of life, a singer of songs,
> A farmer of food and a righter of wrongs.
> It could have been me, but instead it was you.
> And it may be my dear sisters and brothers before we are through.
> But if you can fight for freedom, freedom, freedom, freedom,
> If you can fight for freedom, I can too.
> —Holly Near

It was your hair, comrade. Somebody around that fucking bank spotted you with that hair like Carol Newland, and the Feds came and staked out that bank waiting for you to come back. And you did, and now they've got you. Zip, just like that another one of our strongest fighters is locked up. They must have tried to follow you home from your walk on the beach with the dog, and you spotted them and doubled back away from the house insuring your capture and our safety.

We heard about it on the scanner when 2 Adam 23 was sent to "meet the FBI agent at 175th and Aurora" and impound our vehicle. Since we had neglected to remove Dillinger's (our dog—also in the slammer now) rabies tag, we realized that it wouldn't take the Feds long to trace it back to our house.

That was about 3:30 in the afternoon. Frank[63] was out in the Dodge and wasn't due to call or be home until about five. The people left in the house spent the next hour and a half trying to determine from the scanner whether you were still being held at 175th and Aurora and could use some help, trying to locate Frank who had the only usable vehicle, and trying to judge how much time they had before the Feds showed up. Just before 5:00 they decided they could wait no longer. They burned some shit, left a cryptic note for Frank, gathered up all the weapons and ammunition and tried to walk away.

They had to turn back after one block because the equipment was too heavy. About this time, Frank got home with the car, so we loaded it up with weapons and ammunition and a bare minimum of clothing and other equipment and left. By the time we got to a safe place and unloaded, it was only about 5:30 or 6:00 pm, just four or five hours since you were nailed, so Nora[64] and Frank took the car back to the house to try to get one more carload of equipment out.

They did an area check approach to the house and discovered four or five suspicious cars apparently meeting in the school parking lot that faces Meridian (just where we always figured the police would use as a staging area to raid our house). Nora and Frank drove by these cars twice and were able to confirm that they were Feds by following one of them (a big, dark four door, Inspector Erskine type sedan) as it moved into position behind and to the North of our house. Its license number (IVU 004) was almost the same as the license number of an almost identical Fed car we had spotted downtown some time ago (IVU 001). Nora and Frank left the area just as the raid began.

So now we're in the process of summing up our mistakes and beginning to rebuild, once again from close to the ground.

We have so far identified the following specific mistakes that led to your capture and the raid on our house:

1. We failed to take your day to day appearance seriously enough and didn't realize how distinctive your hairstyle was and how closely it resembled a picture we knew the Feds had of you. This mistake cost us you, our greatest loss, both materially and conditionally, in a long time.

2. Although we had sense enough to remove the dog's license tag anytime anyone went out with him, it never occurred to us to remove his rabies tag. This mistake cost us our base.

3. We overestimated the security of our house and failed to develop clear emergency plans that would have allowed us to evacuate the most valuable equipment, tools, clothes and supplies first. This mistake cost us 90% of our supplies and equipment.

We seem to pay dearly for small mistakes in this work.

Overall, we made the mistake of too much doing with too little thinking and discussion. Since returning from Oregon, we quadrupled our workload with little or no change in our methods of work. During the last two months we did two bank robberies, four or five bombings, a thirty page political statement, a major criticism of John Brown Book Club, and worked throughout on putting together another bank robbery. We were also working on a couple of other major actions that we can't talk about for security reasons.[65] We also did four or five full tune ups on our vehicles, built a canopy for our truck and did all the shit work maintenance that takes two or three hours out of every day.

During this period we had almost no division of labor; tasks were completed on a pretty much hit or miss basis of who was free and capable of doing them. By and large, the tasks themselves were identified and defined spontaneously, as they came up, with very little advance planning.

We worked six days a week, a minimum of nine or ten hours a day, and our discussions were always the "minimum," which usually meant brief reports on today's tasks and assignment of tomorrow's. We took no time for serious discussion and analysis of the kind of problem that led to your arrest and the raid on our house.

We will correct these errors. As we rebuild our base, we will incorporate the following changes in our day to day methods of work:

1. We will develop and implement a realistic division of labor based on the number of people we have and logical definitions of areas of responsibility in our work. In this way, we will have clearly defined responsibility for such things as security practice and will be much less likely to make the kind of stupid mistakes that came from relying on spontaneous insight (for example, to remove the dog's rabies tag).

2. We will unfailingly set aside one day each week solely for meeting. We will use these meetings for political struggle, for discussion and analysis of our strategic development, and for reports, practical criticism, and planning of next weeks tasks.

3. We will immediately develop a set of evacuation plans, establish priorities for the removal of supplies and equipment, and will, from time to time, conduct evacuation drills so that we all understand what is to be taken, and how, for every possible situation.

Throughout the period of rebuilding, we will continue the process of analyzing and defining the mistakes that led to this defeat. In this way, we will transform the raid and your capture from a defeat into a solid foundation for the new base.

Mao Tse Tung says that to be attacked by the enemy is a good thing because it makes clear the distinction between us and the oppressor, and because it illuminates our weaknesses and provides us with knowledge gained from criticism/self-criticism to move forward and grow stronger. He says that we learn a thousand times more from a defeat than we do from a victory. This is true, but only to the extent that we make it true in our practice. And we will make it true because we love you, and we love freedom, and because we are part of the masses of people and a handful of sleazy capitalists and their lackeys are no match for us.

So take care of yourself and hold on. Victory is certain.

> The wheel of law turns without pause . . .
> after winter comes spring . . .
> What could be more natural,
> after sorrow comes joy.

> Love and Struggle,
> The George Jackson Brigade
> November 1977

· · ·

To Bo, Wherever We May Find Her

They snatched you
Leaving that hollow empty gap
TUGs know[66]
My pillow is drying
Spent grief is turning into rage

Eyes, lips, hips, thighs, flower
Arms enfold me
Remembering you on the beach
(Your first boat ride)
Halloween painted faces
Laughter, tears and
Good loving
My lover no longer shoots pool
with a .357
But you still make me feel like dancing

Aches turn to comfort
Bodacious sister woman you are
In my mind as I
Plant bombs, rob banks
Your strength and discipline will
Keep me fighting

—Jory[67]

OPEN LETTER TO JAILERS SPELLMAN AND WALDT

The following appeared under the title "Horse's mouth" in Seattle Sun, December 28, 1977, 2, and in Orca, no. 2, Winter 1977–1978, 22–25.

John D. Spellman
King County Executive
7048 51st Ave. N.E.
Seattle, WA

Lawrence G. Waldt
Sheriff-Director, King County
Dept. of Public Safety
6535 Seaview Ave. NE #709B
Seattle, WA

Jailers Spellman and Waldt:

Tonight we bombed the transformer supplying power to Southcenter and the Andover Park Industrial Complex to protest the criminal and inhuman conditions at the King County Jail. Southcenter/Andover Park Industrial Complex was chosen because it is a center of capitalist activity in King County. Capitalism causes crime with unemployment, poverty and oppression, and the capitalists are responsible for the conditions in their jails.

The media has been reporting on the dehumanizing and overcrowded in the King County jail for some time now. Even the King County Superior Court judges snivel about the "outdated, overworked, and vastly overcrowded" conditions in a jail designed for a maximum of 550, and now confining over 700 people. The jail also is in gross violation of the Fire Code, refuses to correct these violations, and is a potential death trap for those imprisoned there.

It is clear that King County intends to do nothing about these conditions. A bond issue for possible improvement funds won't even be considered until a year from now, if at all.

Further exposure of the brutal conditions and practices at the jail are contained in a letter from Mark Cook in the November 14 issue of the *Northwest Passage*. Mark Cook has been confined in segregation in the King County Jail since March 12, 1976.

> I am kept in segregation, isolated from other 'mainline' prisoners because I am a political threat to the 'order and security of the jail.' Although the keepers admit I have broken no jail rules and regulations, and have caused no disturbance to warrant being kept in disciplinary cells, I have been in such confinement for twenty months . . .

I spend twenty-three hours a day in my cell (six feet by seven feet): I am given midnight showers every two or three days: no daylight enters the cell; cell lighting is poor: there is no ventilation: there is no hot water: there is a sink and a toilet: I eat my meals on the floor (there is no table). I have suffered various harassments from jailers and jail authorities (people in the news media who intervened in my behalf didn't want to believe what was happening). Fellow prisoners in adjoining cells are mostly the uncontrollable psychotics who are locked back here without supervision. They often rage for hours at a time, flood their cells, set their cells on fire; a few have played in and eaten their own feces. Under these and other pressures at times I have reacted futilely, but my awareness of the incompetent and oppressive controls of the state seeps through and I quiet down, struggling inwardly with repressed anger.

I am an African, descendant of Africans trapped here in North America in the slave colonies. I am of the working class, an upholsterer and common laborer when I have to be. So the contempt and indignities I suffer at the hands of the government, though directed at me in this instance, are a sample of the indignity and contempt the government feels for African and working class people who are 'politically suspect.'

Mark Cook is a black, ex-convict prison organizer who was convicted of participation in Brigade activities on the testimony of a bribed heroin addict. His trials were and continue to be marked by government misconduct and deceit. Mark Cook has steadfastly maintained his innocence throughout. His case is still being appealed.

Ed Mead, an admitted GJB member, is in general population at the state penitentiary at Walla Walla. Rita Brown, an alleged member of the GJB charged with numerous bank robberies, is in general population at the Marion County Jail in Oregon. Mark Cook, who denies complicity with the Brigade and has a history of clearly non-violent political activity, had been held in solitary confinement in the most brutal of dungeons in the King County Jail for over twenty one months. Both Rita and Ed are white. Mark Cook is black. His black skin is the sole "justification" for the arbitrary and degrading treatment he is subjected to. This kind of blatant racism is [an] all too common practice by the ruling class generally, and in their prisons and jails in particular.

You should inform your ruling class bosses of the following initial demands:

1. Release Mark Cook into general population with full "privileges" immediately.

2. Publish in the two major Seattle newspapers a *detailed* report of exactly what fire codes are being violated, and what is being done to correct them and bring the jail up to code.

3. Publish in the two major Seattle newspapers *detailed* plans for the emergency evacuation and rescue of prisoners in the jail in case of fire.

4. Make an examination by licensed medical personnel from outside the jail available to all of the people in segregation. Have licensed medical personnel from outside the jail do a thorough investigation of the medical conditions in segregation and publish a *detailed* report of their findings in the two major Seattle newspapers. This group should include people from at least the following medical disciplines: internal medicine, neurology, opthamology, and psychiatry. This group must also include people from the alternative medical community.

You should inform your capitalist bosses that we hold them responsible for these demands, and that if they are not met within a month's time, we will continue attacking ruling class institutions, capital equipment, and persons throughout the Pacific Northwest. These attacks will continue until these reasonable demands are met.

We urge all progressive people in Oregon and Washington to join with us in this campaign to bring King County Jail up to minimum standards of human decency. Some specific things that people can do include:

1. Call Spellman (344-4040) and Waldt (344-3855) daily and harass them about these demands.

2. Continually call the King County Jail (344-2641) and ask if Mark Cook is in general population yet—and why not.

3. Write to Spellman and Waldt; stop by their homes and discuss these demands with them (see addresses at the top of this letter).

4. Call the Fire Marshall (County—344-2573; City 625-4077) and demand to know why they've allowed the jail to remain in operation when it's in violation of the Fire Code. Demand that they enforce the Code at the jail. (If our homes were in violation of the Fire Code, we'd be thrown out of them for not correcting violations.)

5. Call the Health Department (County—344-5210; City 625-2161) and demand that they take action to correct the lack of medical attention for those in segregation.

6. Sabotage Spellman and Waldt's offices, homes, cars, etc.

7. Call and lodge a citizen's complaint with the County (344-3452) and City (625-2161) Ombudsman.

8. Sabotage (Superglue for example) any and all ruling class institutions (banks, supermarkets, insurance companies, etc.) and their capital equipment until these demands are met.

These actions are by no means petty. If they are taken up by enough of us, they would mean a hundred times more than any bomb. *Mass* activity will make the difference.

CAPITALISM IS ORGANIZED CRIME
JAIL THE JAILERS

Love and Struggle
The George Jackson Brigade
December 23, 1977

Bust the Union Busters

The following communiqué appeared in Orca, *no. 2, Winter 1977–1978, 20–21.*

Tonight we bombed a railroad car containing new cars at the Convoy Transport Company in Kent, Washington. New cars are brought by railroad to Convoy and transported from there to new car dealerships in King County. This action was in support of the seven month long strike by the Automotive Machinists Union, Local 289, against the King County Automobile Dealers' Association.

From the start of this strike, the bosses have clearly been attempting to bust the Automotive Machinists Union as a part of their continuing drive to get more profits for themselves at the expense of workers. Their tactics have included slanderous attacks against the machinist in the news media, and court injunctions against mass actions at some dealerships. More recently, they have conspired with the news media in trying to suppress any mention of the continuing strike.

The local union hacks haven't done much better than the dealers. They have limited the "official" battle to picketing, while neglecting to publicize rallies and mass actions, or to spread the word about the strike among other unions. The hacks on the King County Labor Council didn't even bother to put the struck dealers on their unfair [practices] list until after the machinists had been on strike for six months.

But the workers have stood firm against these attacks and continued to build support for the struggle throughout their long and courageous strike. In August, over 800 workers marched in the streets of Seattle in support of the striking auto machinists. The machinists held a mass labor rally November 12 outside the dealer-sponsored Auto Show at the Kingdome. Striking machinists have frequently been joined on their picket lines by workers on strike against Boeing, and by the Firstbank Independent Employees' Association (Seafirst Bank Union), as well as others. Workers in the American Postal Workers Union and the Meatcutters Local 81 proposed and passed resolutions in support of the machinists. On November 17, a mass celebration was held at the Westlake Chevrolet picket line, where machinists "celebrated" having been on strike for six months and vowed to continue sticking it out. On November 23, a group of striking machinists picketed City Hall in an attempt to get the news media to cover their strike.

This attempt at union busting by the Dealers' Association is not an isolated event. Because capitalism (like an old Ford that's been patched up once too often) is falling apart again, there have been more and more attempts at union busting by bosses everywhere. As the capitalists scramble to increase their declining profits, strikes everywhere are becoming longer and harder fought. Currently in Seattle, Seafirst National Bank is attempting to bust the Firstbank Independent Employees' Association, which has been without a contract since August 1. The unions in auto dealerships in Portland, Oregon, were busted out two years ago. Spokane has one union left in a dealership after the rest were busted out five years ago. Southern California has no auto machinists unions left at all.

But the striking auto machinists have drawn the line against union busting, and have been joined in their common battle by workers throughout the King County area. The best strategy against the Dealers' union-busting attempt is to cost the bosses more than they gain by employing scabs. We therefore continue to encourage all people to support this workers' struggle. There are many ways to express support. Choose any of the following and act:

1. Don't patronize the struck dealers. Don't cross a picket line for any reason! Take your business elsewhere or wait until the strike is over.

2. Tie up the dealers' phones! Call in as a concerned person and complain, or call from a phone booth and leave the line hanging.

3. Put sugar in the gas tanks of the dealers' new cars, or potatoes in the tailpipes! This will destroy the engine.

4. Break the dealers' windows! Use bricks, slingshots, small arms, etc. Smash their tires, too!

5. Lock the bosses out! Put Superglue in any and all locks of buildings or cars. (This is easy and it works great!)

6. Call and harass the various news media until they give adequate news coverage to the strike and the real issues involved.

At this time, the unions which our parents and grandparents fought and died for are one of working people's strongest and only protections against attacks by the bosses. In the end, the bosses' attacks can only be overcome by doing away with the bosses and their rotten system. In the meantime:

BUST THE UNION BUSTERS AND KEEP SEATTLE A UNION TOWN! AN ATTACK AGAINST ONE OF US IS AN ATTACK AGAINST ALL OF US!

THE BOSSES NEED US, BUT WE *DON'T* NEED THE BOSSES!

Love and Struggle,
The George Jackson Brigade
December 24, 1977

"OUR LOSSES ARE HEAVY
BUT WE ARE STILL HERE
AND WE INTEND TO KEEP ON FIGHTING!"

Captured	Recaptured	Captured

Therese Coupez	**John Sherman**	**Janine Bertram**

"The Brigade is composed of women and men working together toward revolution. At least 50% of our members are women; at least half of the women are lesbians; at least half of the leadership and decision-making comes from women; at least 50% of the planning and participation in all actions is done by women. We have no 'Mastermind' and no single leader. Rather, we operate in a collective and democratic manner, using and developing the skills and capabilities of all of us. We share skills and jobs so that all of us are working toward being capable of performing any of the tasks, mental and manual, that our work requires."

George Jackson Brigade Political Statement
November, 1977

The ruling class and its authoritarian, sexist media can't understand this. All they know is "command and obey", bosses and sheep, masterminds and followers, superstars and groupies. They desperately want to believe that in capturing our comrade John Sherman they have destroyed us. But, *the power of the people is the force of life* and the revolution is the power of the people.

Our losses are heavy but we are still here and we intend to keep on fighting! We send all our love and strength to our locked-down comrades.

On the night of the Tacoma bust, a couple of us went to the safe house to clean up. We didn't have the key so we got in by breaking the glass in the patio door. We had no idea if the Feds were onto the location so we had to hurry but we got everything that was important: the weapons, the equipment, the important documents. Everything but the cat which we couldn't find.

The Feds found the house on Thursday. The media has said nothing about it being cleaned-out. They desperately want this to be the end of the Brigade but the GJB won't die. As long as there are rich and poor, as long as people are starving, rotting in prisons and being shot on the street, as long as we are denied the power to control our own lives, the GJB will live!

There is a lot of anger being felt these days. Other folks have been taking action, like the stuff that happened on International Women's Day. We have decided that the focus of our work right now will be to encourage that anger, to get more folks in touch with it, and to share in expressing it whenever possible.

We are filled with love and rage, fire and smoke.

Seattle - Easter Sunday - 1978

Love and Struggle,
The George Jackson Brigade
(The rest of us)

Flyer produced by Brigade supporters after the arrest of the last members, Coupez, Sherman, and Bertram. The photograph of Coupez has been removed at her request.

Part III

The Power of the People Is the Source of Life: Political Statement of the George Jackson Brigade

The Brigade's political statement surfaced just days after the arrest of Rita Brown. It claimed a number of actions not previously linked definitively to the Brigade, thus complicating Brown's prospects for a successful defense. Aboveground supporters printed it and made it available at Left Bank Books and other sites of radical convergence in the city. *Northwest Passage* collective member Jim Hansen selected portions of the political statement as "an appetizer" for readers. He editorialized: "My intent is that you obtain a copy and evaluate it for yourselves, using it as a focal point for political discourse."[1] As the last three Brigade members would be arrested three months after its release, and since the Brigade's most spectacular actions were already behind it, it caused less of a stir than it would have in 1975 or 1976, before the collective had internally clarified many of the positions set out in this document.

THE POWER OF THE PEOPLE IS THE FORCE OF LIFE:
POLITICAL STATEMENT OF THE GEORGE JACKSON BRIGADE

> . . . a revolutionary liberation movement must deal with the en-
> emy concurrently on all levels, including armed violence. Otherwise
> when the inevitable showdown with the ruling class comes, the rev-
> olution will be left defenseless and the lives of our beloved com-
> rades needlessly sacrificed.
> —Martin Sostre

The George Jackson Brigade has been around for more than two years now, and we have not as yet issued an overall statement of our political philosophy and principles. There have been three issues of *The Angry Turkey*,[2] but these have been written by individual Brigade members reflecting their individual political development and were never intended to represent the unity of the Brigade as a whole. We think *The Angry Turkey* is extremely valuable as a basis for discussion and struggle on the questions raised in armed work and we urge people to use them for that purpose. But people have correctly criticized us for failing to make a clear statement of our political unity as a group, and we hope that this document will provide that.

We dedicate this Statement to the memory of our comrade, Bruce Seidel. Bruce was murdered by police hoodlums as he tried to surrender during the Brigade's January 23, 1976, attempt to expropriate a Tukwila bank.

Bruce saw himself as an inevitable product of the mass movement. He understood the need for a movement with real teeth, and set about changing this understanding into a reality. Unlike so many of his racist counterparts, Bruce did not believe the lives of U.S. communists to be somehow more precious than those of comrades throughout the world who are fighting and dying in the international class war against imperialism.

Bruce not only backed his words with commensurate deeds, he transformed himself as well. He was easy to be with and easy to respect. He gave people everything he had, including large chunks of himself. He taught that each of us has a tremendous revolutionary potential, and that with a little effort we can apply the scientific principles of dialectical and historical materialism to ourselves, thereby enhancing our political growth and productivity. He said the main problem with our movement is people putting themselves first and revolution second.

The death of our comrade still weighs like a mountain on our shoulders. We loved Bruce in life and we love him in death. We don't mourn Bruce; rather we remember his contributions, put his example into practice, and celebrate the joy he brought to our lives.

> CAPITALISM
> crept into my soul
> lunging at my heart
> digging into my throat
> and stabbing at my lungs
> as the blood flowed
> my heart refused to stop
> my voice remained determined
> Then CAPITALISM
> lost its balance
> hopped into his Cadillac
> and retreated back to the police station
> —Bruce Seidel, 1976

History and Summation of Brigade Unity

The Brigade was formed in early 1975 by a small group of unemployed working class communists. In and around the Brigade were working class ex-convicts, ex-students and other more or less permanently jobless people. All of the people publicly associated with the Brigade (B.S., R.B., E.M., & J.S.),[3] and the overwhelming majority of the rest of us,[4] have long histories of involvement in mass political struggle in the Seattle area. In one way or another, it was this involvement in the struggles of women, prisoners, Third World people, gays and young people that led all of us to a commitment to armed struggle.

The Brigade is composed of women and men working together towards revolution. At least 50% of our members are women;[5] at least half of the women are lesbians;[6] at least half of the leadership and decision making comes from women; and at least 50% of the planning and participation in all actions is done by women. We have no "mastermind" and no single leader; rather, we operate in a collective and democratic manner, using and developing the skills and capabilities of all of us. We share skills and jobs so that all of us are working towards being capable of performing any of the tasks, mental and manual, that our work requires.

The main point of unity for the Brigade has always been the determination to fight capitalism—with force of arms—here and now. We reject the notion prevalent in the left that the skills and experience necessary to wage successful revolutionary war will drop from the sky when needed. We do believe that the central task for revolutionaries at this time is mass organizing. We also believe, however, that it is vitally important that some of us begin the complex process of developing the theory and practice of armed struggle. Armed struggle is not the "axis around which all other forms of struggle harmoniously develop," but it is an absolutely essential part of the struggle to destroy capitalism and its heavily armed state.

We also are, and have always been, united on the following points:

The struggle to destroy capitalism provides the foundation for the struggle to end all oppression. The destruction of capitalism is our central strategic goal. It is vital that we unite and mobilize against our common enemy, the international imperialist class. At the same time, we must constantly intensify our struggle against all the forms of special oppression that class society gives rise to.

Although there are several classes and strata that have no objective interest in capitalism (i.e. petty-bourgeoisie, bureaucrats, managers, etc.), the only truly revolutionary class is the proletariat—the working class. That is, all of us who own nothing but our labor and who, as a class, produce everything that gets produced in society. Only when the working class includes all of us, and when we all share equally the responsibility as well as the rewards of production—the heart and soul of society—is there a basis for freedom.

There are millions of people in this country whose lives literally depend on the destruction of capitalism and who are ready and willing to fight it given the opportunity. These are the more or less permanently jobless working class people—prisoners, ex-prisoners, old people, young people, people trapped into the lowest paid, most temporary shit jobs, people forced on welfare and forced to remain there. All of these people are discarded by capitalism in its monstrous development and thrown into its ever-increasing reserve army of labor, which capitalism uses to keep wages at a minimum and as an emergency work force in the event of war and other disasters. It is among these people that armed struggle arises spontaneously and it is here that armed struggle in general, and the GJB in particular, have taken root in this country. We firmly believe that these people will form a powerful revolutionary army and provide the armed force necessary to sweep the capitalist parasites forever into the "dustbin of history." Without their strength and courage we cannot succeed.

We recognize that sexism and the special oppression of women are the most pervasive and fundamental bulwarks of all class society; and that the struggle against the special oppression of women is one of the most potent revolutionary forces in this country. This is not to say that sexism is "more oppressive" than racism, or more anything than anything else, but simply to point out that the special oppression of women was the historical foundation on which class society arose. Sexism is the ideology of the special oppression of women and is a major tool of the ruling class to divide and exploit us. Sexism must be smashed in each of us.

The struggle of oppressed nations within the U.S. (Black people and Native Americans, for example) and around the world for liberation and self-determination is part and parcel of the world revolutionary movement and must be actively supported by North American revolutionaries. Racism is the ideology of national oppression and is a major tool of the ruling class to divide and exploit us. Racism must be smashed in each of us.

The highest form of internationalism for North American revolutionaries is to make revolution here, and destroy U.S. imperialism's base.

We are unalterably opposed to the oppression of gay people. Capitalism contains within it the seeds of fascism, and gay oppression is one of the clearest examples of this. While capitalism promotes gay oppression all the time, in a period of advanced economic deterioration and turmoil the ruling class historically encourages hysterical attacks on gays as a tool for promoting reactionary views and dissension in the working class. It diverts our attention from the real situation and crimes of the ruling class, and lays the foundation for further ruling class attacks on larger and larger segments of the population. We also reject the reactionary and fascist notion put forward by much of the left that gay people cannot be revolutionaries. History and our own practice clearly prove otherwise.

We reject the "foco" and "military vanguard" theories. We see our job as providing armed support for existing mass struggle that has clearly developed to the point where armed struggle can have a positive effect. Whenever possible we determine this by talking to the people actually involved.

In the beginning, the Brigade was also united around the need for socialism and a workers' state (the dictatorship of the proletariat) as a transition to classless society. In fact, the people who formed the Brigade were Marxist-Leninists. They saw the need to fight capitalism with armed force as a necessary step in the struggle to build socialism. They did not, however, require agreement on this for people to participate with them in armed work. And, prior to the Oregon retreat, the Brigade worked with various people from time to time at the minimum possible level of political unity—i.e. the necessity to develop armed struggle here and now, and unity on an action at a time.

The defeat at Tukwila dramatically changed the composition and disrupted the political development of the Brigade. In the aftermath of Tukwila, we had to start all over again to seek out our political unity. We no longer agree on the need for socialism and a workers' state. Although we are sharply divided on this question, we have not as yet found it necessary to resolve it either by reaching unity or disbanding. We have, however, spent a lot of time in the last year and a half struggling to better understand the nature of this division so that we can deal with it correctly when the need does arise in practice. On the question of the need for socialism, the workers' state, and other related questions, there are now essentially two views in the Brigade; these are contained in the two statements attached to this document.

We are firmly united on the eight points of unity listed above, and on the whole of the Brigade's Political Statement.

The Left

> To build up the resistance of the people to the required pitch needs more than guerrilla activity. The aims of the movement must be popularized, the objectives clearly stated, and the world must be informed of what's happening and why.
> —"Notes on Guerilla Warfare," Irish Republican Army

The left includes both formal organizations and independent, progressive people. We recognize both the positive and negative aspects of and roles played by each of these parts in moving the revolutionary struggle forward. We have deep respect for those honest people in all parts of the left who have committed themselves to and are working towards revolution. We do not see support for armed work at this time as a dividing line between honest and dishonest people. There are many honest revolutionaries who do not yet recognize their responsibility to support armed struggle.

But around the question of armed struggle, the organized left has ignored their responsibility to provide leadership and support for armed work; and it is only from progressive independents and ordinary people that we have received any kind of support.

For the most part, the organized left in Seattle has ignored us. Our experience with them has led us to become somewhat cynical about them, so their behavior hasn't bothered us too much. This cynicism is an error we are working to overcome. But their behavior has also forced us to learn the hard lessons of self-reliance: a strength we are proud of and will continue to develop.

At the same time, we recognize the important contributions made by those few independent segments of the left, and the ordinary people, who have supported us, whether verbally or materially. It was the support that was given, knowingly and unknowingly, that made it possible for us to survive long enough to learn self-reliance.

The aboveground left can and will be a mighty weapon in the hands of the people. This can be seen very clearly in their work during the Viet Nam war. They played a leading role in exposing its true imperialist and aggressive character and in helping to unite and mobilize people to oppose it. The Vietnamese people have publicly stated their recognition of the key role this resistance played in helping to end that war. We are confident that the vast majority of people and organizations in the left will come to see just as clearly their responsibility around armed struggle in this country. It is those people who critically support armed struggle now who are providing leadership examples for the rest of the left around this responsibility.

Weather Influence

When we first came together, we were heavily influenced by the Weather Underground Organization and its politics. Practice with local Weather support people, however, soon exposed to us their cowardice and hypocrisy. Both Bruce and Ed have written denunciations of Weather and we fully support these documents.[7] But we feel that no mere practical criticism can succeed in revolutionizing that organization, and that the entire thrust of Weather politics is wrong and opportunist.

Weather played an important and progressive role in its beginning because they took up the question of armed struggle in the United States at a time when most "revolutionaries" seemed to think that it was something that happened somewhere (anywhere) else. We feel as much comradeship and respect for honest rank and file Weather people as we do contempt for its opportunist leadership—leadership that brought us, for example, dope dealing and turning oneself in to the police as revolutionary tactics.

We do not believe that this opportunism is an accident—it flows directly from their view that revolution itself is something that happens elsewhere and that the only role for the North American people is to be a rooting section and fifth column in national liberation struggles against U.S. imperialism. Weather's view that people in this country are too fucked up; too fucked over; too backward; too whatever to make revolution is nothing more than an excuse for ignoring Weather's own class background. Both these views clearly underlie *Prairie Fire*[8] and everything else Weather has written, including stuff from the so-called "revolutionary committee." The majority of Weather leadership comes from the upper classes and they refuse or fear to give up their privileges. They use their politics to liquidate class struggle and allow themselves to refuse to change.

We don't think the latest spectacle WUO has provided for us, "The Split," means very much. We think the only way the "revolutionary committee" can live up to its name is to repudiate *Prairie Fire* politics and turn their energy to building revolution in this country. Instead the main issue in the split is, so far as we can tell, that the "revolutionary committee" claims to be "more *Prairie Fire* than thou."

> . . . I should just like to make one last point about solidarity between the international working class movement and our national liberation struggle . . . The main aspect of our solidarity is extremely simple: it is to fight . . . We are struggling in Guinea with guns in our hands, you must struggle in your countries as well—I don't say with guns in your hands . . . but you must find the best means and the best forms of fighting against our common enemy: this is the best form of solidarity.
> —Amilcar Cabral, 1964

The Police (and Other Backward Elements)

The police in this country divide pretty sharply into two. (Here we are talking primarily about rank and file patrol people, dispatchers, etc., and not the FBI, ATF, supervisors and other elite corps.) The police are the most visible and oppressive arm of the ruling class: armed and extremely dangerous strikebreakers, thugs, hostage takers and murderers for capitalism. Backed up by the courts, prison structure, social services and the rest of the state apparatus that enforces the control and oppression of people who are poor, sick, too old, too young, or unemployed, the police are the front line troops of capitalism. Also, their consciousness, is (obviously, given the reality of their day-to-day lives) overwhelmingly reactionary and resistant to change.

But the police have no objective interest in maintaining capitalism, and they are not the enemy. The police do not profit directly from the exploitation of labor, but are themselves exploited workers, denied even the right to strike. The police have one of capitalism's shittiest jobs. A good 70% of their time is taken up with socially necessary but mindless and tedious shit work like directing traffic, putting tickets on abandoned cars, getting dead animals off the road, and writing inane reports about all of this. (We know this to be true because for the past two years a healthy percentage of our lives has been spent listening to them on a police scanner.) For the rest they are charged with standing right up there on the front lines and keeping the lid on the volcano of violence and discontent capitalism produces. It's little wonder that so many of them turn to booze and other forms of self-destruction. A central dilemma in police officers' lives is that they have more in common with the day-to-day street criminals they send to jail than with the bosses they do it for. This is more or less openly understood by both the police and the street criminals.

Given all this it seems pretty clear that, as the contradictions sharpen, more and more of the police will come to see the truth and come over to the side of the working class where they belong. We should be prepared to welcome them—very cautiously. At the same time, we must make it very clear in our practice that individual police officers are fully responsible for the murders and torture they commit, and for the general torment they cause people. This means that people should retaliate against police crimes.

We think it is completely wrong and one-sided to view the police, state bureaucrats, bureaucrat capitalists (managers), foremen, etc., as nothing more than flunkies of the ruling class. Although for the most part these strata play a backward and reactionary role at this time and must be dealt with [with] extreme caution, they should not be summarily rejected by revolutionaries. In the long run, capitalism holds nothing but grief for any of them and they should be struggled with to see this, to change their class stand and come over to the side of the working class.

Terrorism

The bourgeois media gets a lot of mileage from calling us terrorists—as if that were the obvious truth, not open to question. In fact, we are opposed to terrorism.

Terror is a tactic, no more and no less. People employ terror to strike fear and confusion in the minds of their enemies. Terror, like most any other tactic, can be revolutionary or not depending on concrete conditions.

Terrorism, on the other hand, is never revolutionary. Terrorism is the view that the use of terror alone is the strategy for revolution: that through the use of terror alone, we can sweep the strongest oppressive force in history from the face of the earth. We think not.

Terrorism is the flip side of reformism. Terrorism, like reformism, operates on the absurd notion that capitalists and capitalism can change, given the right motivation. For reformism, this motivation is reason and/or parliamentary activity. For terrorists, the motivation is terror. But they are united in the belief that they can change capitalism without destroying it. Capitalism cannot change for the better. It operates on laws of historical development that are outside the will of terrorists, reformists, the people, and even the capitalists themselves. Capitalism can only be overthrown—by the masses of people, armed, organized and united in their own interests. Armed struggle is valid only to the extent that it supports and enhances mass struggle.

Terrorism results from the capitalist sicknesses of individualism and self-service. Underlying terrorism is an abiding contempt for the masses of people. Terror is an extremely easy tactic to use. It requires no special investigation to shed light on the possible effects of your actions; it requires no effort to be responsible for your actions, or accountable to anyone. Terrorism requires no principles to speak of and very little work. Pretty much all you need to be a terrorist is the ability to hit a target about the size of your back door at 50 or 60 yards, and a sufficiently strong arm to toss a bottle of gasoline across the street. Revolution will come here only when the force and enthusiasm for it reach throughout the country, and when the vast majority of us are taking part in it—terrorism will not bring that day one second closer. We reject terrorism and the notion of contempt for the masses which underlies it. We also think that the tactic of terror itself is dangerous and should be used very sparingly, if at all, in this country.

For people fighting against extinction, such as the Palestinian people, the use of terror is an entirely different question, however, and we support peoples' right in such struggles to use whatever means are necessary to insure their survival.

The Road Forward—Strategy

> Settle your quarrels, come together, understand the reality of our situation . . . that people are already dying you could have saved, that generations more will die or live poor butchered half-lives if you fail to act. Do what must be done, discover your humanity and your life in revolution. Pass on the torch. Join us, give up your life for the people . . . Take care of yourself and hold on.
> —George Jackson

We've learned a lot about armed struggle in the past year and a half. We have become pretty proficient tactically, and we've identified and started to resolve some of our main strategic weaknesses. Tactical problems and questions continuously come up in the course of our work. We've made it our policy to try to develop dialogue with people about our tactical problems as they arise. An example of this is the bombing questions raised in our July 4 [1977] communique.

We believe that the main task of the urban guerrilla at this time is to master the art and science of revolutionary war. We can do this only by doing it—summing up our lessons—and doing it some more. We are more than ever committed to taking part in this education by practicing revolutionary armed struggle.

Our practice has confirmed for us three critical strategic goals:

1. BREAKING DOWN OUR ISOLATION: We have come to believe that the main obstacle to developing armed struggle here is the isolation of underground fighters from the rest of the world. This problem is particularly acute for fugitives. This contradiction arises from the need for security and it must be resolved within that context so that we can survive and keep on fighting. The contradiction has two parts:

Most importantly, we are isolated from the masses of ordinary people who are the revolution. On the one hand, we are weak and vulnerable and cannot go out among the people to do investigation and learn from them as much as we need to. The simple mechanical task of growth—recruitment—represents an enormous security problem for us. On the other hand we cannot survive for long, much less be successful, unless we can find ways to do these things. We need to develop creative and concrete methods for reaching people. One example of this that we're starting to look into is citizens band (CB) radios. Once we solve the security problems around it, we can use CB radio to reach really broad segments of the population. We can talk to people, listen and respond to their criticisms, and in time develop a valuable dialogue.[9]

Secondly, we are isolated from the aboveground left. This problem isn't nearly so deep as our isolation from the masses of people, but resolving it can provide a basis for breaking down our isolation from the rest of the world. The aboveground left at this time represents our main (even though indirect) contact with the masses and with the development of the revolution. We learn what's happening from them through their publications and other media, and, to a certain extent, they help us distribute our communications to the people. Also, we believe that only by deepening our ties with people doing mass political work can we avoid for long "putting the military in command." This means that if we don't get input and direction from other people, we will be making all these decisions ourselves. Since we are military workers, this is precisely "putting the military in command."

We seek to unite with all who can be united around the eight points of unity put forward in this document. We are anxious to work with—develop organizational ties with/talk with/whatever with—all progressive people who can agree with our eight points of unity.

2. ENLARGEMENT OF THE ARMED STRUGGLE: Enlargement of the armed struggle can occur on two levels. First by enlarging the Brigade itself through recruitment, etc. Both the problems and the advantages of this are pretty obvious, and we don't want to talk about it too much for security reasons. The second is by developing ways to take part in unified and coordinated strategies and/or actions with other groups already doing armed work. We are very anxious to explore this, and we hope to have some specific suggestions along these lines in the near future.

3. DEVELOPMENT OF A RURAL BASE: As to the development of a rural base, we see this as an obvious long term need that we should start working on now so that it doesn't catch us unprepared. In the beginning stages, armed struggle can develop only in the cities. This is because of the ready availability of equipment, hiding places, targets, banks, etc. Sooner or later, however, the number of people involved becomes unwieldy and even the problem of finding a place to meet securely becomes insurmountable. In the final analysis, only rural areas can support large-scale armed struggle.

This shift can begin very simply by finding isolated areas for equipment stashes, meetings, target practice, weapons testing and so forth. We will continue to live and work entirely in the city for some time, but we must start soon to develop our ability to go to the country, hide there and attack from there.

A common argument against armed work in the U.S. at this time is that armed work has no place during a non-revolutionary period. We disagree. A revolutionary period is when: (1) the contradictions of capitalism grow so intense that the ruling class cannot continue to govern and maintain its control in the same old way; (2) the people cannot continue to live and work as they have; and (3) the people are sufficiently organized to exploit the situation and carry through the revolution. Revolutionary periods are characterized by massive upheavals, world-wide depression, imperialist war, and the general deterioration of ruling class control.

Although we agree that North America is not in a revolutionary period, it is in our future like a ship on the horizon. This is the time to get ready, to intensify aboveground mass organizing and to begin to learn the military skills we will need to prevail. A revolutionary situation can end in only one of two ways: either we will win, or they will. Their victory this time will mean either full blown fascism, or the wholesale murder of the working class through world war. Or both.

We can only win if we develop as evenly as possible both mass organization with the depth and breadth necessary to demand an end to capitalism, and the armed force necessary to enforce that demand. We firmly believe that revolution will come to this country in the form of protracted and bloody warfare and we are determined to start learning how to fight. This time it will be them and not us that bite the dust—forever.

None of this is to say that armed struggle is just practice for later. Guerrilla actions do cause material damage to the ruling class. We help to break down their class power by clearly supporting mass struggle or by punitive actions against them. Also, we help destroy the myth of their invincibility and our powerlessness. We are a small example of the potential power, strength, and determination of the people.

We urge people doing legal, aboveground work at this time to participate in this process of learning to fight by arming themselves, learning to use their weapons, and doing "armed" actions against the enemy.

Tactics

> "It's an historical reality that the easiest way to arm the revolution is by taking weapons from the enemy—likewise the most scientific way to finance revolution is by expropriating capitalist banks. The pigs have the guns and the banks have the money."
> —Black Liberation Army

The main tactics available to the urban guerrilla are as follows:

1. Expropriation and confiscation.
2. Taking prisoners.
3. Liberating prisoners.
4. Enforcing revolutionary justice.
5. Bombing and sabotage. (This can be either punitive in nature or in support of peoples' struggles.)
6. Propaganda and counter-propaganda.

The four main political principles that should guide the urban guerrilla in using and developing these tactics are:

1. Take nothing from the people; destroy nothing belonging to the people—"not so much as a thread." In the event anyone other than the ruling class or its state loses anything as a result of a guerrilla attack, they must be reimbursed immediately and fully.
2. Oppose terrorism, reformism, and all other forms of contempt for the masses.
3. Politics in command—rely on the people. This means that guerrillas must develop ways to take their leadership from the masses of people and from people doing aboveground, mass political work. This also means that we have a responsibility to be accountable to the people. Communiques are our tool for doing this. Through them we explain to people what we are doing and why; and counter the mystification and lies spread by the bourgeois media.
4. The ruling class is made up of real people, who conspire and plan their crimes behind closed doors and behind the facade of interlocking directorates and the like. Our task is to seek out the enemy behind all his fronts and attack him here. We must expose to people the thousands of threads that bind the ruling class together and to its state. This means that we do not limit ourselves only to the most

immediately obvious targets, but that we should in fact always try to demonstrate the class character of the enemy.

The main tactical principles we follow are:

1. We see propaganda and counter-propaganda (important as they are) as secondary aspects of our work. Primarily we strive for our actions to have a material effect on the world.

2. We concentrate our forces on the enemy's weaknesses. We choose when, where, and how we will attack; this is our main tactical advantage. Where necessary, we divert the police away from the target.

3. Overall, we are in a period of defense and consolidation, and we avoid actual confrontation and battle if at all possible. By choosing areas of low police concentration, we try to insure that if we are taken by surprise and have to fight, the outcome will not be in question.

4. We develop our tactics so as to keep the initiative. That is, to keep the enemy reacting and guessing, never quite sure where we are, who we are, or where we will strike next. In this way we deny them the space to develop an effective plan against us.

5. The Compton Massacre of the SLA clearly shows that the police are more than willing to use terror and murder when it suits them. If taken by surprise by a superior force, we will make a positive effort to surrender—we see no advantage to more freedom fighters being fried on the six o'clock news.

6. On the question of security, consciousness is primary and determines whether or not security will be upheld; specific security measures are secondary. Consciousness, however, develops and comes from the practice of specific measures and techniques. Security is a state of mind. Being security conscious requires that we integrate security into our whole lives; into everything we do. It doesn't apply just during certain meetings, or with particular people or when the heat is around.

Overall, security practice is common sense. Concrete methods must be different for different circumstances. We think people should develop and apply concrete security practices based on the following principles. We have developed and confirmed these principles in our practice and they have served us well:

a. Security is very important to our work; it provides the context in which we survive and act. Action, however, is primary. In the end, any contradiction between security and action must be resolved in favor of acting.

b. No matter who or what the circumstances, DON'T TELL ANYONE ANYTHING THEY DON'T NEED TO KNOW.

c. Who to trust: "Trust" NO ONE. "Trust" as a subjective judgment should not enter into security decisions. Assume anyone could be a potential informant unless you've had long (years) experience with them, or have thoroughly checked them out. This way no one questionable will see or hear anything they shouldn't.

d. When doing secure work with other people, form an organization so you'll have a vehicle for excluding people and/or thoroughly checking backgrounds when necessary.

e. Do background checks if you have a reason to question anyone. Be thorough and positive before trusting anyone you don't have common experience with.

f. Struggle against paranoia. Paranoia is unreasoning and counterproductive to security. It's a tool the enemy uses to keep us inactive. Adopt good security practices and develop an all-sided, realistic view of the world.

g. Assume the enemy knows nothing and that he knows everything he could possibly know. Operating on both these assumptions means that, on the one hand, we will be as careful as possible to deny him access to all sensitive information. We will avoid the laxness that comes from thinking that he must already know such and such so it isn't worth the trouble to keep it secret. If at the same time we assume he already knows everything he could know, we will avoid being lulled into a false sense of security and will be constantly vigilant.

7. Good intelligence is the foundation of a successful guerrilla organization. The vast majority of intelligence work involves the gathering and organization of readily available pieces of information. Although this is mostly shit work, there is no way to overstate its importance.

(An important task for people who want to remain aboveground while participating in and supporting armed struggle would be to develop these skills. Start files on developing mass struggle[s]; pay particular attention to the organization of the ruling class as it opposes them; investigate the police and strive to understand their strengths and weaknesses [start by getting a police scanner]; develop target information: suggestions, terrain, weak spots, etc.; talk to the masses about armed struggle; publish the results of these investigations so that underground fighters and everybody else can see them.)

8. Seattle is our main area of work. There are two reasons for this: First, Seattle is where we have all worked, lived and fought before. It is where we understand best. It is where our roots and our base and our debts are. Second, for as long as we can remain free and fighting where we choose, we attack for all to see the myth of police invincibility.

At the same time, we have to stay vigilant and alert to the progress the police are making in tracking us down, and be prepared to retreat at a moment's notice to a safer rear area where we can recuperate, lick our wounds, build back our strength and wait for the heat to die down so that we can return again. Our year and a half in Oregon is an example of this. The entire rest of the country is a potential rear area for us. We are trying to develop the ability to make these retreats in a planned way, and on our own initiative.

• • •

This Political Statement is a summation of our present political unity. It is the result of over two years of practicing armed work. We are in a process of constant struggle and gravity, and do not see these views as static or final. Rather, they will continue to change and develop as our experiences and the development of the revolutionary movement lead us to a deeper understanding of revolution, and the role of armed struggle.

We remind people that, in this Statement, we have not given up any specific information to the police. Rather we have let the people know as much of the specifics about us as the police already know, and are hiding from people.[10]

We encourage people to respond to this Statement. We will do our best to reply to the criticisms, comments, ideas that folks have about any parts of this Statement, our work, or questions raised in our communiques. It should be understood that responses need to be distributed publicly if they are to reach us; and that we don't see things as soon as they appear. For example, we've just recently seen "A Response to the George Jackson Brigade" by the Stagecoach Mary Collective (August 10, 1977), and are now in the process of responding to it.[11]

In the spirit of support, criticism, and understanding, we send revolutionary greetings to Stagecoach Mary Collective, Walla Walla Brothers, Left Bank Books, *Open Road* (Canada), BARC (San Francisco),[12] New World Liberation Front, Black Liberation Army, Assata Shakur (BLA), Sundiati Acoli (BLA), Red Guerilla Family,[13] *Fifth Estate*,[14] Martin Sostre, Attica Brothers, Dacajewah (John Hill, Attica),[15] *Bar None*,[16]

Fred Hampton Unit (Maine), Sam Melville-Jonathon Jackson Unit (Massachusetts), FALN,[17] Puerto Rican Socialist Party, Lolita Lebron, Irving Flores, Rafael Cancel Miranda, Andres Figueroa Cordero, Oscar Collazo, CATSHIT (Leavenworth Federal Penitentiary), Emily Harris,[18] Joe Remiro, Russ Little,[19] Bill Harris, *Midnight Special*,[20] Eddie Sanchez, Carol Crooks, Marilyn Buck, Cameron Bishop,[21] Susan Saxe, Kathy Power,[22] American Indian Movement, Leonard Peltier, Red Army Faction (Germany), ETA (Basque guerrillas),[23] Red Brigades (Italy),[24] Red Armor (Mexico), Japanese Red Army,[25] IRA (Ireland), Montoneros (Argentina), FRETILIN (Timor), International Che Guevara Brigade, Committee for the Self Defense of Society (KSS, Poland), our comrade Ed Mead, and all other groups and individuals who are involved in the practice or discussion of armed struggle against imperialism.

> hurl me
> into the next existence
> the descent into hell
> won't turn me
> i'll crawl back
> to dog his tail
> forever
>
> i'm part of the
> righteous people
> who anger slowly
> but raged undammed
> we'll gather at his door
> in such a number
> that the
>
> RUMBLING
>
> of our feet
> will make the earth tremble.
> —George Jackson

STILL AIN'T SATISFIED
DARE TO STRUGGLE, DARE TO WIN

Love and Struggle,
The George Jackson Brigade
November 1977

ANTI-AUTHORITARIAN STATEMENT[26]

The most obvious task (often the hardest to see or act on) of revolutionaries in ameriKKKa is to smash the state. Only by destroying this capitalist/imperialist economic power and its institutions can we strike a total blow to the ruling class and the state (u.s. government) which protects and maintains it. It is also obvious that if we recognize a ruling class, we must recognize a working class. This working class knows no boundaries of color, age, or sex. This does not mean that the working class does not have problems (e.g., rape, lynching, and child molestation) that are as serious as the boundary between those that got and those that ain't. But it is certain that only by destroying capitalism can we complete the changes necessary to our survival as peoples of dignity and respect. We do not believe that the majority of working people are stupid or unfeeling—in fact [we believe] just the opposite based on historical and personal knowledge. We are certain that the people will overcome all of these problems and the many others that exist.

Most of us are born, educated, work our lives away and die as part of the working class necessary to maintain capitalist economy in ameriKKKa. The economy of profits for a few, consumers and consumed, inflation, unemployment, phony shortages, never enough wages, welfare and food stamps, abortions only for the rich or purposes of genocide. The economy of increasing illiteracy; where upwards to 50% of high school graduates cannot read or write. The civil rights and/or equal rights of today can only produce tokenism in a system that depends on slavery. Wage slaves and free slaves (e.g., housewives and children) cannot be collectively unshackled until all systems that continue to create them are totally destroyed.

We should learn from all present struggles as well as the revolutionary history of peoples around the world. We should also recognize that ours is an advanced industrial society, unlike many countries where revolution has happened or is happening. Advanced industrial society in ameriKKKa also means advanced divisions, advanced isolation, and advanced lack of trust. It is time to stop believing in the "ameriKKKan dream," that we are the smartest and best. We need to deal with reality as it is; recognizing differences that exist and begin to work to build respect thru unity whenever possible.

Organizational forms that will realistically deal with the advanced ills of capitalism in ameriKKKa must be developed from our own concrete conditions and experiences. Perhaps some will be the same as those used in other places and times, but we must never deny the possibility of new ideas and forms. All of us who labor in a million different ways will decide what to do. No idealistic vanguard will lead us; we will lead ourselves. We are very unsure of the "need" for a centralized government at any time under any conditions except maybe severe famine or plague. Famine or plague can not occur very easily nowadays as we have the technology for eliminating most human ills and suffering almost immediately; or at least the capability to develop such rapidly by redirecting research efforts. It seems to us that centralized government almost always means centralized power. All the power in one place/group can only fester like a boil and eventually corrupt even those who started out with good intentions. Decentralization (spreading the authority and power as thin as possible) seem to us to be a better, safer, healthier concept. This would mean less possibility of any group or individual becoming too entrenched in positions of influence and thus, over time, power. Abolish power. We must make every effort possible to encourage all of us to develop our imaginations and to expand the people's creativity.

Serious revolutionaries must devote time and energy into the creation and implementation of organizational forms that will guarantee all of us who choose to fight equal participation in bringing the ruling class to its knees. Internal workings and how we relate are just as necessary as smashing the state. If we don't do this, smashing the state will serve no purpose. The reformists and "capitalist roaders" could easily regain control by playing on the weaknesses of traditional capitalist attitudes and conditioning. The people are the revolution. Because this is so they will have, as one of their strongest weapons, revolutionary consciousness. You cannot buy the revolution. You cannot make the revolution. You can only be the revolution. It is in your spirit or it is nowhere. Without revolutionary consciousness (the basic understanding of all oppressions), there will be no revolution, only a changing of the guard. This revolutionary consciousness is vital and must grow on, thru, and far beyond the smashing of capitalism/imperialism.

The power necessary to destroy ameriKKKan capitalism/imperialism is an awesome authority. But our new classless society will not be patriarchal or hierarchical, nor should our struggle to build it. The only way for the revolution to be ripped off from the people is if elitist leaders gain control at any point. We don't believe that the transition period from capitalism to communism need be a long or closely regulated one. The people will be armed and have a fairly clear idea of life as it should be or they will not have the love and determination necessary to smash the state. Philosophies are set up to be fulfilled; if some say a transition will be long, then they must work for it to be long or their philosophy will not be fulfilled. Our belief/goal is to be rid of any state as quickly as we can. Only a state can develop bureaucrats who close their doors to the people. Authority can't be destroyed by any movement which is in itself based on authority. Patriarchal, capital and state power can never be overthrown by organizations that are themselves hierarchical and authoritarian (of, relating to, or favoring a political system that concentrates power in the hands of a "leader" or small groups). Instead revolutionary organizations must mirror the organization of the future.

One form which has been developing in recent years is small, tightly knit, autonomous (the freedom to act in your own and others' interests in agreed upon matters without special approval, permission, or quorum) collectives; co-operating and supporting each other in as many ways as possible. (This idea is not a new one to this era; it has quite the world history). This form guards against police infiltration and the domination of the majority by a few "leaders." It just ain't possible to be a snitch or a boss where people know (have checked) where you come from and talk and work together on a regular basis.

These groups should focus on identifying leadership when it occurs and making sure it is temporary or for a particular task. All should be encouraged to assume such leadership for short-term jobs. How else can we learn to have confidence in ourselves? Skills have to be shared and tasks rotated, except in periods of extreme crisis. Rotation of all jobs is as vital as no special pay, privileges, or titles; all these help eliminate experts. We fail to see how rotation of all jobs can be anything but strengthening—as we all learn only then can we all be stronger. When we all are strong with skills and knowledge there can be no professional class of leaders. Non-oppressive ways of relating must be found and used daily. We've all had a lifetime of learning overt and subtle ways of manipulating others. Only with practice and struggle can we overcome our bourgeois socialization and relate to comrades and allies on an equal and honest basis. "None of us is better than all of us."[27]

At the same time, the groups should learn how to work and cooperate with other groups toward the common goal of smashing the state. What seems to logically come out of all this is a federation of some type as described in the SLA communique #5:

"5. To place the control of all the institutions and industries of each nation into the hands of its people. To aid sovereign nations of the federation to build nations where work contributes concretely to the full interests and needs of its workers and the communal interests of its communities and its people and the mutual interest of all with in the federation of nations . . . 15. To build a federation of nations, who shall formulate programs and unions of actions and interests that will destroy the capitalist value system and other anti-human institutions and who will be able to do this by meeting all the basic needs of all of the people and their nations. For they will be able to do this because each nation will have full control of all its industries and institutions and does not run them for profit, but in the full interest of all of the people of its nation . . . 16. To destroy all forms and institutions of Racism, Sexism, Ageism, Capitalism, Fascism, Individualism, Possessiveness, Competitiveness and all other such institutions that have made and sustained capitalism and the capitalist's class system that has oppressed and exploited all of the people of our history." (We encourage all folks to read and discuss the rest of this communique and any others you can find by the SLA.)[28]

As groups increase in size and number, they would collectively decide how to co-operate (e.g., trade) and defend themselves and each other without losing their self-determination. We think this is a very high degree of unity—trading and defending ain't small things! It means determining an economic system that is not based on profits and combating the enemy in all his hiding places. A federation seems to be a working method for recognizing existing differences, respecting them, and struggling toward overcoming them.

Although it's much to early to tell, this federation form could probably be expanded and used before, during, and after the smashing of state power. It seems to be a common view among Marxist-Leninists that anti-authoritarians, and other such opportunist, slanderous rabble don't care about "the baby" and are foolishly simple enough to throw out the dearest thing we have, the infant of tomorrow. We would prefer to not drown "the baby" nor to smother it in our bosom; but to teach it to be strong, self-reliant, and uninhibited. It's true there are several questions that need answering. We encourage folks to be thinking about the following: What happens when the revolution involves upwards to 200 million people? How will the people determine sections of the federation? Special oppression? Production? Geography? We are just beginning to form thoughts on these questions and would like plenty more input. We need to hear your ideas.

A current example of this form at work is the recent birth of 3rd World gay organizations in the San Francisco Bay area. These sisters and brothers no doubt encountered many obvious and presently unsolvable contradictions trying to work with predominately straight 3rd World groups and predominately white gay groups. The solution has been to build several (Black, Asian, and Native American that we've heard about) autonomous 3rd World gay organizations. This enables them to do their work without a lot of bullshit and also insures that the needs relating to their special oppressions will be met. Another thing this form gives is a real base of support developing from 3rd World gays' concrete conditions and experiences. No oppressor can fully understand the pain, anger, or uncertainty of being oppressed. White people cannot understand what it's like to be a person of color in ameriKKKa, nor can heterosexuals understand what it is to be an ameriKKKan lesbian or faggot.

The time for fighting this revolution is never tomorrow; whatever tool/forms are necessary must be learned and used today. Communication is an example of one of the most important areas of what we need to do well and quickly. Regardless of structure, any time expansion occurs, keeping in touch with reality/others becomes a real problem. The responsibility is two way: to let others know where we are and to find out about other peoples. Working coalitions of oppressed peoples are a necessity in every job from painting picket signs to building and planting bombs. But they can only last a short time unless all involved are treated as equals. This means listening to and struggling with each other in an atmosphere of sincere support. This is known as respect; a necessity for all of us and something that is missing in the lives of ameriKKKa's oppressed peoples. We have to learn to take control over our own lives now, and how to develop a collective power base without fucking over each other. We have a job to do here in the belly of the beast, to destroy capitalism/imperialism at its roots. Let's get on with it!

p.s. cooperating, autonomous groups of mosquitoes can drive an elephant insane.

SERVE THE PEOPLE—FIGHT FOR SOCIALISM
From the George Jackson Brigade Marxist Leninists[29]

As communists, we fully agree with the final goal of liberation and a classless, stateless society put forward by our comrades in their statement: that goal is our reason for being here. We also share the same deep concern and determination that our revolution not be ripped off by capitalists, patriarchs, hierarchists, or any of the other forces of evil that serve the international ruling class. There is no disagreement within the Brigade over the need to build structures that mirror our revolutionary goals; the necessity of involving all of us in making revolution; the need for people to be nurturing and respectful of each other, etc. Our disagreement is on how to achieve all of this. In this statement, we will limit ourselves to discussion of our differences.

Our differences are in effect a disagreement between anarchism and communism. Anarchism develops in honest people because of an honest and righteous concern that democracy, individual initiative and the power of the people be upheld. Anarchist solutions, however, unrealistically deal with only one side of the complex set of contradictions facing us. In this statement, we are not denying any side of any contradiction, but merely pointing out in each case the side that is ignored by anarchism. In each case here, that part is also clearly primary.

There is nothing especially new in anarchism. Every pre-revolutionary period in capitalism has seen the re-emergence of anarchist as well as Marxist-Leninist ideas. Although anarchism has assumed various names and forms throughout the years (Anarchism, Antiauthoritarianism, Anarcho-such and such, etc.), its central characteristic has always been a confused and paranoid view of the state.

The state (any state) is an instrument of class rule—no more and no less. It is, therefore, state agencies who are the visible agents of oppression now: police, prisons, courts, schools, welfare, etc. If we take this superficial appearance and accept it as the true nature of things, we would naturally conclude that it is the government itself that causes oppression, and that the key to ending oppression and exploitation is to do away with government. Nothing could be further from the truth. Government is itself the result (and often the form) of the oppression that class society produces. Doing away with government will be the result of doing away with class society, and not the other way around. We seek to destroy capitalism because it stands in the way of liberation and an end to oppression. We smash the bourgeois state, not because smashing the state will automatically produce freedom, but because if we are to destroy capitalism and its ruling class we must first destroy the means by which it rules.

Since the state is no more or less then the instrument of class rule, the state will continue to exist, no matter what we might prefer, for as long as class society exists. And a revolution cannot immediately do away with class society, it can only replace one ruling class with another. What's unique about this historical period is that the new ruling class will be the masses of laborers instead of a few bosses.

We want to state as clearly as possible that, although we do not believe that anarchists are "opportunistic, slanderous rabble," we do firmly believe that anarchism is grounded in the ideology of the capitalists, and that its persistence in honest people is the clearest example we can think of just how deep that ideology is driven into all of us. The real danger of anarchism is that it saps the strength of honest revolutionaries, and diverts revolutionary energy away from concrete, realistic goals. The following seven points represent the main areas of struggle between anarchism and communism within the Brigade.

1. Not even the anarchists can completely ignore reality, and when pushed to the wall, they often start talking about a federation of small "affinity" groups as a solution to the problem of transition from capitalism to communism. This is because they view (and fear) centralism, the dictatorship of the proletariat, and revolutionary leadership as things in themselves, divorced from the concrete reality in which they exist and out of which they flow. This is at the heart of the disagreement within the Brigade.

Centralism, like anything else, serves one class interest or another. Airplanes, tanks, bombs, guns, all of these [are] terrible things in the service of the imperialists. In the hands of the people, however, they are tools of liberation. Centralism, in the service of imperialism, is a terrible thing. In the hands of the people, centralism is a tool of liberation no less than any other weapon. Anything is "good" or "bad" depending only on how and in whose interest it is used. To jump to the simplistic and one-sided view that the abstract concepts of centralism, the dictatorship of the proletariat and revolutionary leadership are "bad" and must be rejected is to throw the baby out with the bath water. Seeing things as abstract, divorced from the reality surrounding them, is the way the bourgeoisie teaches us to view the world.

Not that we have any choice in the matter. The briefest glance at the reality that exists in this country leaves no room for doubt as to whether our new government will be centralized or fragmented. When we abolish private ownership of the means of production in this country, we will come into control of a huge, immensely complex, integrated and unified system of production. The reality before us includes an international bourgeoisie (the present ruling class), with its own organizations; a socialized and integrated national and international economy; twenty million "white collar" bureaucrats; a highly centralized and effective police and military apparatus; etc. Even assuming there were some justification for dividing us into small, autonomous groups (which there is not), the mind boggles at the problem of separating out areas of responsibility and control from the vast system of production in this country and assuring that each affinity group fully acts in the interests of everybody in each of the other "affinity" groups; in a federation. We think it's absurd on the face of it.

The immense task of transforming society will require the collective input of everybody; democratic centralism is the tool for assuring that everybody is represented, and that our representation has an effect on the world we seek to change. Democratic centralism combines the strength and diversity of democracy with the strength and unity of centralism. Revolutionary democratic centralism is not hierarchy and power vested in a few leaders over the rest of us. The democratically centralist proletarian state is precisely power seated in the whole of the people, united. Proletarian democratic centralism is a weapon to do away with hierarchy and guarantee the widest possible participation in revolution.

Because of the lack of unity and communication, federation may well be a necessary tactical step at this time—particularly for groups engaged in armed work. In a period when we don't have enough political unity to form one organization, this would allow us to achieve unity of action while preserving small group autonomy. But we believe that federation should be seen as a temporary step, required because of our weaknesses. Federation is a necessary evil that promotes and perpetuates our divisions and it should be discarded as soon as possible. Instead of building unity, federation institutionalizes our differences.

Socialism is the general form we will use to rid society, ourselves and our children of the cancer of bourgeois practice and ideology. It's hard for us to see how this could be accomplished within small autonomous affinity groups. What if, for example, the Black Flag Tractor factory in

Ogden, Utah decided that the sexual division of labor was perfectly natural, and correct; that woman's place was in the home, and that they were not going to mess with the "natural order of things"? Is this their right as an autonomous affinity group if the majority of them agree? We think not. What if the Red Star Locomotive company in Santa Fe, New Mexico, decided that, due to their strategic location in the nation's transportation system they could hold the rest of us up for an exorbitant price for their services? Would this be liberation or extortion?

None of this means that we should ignore the problems that special oppression and the longstanding divisions that have been imposed on our class have produced. The struggle to rid ourselves of our oppressive notions and behaviour, and learn new, revolutionary ways of being, will be a long and hard one. And we recognize the need, both before and during socialism, for separate organizations of specially oppressed people. But these separate organizations will not be independent governments; rather their function will be to lead all of us in our common fight to overcome all forms of special oppression. They would have the same goal as the socialist state of which they are a part: to do away with the reason for their existence; to reach a time of real unity and communism.

We are fundamentally opposed to a federation of small "affinity" groups as a revolutionary goal; clearly a system that requires not one but numerous bureaucracies, governments and bureaucrats is much easier to rip off. If it is true (and we believe it is) that the working class "knows no boundaries of color, sex or age," that "all who depend on their labor (paid or unpaid) for survival are members," then any attempts to divide us into small groups is doomed to fail.

The sole exception to this is in the case of oppressed nations within the United States. We fully support the right of oppressed nationalities to secure territory within North America, form their own governments and determine their own destinies.

2. We disagree with the view implicit in anarchism, and explicit in our comrades' statement, that the transition from full-blown capitalism to a classless, stateless society will take a relatively brief period of time. The overthrow of capitalism will take a considerably long time; and the road there will have many twists and turns, false starts, backtracks, etc. But this task, long and arduous though it will be, represents only the first and simplest step in our struggle to be free. We need clearly to understand the distinction between the overthrow of

capitalism (the seizure of state power), and the advent of a classless, stateless society. The former is only the first, tiny step in a journey that will take many years, perhaps generations. It's very important to be clear on this question. Otherwise, not only will we be out of step with reality on the question of what is to replace capitalism; we will very likely pass up the opportunity to destroy capitalism when it arises. Lenin once said that the difference between the Bolsheviks and the anarchists was that the anarchists wanted the revolution to wait until people were different, while the Bolsheviks wanted the revolution now, with people as they are. Ain't it the truth.

3. Revolutionary leadership occurs when the development of the revolution produces people with the experience and clarity of insight necessary to sum up the collective experience of the entire class and identify the way forward. Revolutionary leadership is a product and a weapon of the revolution, and if we are to succeed, we must learn to identify it and encourage it among us. At the same time, we must learn to be vigilant and to distinguish between revolutionary leadership and self-serving opportunism; we must strip leadership positions of all privilege and permanence; and we must never allow power to rest in the hands of state or party officials. The key to developing responsible leadership is to encourage the initiative of the masses of people. Only the masses of people, armed, organized and conscious of our class and our role in society can for long guarantee responsible, revolutionary leadership. We oppose the arbitrary "rotation" of leadership positions because we believe it weakens the revolutionary struggle. The masses of people will choose people for leadership positions based on their practice, experience, and grasp of reality; and they will change them when they see fit.

4. American exceptionalism is nothing new. Traditionally, however, it's been used to deny the need for armed struggle in the U.S., i.e. "America has a long history of democracy, almost universal literacy, universal suffrage, and a tradition of encouraging, at least in words, civil dissent. Therefore, American bourgeois democracy is much more unstable in its class character, and socialism can be snuck into America without the ugly necessity of armed struggle." And so on.

Our comrades' brand of American exceptionalism is a little more subtle. They turn the premise on its head and persistently claim that since the American working class (although "not stupid or unfeeling") is so fucked up, individualized, competitive, racist, sexist, etc., the centralization and unity of socialism is unnecessary or dangerous or something. If all this slander were true (which it is not), we would expect to find anarchists arguing for more centralization to keep all these fucked up people from ripping off their own revolution.

5. While it is true that security is much easier in very small, tightly knit groups that are isolated from each other, it's also true that small, tightly knit autonomous groupings can't be very effective against a united, monolithic force like the U.S. Army. There is a contradiction between the revolutionary goals of developing individual initiative and promoting the fullest possible democracy on the one hand, and the need for strength and unity of action that comes from centralized organization on the other. Anarchism's view of this is too one-sided; it completely ignores the second part of the contradiction. They would have us take on an (already "insane") elephant with a gang of mosquitoes.

6. "A revolution is certainly the most authoritarian thing there is; it is the act whereby one part of the population imposes its will upon the other part by means of rifles, bayonets, and cannon—authoritarian means, if such there be at all . . ." (V.I. Lenin, *State and Revolution*). This seems pretty obvious and we don't understand how anarchists propose to accomplish a non-authoritarian revolution—it seems a contradiction in terms. If what they mean is a revolution that is non-authoritarian toward the toiling masses, while being ruthlessly authoritarian toward the ex-oppressors, then we would agree with them 100%. That is a definition of the dictatorship of the proletariat.

7. We have used the phrase "the masses" extensively throughout this statement, and we'd like to clarify what we mean by that. Very simply, we mean the whole of the people (excluding the ruling class and its agents, and including ourselves) as a whole; as distinct from any of its parts. No part of the people will carry through the revolution by themselves—not the industrial working class, not women, not men, not oppressed nationalities, not gay people, not communists, not anarchists, not anyone by themselves—only all of us, massed together, can win. Only when each of us has truly integrated the slogan "serve the masses" into our thought and practice; only when each of us truly sees our individual interests, needs and desires as secondary to

the interests, needs and desires of all of us will the revolution be completed. This is the heart of revolutionizing our consciousness.

A struggle recently occurred in the Brigade over the phrase and the idea that our work should be "in the service of the people." This phrase was omitted from the Brigade's statement of unity because the anarchists among us held that we are "the people," or at least part of them, and that this idea therefore falsely sets us above everybody else and is elitist. If we are to have any hope of putting our own interests, needs and desires secondary to those of all of us, we had better understand clearly that being a part of the people is much different from being "the people."

> Our point of departure is to serve the people wholeheartedly and never for a moment divorce ourselves from the masses, to proceed in all cases from the interests of the people and not from one's self-interest or from the interests of a small group . . .
> —Mao Tse Tung, 1945

As communists, our goal is to see the masses of working people in full ownership and control of all of society and all that society produces. In order to accomplish this, we must smash the bourgeois state and replace it with a fully democratic workers' government.

It is impossible to leap in one bound from capitalism to a classless, stateless society. The resistance of the international ruling class (the bourgeoisie) will not disappear simply because we destroy the oppressors' state apparatus. Far from it. In fact, their resistance and determination to regain their power will increase a thousand-fold. Given half a chance, they will succeed, as they have in the Soviet Union. This is one of the clearest and most important lessons passed onto us by the Russian Revolution.

The bourgeoisie have vast international connections with almost unlimited money and resources. Most importantly, they have our deep force of habit passively to accept bourgeois ways of thought, relationships and social organization. Day to day life in their system (capitalism) has created and constantly reinforces this in all of us. While we must begin transforming our consciousness now, it seems no more than common sense to us that this ideology cannot be fully overcome within capitalism, since capitalism is its source. Only years of practice and prolonged struggle within a non-exploitive social context can finally and completely overcome it.

Socialism—a workers' state—is necessary to make the transition from capitalism to communism (classless society). This workers' democracy will have a twofold purpose. First, it will be the weapon whereby people will eliminate private ownership of the means of production and the unemployment, poverty, destruction of the environment, war, and all the misery capitalism produces in the name of profit. It is only within this context that we will all be able completely to transform ourselves and throw off the shackles of "traditional capitalist attitudes and conditioning" that blind and cripple us. Second, it will safeguard and defend our revolution by ruthlessly suppressing the attempts of the international bourgeoisie to restore their system of greed and human misery.

The principles of socialism and the workers' state were not "invented" by Marx, Lenin, or anyone else. They were discovered, by the people, in bloody struggle against the bourgeoisie; and they have been used and refined in every anti-capitalist revolution since the Paris Commune of 1871. There are lots of positive as well as negative lessons to learn from these experiences. This is not to say that some "blueprint" for revolution is mechanically passed on to us. Revolution is much harder work than that. Marxism-Leninism is a science that analyzes reality as it exists, and which changes as historical reality changes. Marxism-Leninism is the concrete analysis of concrete conditions. Concrete conditions are different here than they have been anywhere else—but that's been true everywhere. Concrete conditions in China were vastly different from those in the Paris Commune; those in Vietnam much different from the Soviet Union; and so on. And the specific forms of socialism in these countries have reflected these differences. The specific forms of socialism in the United States will be very different from anywhere else, and will be discovered by the people here in the process of struggle and practice. The way to assure that our revolution will meet the needs and represent the interests of all of us, is for all of us to participate in the leadership of our revolution. To be successful demands that we also be firmly rooted in reality, and learn from and use the lessons of history and our own experience, to develop a successful strategy for revolution here.

Socialist Revolution is the "self-conscious, independent movement of the immense majority in the interest of the immense majority." (Karl Marx)

Obviously, the reaction of bourgeois elements to these statements of differences will be to play them up as some kind of a split. We think people should struggle against this sleazy divisiveness when it occurs. We are firmly united on the eight points of unity and on the whole of the Brigade's Political Statement. Our political differences are not around questions that are primary at this time (although they will in the future mean the difference between success and failure for revolution in this country). Our political differences are theoretical at this time, and have no effect on our work. We intend to be together and fighting for a long time to come! The answers to these questions will be resolved in practice and decided by the masses of people in this country and around the world in the process of making revolution.

We encourage people to deal with the question of armed struggle in this country at this time, and to fully discuss, criticize and respond to the Brigade's Political Statement and our work. We need this response and criticism. Discussion of our theoretical differences is plentiful and ongoing in existing Marxist-Leninist and anarchist writings, while discussion of the issues raised in this document and our work is almost nonexistent. In any event, we are not interested in and will not respond to any comments on our statements of differences for at least six months.

COMBAT BOURGEOIS DIVISIVENESS AND SENSATIONALISM!

CHRONOLOGY OF BRIGADE ACTIONS

Early Spring 1975—Firebombed Seattle Contractor
Firebombed and destroyed the offices of a local contractor in support of a local struggle to win jobs for Black people in the construction industry. This was a prolonged struggle that had received wide support in the community. Throughout the struggle there were mass demonstrations and many demonstrators were arrested. This action was unclaimed at the time because we didn't want to draw attention away from the jobs issue; it was also receiving extensive media coverage because of its mass character. Just after the action, we did privately circulate a criticism of the leaderships' strategy of pitting Blacks against whites for jobs, instead of uniting around the demand of jobs for all.[30]

Late Spring 1975—Sabotage And Destruction Of Heavy Equipment At Contractor's
Sabotaged several pieces of equipment, burned and destroyed a large truck and heavily damaged a D G Cat belonging to the contractor referred to above. This action occurred just prior to the trials of people charged in connection with the mass demonstrations around the struggle for Black construction jobs. After the action, charges against the protesters were dropped because the contractor refused to testify. He told reporters his refusal was based on the tens of thousands of dollars of damage suffered and he wanted no more trouble.[31] This action was also unclaimed at the time.

June 1, 1975[32]—Pipebombed Washington State Department Of Corrections Offices, Olympia
In January of 1975,[33] prisoners at Walla Walla state prison took hostages, seized the prison hospital and a wing of the prison to put forward a number of just demands including: a halt to behavior modification programs, particularly the brutal one in the prison's Mental Health Unit; an end to involuntary transfers; and firing the director and several abusive employees of the Mental Health Unit. This rebellion occurred after lengthy peaceful negotiations with prison officials failed to produce any results. The rebellion was crushed, a complete media blackout imposed, and the prison bureaucrats continued to ignore the prisoners' demands.

On June 1, the Brigade burglarized and pipebombed the main office of the Washington State Department of Corrections in Olympia. The bomb destroyed the office of the deputy director of Corrections, damaged much of the east wing on the second floor and part of the first floor. Damage exceeded $100,000. This action was in support of the demands raised by Walla Walla prisoners' six months earlier. This action also publicly announced the existence of the Brigade. (Communique issued)

August 1975—Pipebombed Federal Bureau of Investigation & Bureau of Indian Affairs
We simultaneously bombed the FBI office in Tacoma and the BIA offices in Everett, Washington, in response to FBI terrorism at the Rosebud and Pine Ridge reservations in North Dakota. We had the action to coincide with a 100 mile mass march from Seattle to Portland organized by local Native American leaders. This action was unclaimed at the time because we didn't want to draw attention away from the primary issue of FBI terrorism against Native Americans.[34]

September 18, 1975—Pipebombed Capital Hill Safeway Store
Bombed a 50 pound bag of dog food inside the Capital Hill Safeway store in Seattle. This action was intended to show love and solidarity with a man who, in an independent action, had died four days earlier attempting to arm a bomb behind the same Safeway store.[35] On the day our bomb was to be planted, we received word of the SLA capture,[36] and our rage increased. Although Safeway is a perpetual target because of the super-exploitation of farm workers, Safeways' use of poisonous pesticides and chemicals for profit, and monopolistic practices that squeeze every last penny out of their customers, this was the closest thing to a spontaneous action ever indulged in by the Brigade.

Our bomb caused minor injuries to several customers. This action was *wrong* because we brought violence and terror to a poor neighborhood, and we have thoroughly criticized ourselves and changed our practice. (Communique issued)

January 1, 1976—Pipebombed Safeway's Main Office & The Laurelhurst Transformer
Exploded two bombs at Safeway's main office for the Seattle area in Bellevue—one under a coolant tank, and one in a construction site at their administrative offices. Simultaneously, we destroyed the main transformer supplying power to the rich Laurelhurst suburb of Seattle. The Safeway bombs were intended to be a self-criticism in practice of the Capitol Hill Safeway bombing, as well as a continuation of the attack against Safeway. Damage was apparently minimal.

The Laurelhurst bomb was in support of a long and courageous strike by City Light workers in Seattle. The $250,000 substation was completely destroyed. Striking workers refused to perform emergency repairs on the substation and picketed it so as to prevent scabs or supervisors from repairing it during their strike. ("New Year 1976" communique issued)

January 23, 1976—Tukwila Bank Robbery Attempt
Unsuccessfully attempted to expropriate $43,000 from the Tukwila branch of the Pacific National Bank of Washington. A brutal attack by King County police and Tukwila Police left our comrade Bruce Seidel dead, John Sherman shot in the jaw, and John and Ed Mead in police custody. All other participants successfully escaped after firing on police from the rear in an attempt to aid our comrades in the bank. The expropriation was intended to finance armed work. This action was attempted with insufficient knowledge of the police, armed robbery tactics, and combat training. We paid dearly for our lessons.

March 10, 1976—Prisoner Liberation
We rescued John Sherman from police custody during a doctor's appointment at Harborview Medical Center. During the action it became necessary to shoot and wound a King County police officer because of his failure to cooperate fully with the comrade assigned to him. ("International Women's Day" communique issued)

June 1976 to February 1977—Tactical Retreat
Tukwila nearly destroyed us, and the rescue drained the last of our meager resources. The organized left almost unanimously rejected us, and this forced us to learn to rely on ourselves, ordinary people, and progressive independents in the left. Many ordinary people did help us, knowingly and unknowingly, and this made it possible for us to survive, rebuild our strength, and learn the hard lessons of self-reliance. This move to self-reliance was probably the most important thing we accomplished during the retreat. We also accumulated lots of equipment, experience and knowledge of the police. We did six teller robberies for more than $25,000, and ran checks for survival, equipment and supplies. We later claimed these actions because we are determined to be accountable to the people, and because the police knew we were responsible and were withholding this information for reasons of their own.

After the Tukwila action, the government had launched a massive attack on the left with their Grand Jury. Numerous people were .

subpoenaed, and many of them refused to cooperate. In June 1976, the Brigade sent handwriting samples to help clear a woman falsely accused of signing one of our communiques. Another woman spent six months in jail for refusing to cooperate; and a Black ex-convict prison activist was convicted of participation in Brigade activities on guilt by association with the prison movement, the testimony of a junkie (for which the Feds paid $10,000 and a new identity!), and because of the color of his skin.[37] Our captured comrade Ed Mead was also convicted and sentenced to several lifetimes in the state penitentiary at Walla Walla. While some people fought the Grand Jury only out of narrow, individualistic self-interest (some even cooperated), many others correctly saw it as a collective struggle and based their resistance on that view. Many people took up the fight even though they weren't being directly attacked. In the end, the peoples' united resistance defeated the Grand Jury attack and forced the Feds to turn to other, sneakier tactics. We send our deepest love and support to all those who fought against the Grand Jury, and who were or continue to be attacked by the state.

May 12, 1977—Pipebombed Rainier National Bank
Pipebombs were placed at two Bellevue area Rainier[38] National Bank branches. One failed to explode because of faulty equipment, and the other exploded causing damage to the safe deposit vault and an adjoining wall. This action was to support the longest strike in the history of Washington prisons by maximum security and ISU (the hole) prisoners at Walla Walla state prison, and in response to a series of attacks and empty promises passed off as "changes" by prison bureaucrats. The strike was primarily around brutal conditions in the hole, and (again) behavior modification programs. We chose Rainier National Bank because of its corporate ties to the *Seattle Times*—the leader of the ruling class propaganda against the prisoners.

The ruling class response to this attack was to up the price on the heads of two Brigade comrades.[39] Striking prisoners in the hole at Walla Walla issued a statement fully supporting the action. ("May Day" communique issued)

May 21, 1977—Armed Expropriation
Expropriated $1,300 from the Newport Hills (Bellevue area) state liquor store. This action was to finance armed work.

June 20, 1977—Armed Expropriation
Expropriated $4200 from the Factoria (Bellevue area) branch of

the Rainier National Bank. We chose RNB because of the *Seattle Times'* continued refusal to print any of the truth of the struggle and strike at Walla Walla. This action was to finance armed work. We claimed both of these expropriations because the police were hiding their knowledge that we were responsible for the actions, and we wanted to warn people to be alert to their investigations. ("Summer Solstice" communique issued)

July 4, 1977—Attempted Bombing, Olympia
Unsuccessfully attempted to destroy the main substation supplying power to the State Capitol complex in Olympia. The thirty-minute warning given police to allow them ample time to evacuate the immediate area also gave them ample time to throw the safety switch and turn off the bomb. The action was in support of the continuing strike by men in the hole at Walla Walla and in support for their demand for decent living conditions and humane treatment.

By August, the long-time, hated warden, bloody B.J. Rhay had been successfully ousted, a new warden appointed, and the hole had been cleaned and painted. The men ended their strike when these minimal demands were met. Subsequently, some other prisoner demands were met, including the release of our comrade Ed Mead and a number of others from their arbitrary and prolonged confinement in the hole. There was and is a complete blackout of this news and continuing prisoner grievances in the Seattle media. ("Tell No Lies, Claim No Easy Victories" communique issued)

September 8, 1977—Armed Expropriation
Expropriated $1100 from the Juanita branch of Old National Bank. This action was to finance armed work.

September 19, 1977—Armed Expropriation
Expropriated $8200 from the Skyway branch of People's National Bank. This action was to finance armed work.

October 6, 1977—Attempted Weapons Test at Car Dealership
Unsuccessfully attempted to test an incendiary bomb on some recreational vehicles at the Westlund Buick new car dealership. This action was in support of a six-month strike by Seattle automotive machinists and several other automotive unions. Westlund was chosen because he is head of the Dealers' Association.

October 12, 1977—Pipebombed Car Dealership

Pipebombed and caused minor damage to the main building of S.L. Savidge new car dealership. This action was in support of the six-month strike by Seattle automotive machinists and other unions. Savidge was chosen because of his role in the union busting attempts of the Dealers' Association. ("Bust the Bosses" communique issued)

October 15, 1977—Firebombed Car Dealership

Firebombed and destroyed several new cars at the BBC Dodge new car dealership. This action was in support of the six-month strike by Seattle automotive machinists and several other automotive unions. The strike continues. (Verification that we were responsible for all three dealership bombings was sent to the Automotive Machinists Union after the dealers publicly accused the union and striking workers of complicity in the actions. Subsequently the union took the offensive and filed a half-million dollar slander suit against the King County Automobile Dealers' Association, and its chairman and former chairman. They also filed an N.L.R.B. complaint charging the Dealers' Association with bad-faith bargaining.)

November 1, 1977—Pipebombed Mercedes-Benz German Car Dealership

Pipebombed and destroyed a $24,000 Mercedes-Benz, and damaged several other new cars and the building at the Phil Smart Mercedes-Benz dealership in Bellevue. This action was to demonstrate support and solidarity with the Red Army Faction in Germany, and the thousands of people fighting in the streets in Europe and around the world in retaliation for the West German government's murders of Red Army Faction guerrillas Gudrun Ensslin, Jan Carl Raspe, and Andreas Baader, in their prison cells. ("You Can Kill A Revolutionary, But You Can't Kill The Revolution" communique issued)

November 3, 1977—The Power Of The People Is The Force Of Life

Issued "The Power Of The People Is The Force Of Life," Political Statement of the George Jackson Brigade.

Community Response
To the George Jackson Brigade
The Valerian Coven

To the George Jackson Brigade:

Dear Comrades,

We are writing you after much discussion and reading of the George Jackson Brigade political statement and communiques issued. We feel this discussion is a good place to start but critical support is more than this. We feel it is important to share our criticism with you in hopes that you'll get the feedback you asked for months ago. We criticize ourselves for the time lag in responding. We realize it is our responsibility to respond to you to help break down the isolation created between aboveground and underground political activity. We also realize that effective, open communication cannot happen unless we respond to what you have put time and energy into writing. We want you to know that we extend to you our support and appreciation for writing the political statement and communiques explaining who you are, and what you see as your work and reasons and decision-making process. We also feel supportive of the risks you have taken and continue to take in the name of revolutionary struggle. We send greetings to Rita and Ed. Stay strong . . . feel our strength on the other side of the walls move through you.

Out of our discussions came serious questions and criticisms about how we see you implementing point of unity #8 in your political statement: "We reject the 'foco' and 'military vanguard' theories. We see our job as providing armed support for existing mass struggle that has clearly developed to the point where armed struggle can have a positive effect. Whenever possible we determine this by talking to the people actually involved." We are in agreement with this point of unity. We also feel this is an area where open communication between above and underground work is vital. We feel more discrimination and investigation must happen in order to evaluate the effectiveness of armed struggle in regards to a particular issue. Some of us feel we cannot support the armed actions around the machinist union strike. Those who don't give the following reasons:

1) There are more issues than striking workers at stake. One of the struck dealers is on property robbed from older poor residents of a neighborhood that is struggling daily to survive and keep big business

from suffocating them out of existence. The visible striking workers are only a small percentage of people affected by the bosses that "we are trying to bust." We criticize you for not taking into account other people who suffer from the greediness of the profitmakers. The residents of that neighborhood are too poor, too old, and too sick to ever walk a picket line and for some ever to hope to see the possibility of having a job to strike at.

2) Most of the machinists walking the picket line are white men. They are making $7–10 an hour. It is very difficult to make your way into the machinists union if you are a woman (white or third world) or a third world man. The sexist ridicule that a woman has to put up with, whether it's talking to a striker, applying for a job or buying parts from the parts department, makes it pretty difficult to support the workers' earning power based on racial and sexual privilege.

3) Though in theory we support your bombings of the dealerships and attacks against bosses, we wonder if you're open enough to hear the non-support from the strikers and re-evaluate your work. This has not been a violent strike. The strikers have not been motivated to fight back or commit any acts of sabotage or self-defense, as in, say, the miner's strike. So where does the armed action fit in? The strikers and union bosses, from what we've read and seen televised, condemn your actions and are not exactly rallying behind them. Some of us feel that for armed support work to be effective it should come at a time when those workers are *themselves* fighting back and underground folk supplementing those actions. Otherwise there is danger in further hampering and alienating workers whose struggles you wish to support. We also see this as a military vanguard attitude saying to the strikers, "follow us, we know best how to win your battles."

We are all in agreement that the communiques, stating specific tasks (armed and unarmed) outlining what folks can do to plug into this long, weary strike were good and clear. One suggestion we would like to make, however, concerning all of your written material is about the heavy use or rhetoric. Without a "revie" dictionary most folks are at a loss in figuring out what you mean. Can you hear that the so-called "masses" don't know what the hell you're talking about when you use terms such as imperialist, nations, vanguard, reactionary, oppression, fascism, etc? It would be helpful if you would define your terms if you feel it's necessary to use rhetorical jargon. Be aware that it turns a lot of folks off and can come off as elitist. We in the aboveground share this responsibility in making ourselves heard and understood. We do feel you were clearly understood when you wrote the jail letter, the May Day communique and the discussion on terrorism in your statement.

We do feel that your most effective work has been around prison issues. We give the following reasons:

1) Violent aggressions call for violent retaliations. The prisons are full of violent dehumanizing conditions. The pipe bombing of the Wash. state Dept. of Corrections offices in Olympia, the 1977 attempted bombing of the main substation supplying power to the State Capitol in Olympia were clearly warranted actions against state institutions and mobilized support for the Walla Walla strike—on both sides of the prison walls.

2) The communiques that followed these actions and the jail letter dated Dec. 23 were excellent examples of effective communication in an area where the aboveground can and is working to end the brutalizing conditions suffered by inmates.

We have some strong disagreements with your analysis of the police and their revolutionary potential. You talked in your political statement about their class origins and ultimate class interest without directly dealing with racism and sexism. Most rank and file police are white males. Many of them spend time beating up queers, shooting black robbery "suspects" in the back, harassing prostitutes, and ignoring, ridiculing and/or actively participating in the life and death struggles of rape victims and battered women. For the police to see these people as their allies in the class struggle would require leaps of consciousness that we don't expect from many of them.

The folks in power, for the most part white rich men, have spent much time and money developing, encouraging, training and giving social license to certain people to express the violence that keeps us all down. This form of violence also protects their precious private property—the source of their power. While we agree that for the most part the police's economic interest is not served by keeping the less powerful down, we must recognize the benefits they do reap from their position. This society gives us all reason to be violent but robs us of the right and power to protect ourselves and retaliate against these constant attacks. Police, on the other hand, are hired and trained to express violence, especially racially and sexually, their lack of power economically would give them all the more reason to hold on to what they've got. But there is much more to an analysis of the police force than along economic lines. We feel you did not analyze the development of the present police force and brutality adequately. We *strongly* urge you and anyone else reading this letter to read and discuss *Iron Fist and Velvet Glove: An Analysis of the Police.*[40]

We'd like to finally comment on "mass struggle." We are aboveground workers and a part of that "mass." We must do our work differently than you do yours. We are employed workers and students who take daily risks in providing services to poor and working class young and old people. We feel we do not confine our politics to meetings and organizations. We take them with us to the job. Which means putting ourselves on the line one day and going back the next to face the consequences of our overt actions. We cannot hide our identity or make hit and run attempts at change. We believe our aboveground work is essential and vital to a revolutionary overthrow of Amerikkka.

We also see underground work as an essential and necessary part of the whole, entire struggle. We need to know if you're into struggling and acknowledging our work. Will our input about the usefulness and timing of armed support for our struggles and work be heeded?

In the destruction of a government that robs us daily of our money, pride, and freedom, we must not overlook the importance of mobilizing and supporting each other in this long struggle. It took us months to get to a place of writing this response. Many of us read the jail letter and said "great communique" and never called the jail or did any of those "good suggestions," feeling it was addressed to those masses. We have since acted on some of the suggestions and are self-critical for the delays. We also are currently re-evaluating our work and trying to find more effective ways of supporting each other. This is one attempt. We urge folks to examine what it is we mean when we say we are "critically supportive" or "politically active." Because if we can't organize, communicate, or mobilize ourselves, how the hell do we expect to do the same with the masses of people we hope to reach out for and work with?

Love and Struggle,
The Valerian Coven

Part IV

WHEN *IS* THE TIME?
THE LEFT COMMUNITY DEBATES ARMED ACTION

The selections in this section originally appeared in *Northwest Passage*, an antiestablishment, countercultural periodical based in both Bellingham and Seattle from the late 1960s on into the 1980s. The first five pieces reflect what was—despite the Brigade's complaints of being ignored—a concerted effort to explore the implications of a guerrilla presence in the Pacific Northwest.

The pieces were timely. In an editorial after the first installment a member of the *Passage* editorial collective remarked with ironic ambivalence: "The Forum on Armed Struggle/Terrorism has sparked the hottest debate from our readers since the legendary *Passage* debate over two years ago on the subject of Monogamy. Does this represent progress? Perhaps." She continued: "Already we have received more letters than we can print on the topic . . . We only wish that this amount of enthusiasm and input could be generated around other topics as well . . ."[1]

The *Passage*'s coverage of the Brigade begins with an interview with cofounder Ed Mead conducted in the King County Jail. Mead was captured on January 23, 1976, in the course of an over-ambitious robbery attempt at the Pacific National Bank in the south Seattle suburb of Tukwila; the same event which left Bruce Seidel dead and John Sherman wounded and in custody. After Sherman was freed by remaining Brigade members on March 10, Mead became the Brigade's de facto spokesperson. As he was already planning a political defense that would not substantially challenge the circumstantial evidence arrayed against him, he felt little incentive to keep quiet.

In the next article, Roxanne Park, one of Mead's interviewers from the *Passage*, lays out why she considers the Brigade a liability to the Left community. Michelle Whitnack, a former member of the anarchist Left Bank Collective under subpoena by the grand jury investigating the Brigade, took exception to Park's piece, as did the Left Bank Collective itself. Mead, too, responded forcefully to Park's apologia for the status quo.

The campaign against the grand jury produced the next article, an interview with three subpoenees, Brenda Carter, Kathy Hubenet, and

Katie Mitchell. Carter had been the girlfriend of Ralph "Po" Ford (another Left Bank member) before he died setting a pipe bomb behind the Capitol Hill Safeway; the same one the Brigade bombed three days later. Hubenet and Mitchell were pulled into the investigative net by virtue of living with (Mitchell) or *having* lived with (Hubenet) Carter and, thus, in the prosecutorial imagination, knowing Ford. The George Jackson Brigade included Ford's friends, investigators reasoned. (Mead had in fact known Ford, though they were not particularly close.)

Nearly two years passed before the next major discussion of the Brigade in the *Passage*. The bimonthly tabloid covered the grand jury inquisition heavily, but found little to say about the Brigade while it "licked its wounds" and robbed banks anonymously in Oregon. When the Brigade returned to Seattle in the summer of 1977, they received much less ink than they had a year earlier, in either antiestablishment papers or the corporate press—evidently bombings could be downplayed and ignored just like every other form of protest the media covered then tired of. The *Passage* did, however, reprint two Brigade communiqués and portions of their political statement, which it encouraged people to read.[2]

The letter from "Papaya" pushing for more clandestine collaboration with the Brigade (by, among other methods, carrying out the illegalities called for in preceding Brigade communiqués) may well have been written by a Brigade member or one of their close supporters.

Janine Bertram, Therese Coupez, and John Sherman—the last three members of the Brigade—were arrested on March 21, 1978, at a drive through burger joint in Tacoma, as they prepared to rob another bank. The final piece is a jailhouse interview that represents one of the last efforts by Seattle's aboveground Left to wrestle with the issues raised by the Brigade while the organization was still an immediate presence in the city. It has a post-operative evaluative tone, in contrast to the insistent "*Which side are you on?*" queries which preceded it.

Ed Mead Speaks from Prison
Interview by John Brockhaus and Roxanne Park
Northwest Passage, May 24–June 7, 1976

Do you happen to know why the [International Women's Day] Communique was signed, because that's the single piece of evidence which is giving them [law enforcement] their heyday right now?

Mead: I don't know why . . . It was a mistake for anybody to have done that unless it was someone like John Sherman, because for him it makes no difference.[3]

The Brigade is being described as a terrorist group. I'd like you to comment on whether you consider yourselves a terrorist group, and what your vision is for armed struggle.

I'm a person who has done years of mass work. I've done mass work inside the prisons . . . and mass work on the outside. As a result of these years of experience, of social practice, I came to the conclusion that something more was needed. That the mass movement by itself could only go so far without the threat or potential threat of revolutionary violence. I joined with others in an attempt to develop this capability. Over a lot of resistance from the Left. My thoughts are constantly changing as I learn things. Initially my thinking was more "you fight fascist terrorism with revolutionary counter-terror." Terrorism is traditionally the weapon of the weak—it's what the Palestinians used. [It's what you use] when you don't have anything else. As the Brigade grew stronger it drew further and further away from terrorist acts— its initial bombings were not accompanied by any warnings.

It's out there, it exists to serve the mass movement. There's a real tendency for people to say: "There's two kinds of people—there's those doing armed work and they can take all the risks and make all the sacrifices and we can sit back and criticize them. We don't have to do any real work, we can just go about our work and revolution is some nebulous hope or passing fad or whatever." I'm not really critical . . . some people have misinterpreted my feelings to the extent that they would say that [I think] everybody should be doing armed work. Which isn't the case. I think that what communists should be doing right now is to strengthen their weakest point and . . . the weakest point right now is the armed front . . . That's not to say that there isn't very important work to be done at the mass level. There is no struggle going on in this town. There's a defensive struggle going on with the grand jury with this recent wave of repression which will probably grow larger. But the mass movement—all the different ethnic groups, all the different political variations—nobody's doing anything, to my knowledge. And that's why I criticize the mass movement.

So you wouldn't describe yourself as a terrorist group then?

I adhere to the teaching of George Jackson that we should meet terror with terror. If it comes to [the ruling class] using terror against the Left, then we should turn it back on them. If there's going to be funerals, there should be funerals on both sides.

Could you imagine a series of events which could cause the Brigade to change its opinion about the validity of armed struggle at this point? Does that seem to you to be a possibility?

Not at all. What I can't understand . . . with welfare just cut back by 50%, with unemployment growing . . . as things continue to decay, how are we going to be able to overturn this thing if not by armed force? Are they going to peaceably give it up? Are we going to go the Chilean route and try to elect a socialist government?

Anybody that's not a revisionist understands the need for armed struggle and the forcible seizure of power. The question seems to be as to whether or not this is the time. I think we're really behind the times . . . I think the reformism and opportunism on the Left is racist. When people are fighting and dying in South Africa, in Angola, in Viet Nam, in South America, against U.S. imperialism, and we here in the United States don't . . . [It's] like we abhor American Exceptionalism yet our practice is exactly that.

Could you explain American Exceptionalism?

American Exceptionalism is the doctrine that says that it's all right to wage armed struggle in other countries, but when it comes to waging armed struggle at home then that's a different thing. That outlook is racist. [It implies] that our lives are more important than those gooks or niggers or whatever.

Or it could be argued that we're in a different situation, the heart of imperialism, and that calls for different tactics.

That is one thing. I don't think that we should define ourselves as anti-imperialists. Our slogan should be more Class War. How long, how long do you think we should wait? Their position is to be murdered and oppressed by U.S. imperialism and they've taken up arms against it. 'Til they invade our borders to destroy the class enemy of all humanity? The best way that we can help the people of Puerto Rico, the people of South Africa, of South America, of all the oppressed people of the world, is not by marching, not by mouthing anti-imperialist slogans, but waging armed struggle against the common enemy.

And by saying this I don't mean that armed struggle is the only level of struggle. I mean that armed struggle as a supplement to the mass movement, but that the mass struggle has clear class orientation, that it's class-defined, and that it directs the brunt of its impact against the class enemy, and not seek reforms—like a "Bicentennial without Colonies"—but rather seeks the seizure and retention of state power by the people.

Do you have any comments on the recent grand jury subpoenas and house search on Capitol Hill?

Good old uncle Ho said that adversity is a true test of a people's fidelity.[4] The adversity experienced by the aboveground community—which has been handled very well—is not so difficult as what might be in the future, with barbed wire, and National Guard patrols on Capitol Hill and the Central Area. House to house searches, doors being kicked in . . . These are the kinds of things that are going to happen and the grand jury struggle is essentially defensive and I'd kinda hate to see people focus on the grand jury as being a token of mass work . . . though it's essential that people . . . who have a boot on their neck be defended.

It's obvious that they're going to be taking more and more hostages from the underground as they're unable to get to the real people. The people that they're going to be going after are those who are the most visible . . . And of course the obvious purpose of this is to scare people from being visible. If people allow this to happen and remain invisible then the people who have stood out become isolated and really vulnerable. That's why it's important that all elements in the community move to support those people who are being persecuted.

You're saying then that they're getting the wrong people, that they're not hitting the people in the Brigade?

(laughs) That's what I'm saying.

There's some questions that I'd like to ask and they might end up being things that you can't answer.

I won't violate security.

Can you comment on whether or not the communique was written in the Capitol Hill house as they're claiming?

I don't have any knowledge . . . I don't know. I'm out of touch with things. But I can say that I don't know those people [who were subpoenaed on May 1]. I know of them, but that's all.

Was Po a member of the Brigade?

No. He was a comrade in that he was attempting to do the same things we were, but he wasn't a member.

Which groups were you influenced by? Were you inspired by the SLA or the Weather Underground?

I personally grew out of Weather. I wanted to go further and I wanted to do more. *Prairie Fire* inspired me. I helped put *Prairie Fire* together—not any of the writing but the shit work. I felt this restlessness, I felt this need to do something more than just talk. I didn't feel good about the level of my political work—my efficiency or productivity. I felt that this was the direction to go, and my friends were not willing to make the move. The SLA inspired me, though as they say, they went too far too fast. The Brigade has tried to go further and faster than Weather, but not to go as far and as fast as the SLA.

To maintain some sort of balance, we always have to be testing the outer limits of struggle: we don't want to go beyond what is sustainable. There's no clear line. The only way to find out what is the sustainable level of struggle is to get your feet wet. I think the Brigade has done a pretty good job of measuring and defining what is sustainable.

What criticisms of the Brigade do you have?

Well, I'm part of the Brigade. And we criticize ourselves. Probably if I were going to cast a vote on a collective decision, I would not have issued that last communique.

The Women's Day one?

Yeah.

Why?

I don't know. Or if I had issued it, I would have tried to ensure that it was issued more carefully or something. I think the Brigade's doing just fine. I can think of nothing I would suggest that they do differently than what they're doing right now. I guess there's always an important line to be drawn between the need for security and the need to educate. It's important that people know that the Brigade is made up of people of different races and sexes. And different sexual orientations within those races and sexes.

What kind of support do you think you have among working and poor people?

Some people think that in order to have the support of people, poor people should organize themselves and march around in circles with signs saying "We support the George Jackson Brigade." That's just another form of rhetoric, and the kind of pattern the Left tends to think in. In terms of food, shelter, guns, money—that's support. And we're getting it. The Brigade couldn't exist without it.

Do you see your criticisms of the Left as being primarily directed at the Seattle area or do you think the same things would have happened in other areas?

I think it would have happened essentially the same. Seattle has traditionally been "laid back," kind of a nice place where lefties go because of the mountains and hiking. The struggle should come other places before it comes here. The Seattle Left has to deal with these things just like the San Francisco community had to learn to deal with them. What I think's going to happen is the Brigade is going to totally bypass the Left—which I think is happening now—and new leaders will emerge.

How do the prisoners here react to you? Do most of them know what you're in for?

I'm locked in what they call the "Annex"—we filed a writ demanding that they give reasons for locking me up and isolating me from the prison population. When I was in the general population I was well-received by the prisoners. One of the reasons that the administration has given for locking me up is because of the influence that I'd have that would be "detrimental" to the prisoners. I wish I was in the general population—the prisoners feel good about me and I feel good about the prisoners. I'm not bullshittin'—I have nothing to lose by telling it like it is and they respect that. The prisoners respect the George Jackson Brigade—more than non-prisoners can ever understand.

One of the biggest criticisms the SLA had of themselves was the way they let the corporate media use them rather than the other way around. How do you think the Jackson Brigade has fared in getting its story out through the media?

I think the Brigade has done really well. If they have been manipulated by the media—do you remember the "Great Gauntlet Challenge" thrown down by Chief Reed of the FBI?[5] He says the Brigade's thrown down this challenge and we're going to pick it up and ram it down their throats. The SLA probably would have responded to that by bombing an FBI office or something. The Brigade is not responding to the media and I think that's a real credit.

What do you expect for yourself in the next few years?

Well, I expect the power of the Left to increase, its power and influence. My options range from going to prison to being murdered (laughs) . . . which I sometimes feel is a possibility. To me . . . what's the difference between the inside and out? I get to fuck on the outside, but I don't do much of that anyway.[6] It's all the same. The work I do is the work I do . . . is the work I do. It doesn't . . . You can do it on the inside as well as on the outside . . . I'd like to survive and I'm going to

do everything in my power to insure that that's the case. Short of re-
nouncing the struggle . . . I don't know what the future has to bring.

Could you describe your political development?

I was raised on a homestead in Alaska, in conditions of poverty, I
guess. Sometimes it became necessary to help myself. I did burglaries,
stole cars, did time in a youth institution. That sort of thing. I would
probably describe my politics—I didn't have any conscious politics—
but I believed in Free Enterprise. My ripping off was just a logical
extension of that conviction: its ultimate expression. My ripping off
didn't have any real class direction; I would just as soon rip off someone poor—well, not someone poor but anyone who had more than me,
which was just about everybody.

When I was about eighteen, I got into doing gas stations. I was in
a different town and needed money to get home. And I broke into a
gas station. I got into the cigarette machine and stole thirty dollars.
I got caught and was sent to Lompoc federal prison in California for
three years . . .

[. . .]⁷

In the process of the struggle, one day I looked at myself and I saw
that I wasn't a criminal anymore. I was something else. I wasn't sure
what that was—the closest I could come to it was radical. I didn't know
if I was an anarchist or a communist—I didn't have a clear understanding. I started reading more. I was offered the choice once at McNeil, to go
to the farm [minimum security camp] and be recommended for parole,
or go to [the United States Penitentiary at] Leavenworth [Kansas] and
have hard times. It all depended on my attitude, what kind of prisoner
I was going to be. We organized a strike; I was shipped to Leavenworth
shortly after that. The struggle continued at Leavenworth . . .

How long were you there?

I was only there for about nine months—I got out on a writ. About
half that time I spent in the slammer. I was writing a book, a prisoner
activist handbook . . . They got into this degrading practice of doing a
digital sodomy trip [rectal search] anytime they'd go to or from court.
They confiscated part of my book and I filed suit claiming I had a First
Amendment right to possess these writings. On the way to the hearing they gave me what they call a "finger wave" and I resisted and they

brought the goon squad and we had a tussle . . . Just constant . . . I was more non-violent than anything.

I came out onto the streets, did work with the Steilacoom prisoners support house.[8] I helped to get them incorporated—non-profit tax status. I came to Seattle and helped to organize the Washington State Prisoners Labor Union. We fought as hard as we could—we organized prisoners on the inside and we organized people on the outside. They worked together to try to bring about real change in the relationship between prisoners and the administration. We took it as far as we could go—and there was another element that was needed. I didn't understand what that was. I knew that armed struggle was necessary, but it was always some distant thing that would some day just naturally evolve without any conscious effort by anybody.

I felt pretty badly . . . My mom has a farm in eastern Washington. She has nine horses, 80 acres, and I went out there; me and Jill.[9] Just kind of laid back and tried to put the whole thing in perspective. We spent nearly a year on the farm. People would come out there from town, go horseback riding and we'd talk some politics now and then. Still the lessons were really hard to learn.

Then the SLA hit town. And I read in the newspaper their Revolutionary War Declaration and I read their program. And I cried. And I wanted to go to San Francisco. Jill said: "No, that's unreasonable, your place is here. We've got this responsibility with the farm that we've got to maintain." So we stayed on the farm a little while longer. Finally I left Jill with the place—she wanted to stay there and she liked it and I came to Seattle. I got involved in various political activities that I won't name for security reasons.

I always tried to move more and more militantly. I went to Buffalo and worked on the Attica Brothers Defense for a while. Then I traveled around the country looking for revolutionary leaders—I was looking for a leader—like where's somebody who knows what's going on here, who knows where we're going. The people I talked to seemed not to have as much understanding as me. Which was really a shock, because they seemed more conservative than me, though given their background they haven't suffered the oppression that people who come from my background have. So it's only natural that the most oppressed—the women, the gays, the Blacks—are the first because their oppression is the greatest. The problem is that communists have a tendency to ignore this and say: "Oh well, he's a prisoner and therefore he's kind of different." Or: "He's queer and that makes him different," or "she's a

Lesbian," or "a Black," and not really examine the conditions of people's oppression that cause them to resist first. That's not to say these are the forces that are going to make the revolution; it's just to say they're initiating the struggle. But communists I think have an obligation to be involved in each of these struggles and to direct them.

TERRORISM AND THE GEORGE JACKSON BRIGADE
Roxanne Park[10]
Northwest Passage, June 7–28, 1976

In the last issue of the *Passage* we carried a jailhouse interview with George Jackson Brigade member Ed Mead. In that interview Mead described his group's political commitment to armed struggle. Following that up, I want to discuss the political ramifications of the George Jackson Brigade's actions, as well as outline some arguments countering their analysis. This criticism is not solely directed at the Brigade; obviously many other individuals and groups in the country share their analysis.

I see this critique as an initial effort, hoping to set some parameters to the discussion. The subject is vital to the Left community today: other people will need to discuss the issues and put forth additional perspectives. We must be able to analyze the events which have grown out of the Brigade's action, giving ourselves guidelines for future work.

Armed Struggle vs. Terrorism

It is necessary to initiate this discussion by making a distinction between armed struggle and terrorism. The Brigade calls its activities armed struggle while others consider them in the realm of terrorism. Determining which label more accurately describes the Brigade involves an analysis of the level of political resistance in the country as a whole.

Usually when people use the term armed struggle they mean a revolutionary effort which is actively using violence as a means for the eventual seizure of state power. Armed struggle implies highly organized, extensive resistance. You must have a sizeable proportion of the people of a country involved in the actions, or at least highly supportive. Vietnam was a good example of a country engaged in armed struggle, and certainly we can find similar armed resistance in Angola, Rhodesia, and the Philippines.

Terrorism is the selective use of symbolic violence (or threat of violence) by a small, clandestine group, aimed at making a political message. Terrorism hopes to convince other people of the vulnerability of the system and to inspire them to similar actions. Terrorism then, usually precedes armed struggle. Therefore, if someone believes that the Brigade is engaging in armed struggle they are also indicating there is a high level of conscious resistance in the country. The Brigade cannot initiate armed struggle as a single unit: the population must support the move for eventual seizure of state power.

I cannot accept that analysis because I do not see this country even close to a state of armed struggle. I believe the Brigade is a terrorist group, and that their use of terrorism up to this point has been highly damaging to the Left. I would like to outline my reasons for this conclusion.

I. At this time, terrorist tactics will not further the struggle for a revolution in this country

First of all, I want to clarify that I am not advocating non-violence as an absolute. I believe that force, or the threat of force, will be the only way a revolution will succeed in this country. The ruling class will not give up power because it recognizes the moral decency of socialism. I am convinced that there will come a time when we need to be ready with arms, with our lives, if we intend to radically transfer power in this country.

The problem with George Jackson Brigade is not, in fact, that they engage in illegal action or are willing to defend their beliefs with guns, or that they commit armed bank robberies, or even that they shoot police. The problem is that these actions, at this point in time in America, will not lead to a revolution. And in fact, they work against a revolution.

In the *Passage* interview, Mead indicated that the objective conditions of this society make it perfectly obvious that we need a revolution and to postpone armed struggle is racist and counter-revolutionary.

A determination of when we should seriously attempt to seize state power through armed struggle requires an analysis of the relative success such an attempt would have. Obviously to start a full-scale war without any chance of winning is suicidal.

When one examines the conditions of the country which might favor such efforts, one needs to look at factors which are *objective* (e.g. inflation, unemployment, crisis in the schools) as well as those which are *subjective—the attitudes* people have toward these conditions. If few people seriously object to unemployment or women's role in our society then a radical obviously needs to raise people's consciousness before there will be enough outrage to generate a move for an alternative government. We could have the most oppressive country in the world, but if most Americans don't view it as such, we don't have a country ready for armed struggle. Similarly, a highly conscious people could revolt under less severe conditions.

I would argue that the subjective conditions in this country are *not* in any way conducive towards armed struggle at this point. The Left has an enormous amount of work to do in simply raising people's awareness of the level of oppression which exists in America. There are vast similarities for our work at this stage to that of Russia in the early 1900s when Lenin wrote: "Calls for terror are merely forms of *evading* the most pressing duties that now rest upon Russian revolutionaries."

II. Terrorism evades the necessary work needed to increase popular support for a revolution

When we asked Mead what support he thought the Brigade had among poor and working people, he answered that it was a tremendous amount. "The people give us food for our mouths, a place to sleep, ammo for our guns and a car for our butts." His vision of support comes from the people hiding the group from the police.

Though this support is necessary to their survival, it does not involve many people. Their choice of illegal actions forces them to only rely on people they can absolutely trust; which can't be very many. Certainly it does not come anywhere near the amount needed to qualify as popular support.

A. Terrorists lack a base of support

The Brigade does *not* have a substantive support base. There do not exist, to my knowledge, groups of people who have been educated and positively influenced by them. Without their bombs, without their robbery, but *most importantly* without the media to publicize their events, they would be unknown.

Terrorists think that they can use the media because of the sensational aspects of their actions, but in the end, the media wins the game because it publishes the story with its own bias. The SLA has criticized itself for getting caught up in the sensationalized portrait the media painted of its organization and then acting in accordance with that myth.

Anyone reading the *Seattle Times* or *P.I.*'s account of the Brigade could see how the media used these events to paint a picture of a dangerous, disturbed group. The *P.I.* carried a three part series on Bruce Seidel, the Brigade member who was killed during the robbery.[11] The story was of a "middle-class college student from a devout family who ended up in a bank with a blazing gun in one hand and a sack of money in the other." He was portrayed as a man who was always trying to compensate for being too short. Does anyone really think that kind of publicity furthers the revolution?

As Walter Laqueur pointed out in an article on the subject, "Terrorists and newspapermen share the naïve assumption that those whose names make the headlines have power, that getting one's name on the front page is a major political achievement."

In one sense, the Brigade members have given everything to the political struggle: they put their lives on the line. On the other hand, the actions they have chosen turn their back to the slow real work which is needed to turn this country around. It is relatively easy to hold up a bank, shoot police, bomb a few buildings. Compare that to changing people's minds about the viability of capitalism, organizing workers, creating a national party that will be able to threaten the other two parties. Compare it to sustaining political activity and interest over the numerous years it is going to take before there is a revolution.

In the Brigade's [International] Women's Day communique, the poem read in part:

> I cannot be one
> acting alone with my
> little toe outside the line
> its both feet
> whole body
> ain't no turning back now
> no more mass meetings, stale mating action

Damn right, no more mass meetings. No more waiting around for others to learn. A lot of the people who lean towards terrorism are those who do not have the energy to sustain their political commitment. They get tired of trying to change things and not having immediate success, so they want to do something BIG, something that will prove they are a real force and need to be feared. This turning to violence out of frustration fits so well into the male tradition of needing to prove power.

B. Terrorists lack a moral community

I remember one individual who hung around the Bellingham community several years ago. He was very interested in terrorism; he talked as if all of us should have hiding places in the hills. When there was a peaceful demonstration, he would start throwing rocks, hoping to incite others to the same activity. If there was one thing we did not need to do at that point it was throw rocks. He had no interest in what led up to the demonstration or what would happen after it. He had no commitment to the day to day lives of the people he supposedly was "helping." He did not have time for anything but the final explosion.

Ramparts published an article a few years ago which emphasized the SLA's lack of a "moral community," characterizing this lack as a serious flaw. The term implies a base in a community to whom a political group has a sense of responsibility. Such a community *personalizes* issues so when decisions are made, real people who might be affected are taken into account. A moral community is what our government needs.

Again, one of the problems of a terrorist group is that they must protect themselves by being isolated. So they don't have easy access to such grounding in a community.

The Brigade has been isolated from poor and working people, but in addition, it has isolated itself from the Left. The Seattle Left has been largely unsupportive of the Brigade's armed struggle analysis, causing the Brigade to become even more hostile/offensive. Listening to Ed Mead I sometimes thought he considered the Left a greater danger than capitalism.

One of the reasons the Left is largely unsupportive is because the Brigade, by taking *their* "politics in command," has seriously harmed other people. The Brigade's actions obviously threaten the entire Left community; the FBI is not going to distinguish them from other radicals.

The Brigade of course does not want any of Seattle's radicals to cooperate with the grand jury investigating the bank robbery. It could mean their death. Because of the structure of the grand jury, a person is [not] excused by simply answering that they do not have personal knowledge of the Brigade. The grand jury intends to ask them questions about any and all Leftists they know, the reasoning being that even if they don't personally know Brigade members they will know someone else who does. So those who refuse to testify end up protecting the Brigade. They also are exercising far more caution and respect for other people than the Brigade has ever done.

In their [International] Women's Day communique, the Brigade speaks critically of the Left and claims that it has bypassed the Left and has instead gone directly to "the people" for support. Later on in that same communique, it encourages "people" not to cooperate with the grand jury and to hold tight. Well, those "people" who are being subpoenaed are people on the Left. It seems like the Brigade members care about "people" if doing so suits their purpose, but not if it gets in the way of their being heroes.

When we asked Mead how he felt about the grand jury subpoena, he made two comments:

> The adversity experienced by the above ground community . . . is not so difficult as what might be expected in the future with barbed wire, and National Guard patrols on Capitol Hill and the Central Area.

(Things aren't as horrible as they could be: so what?)

> I lost my best friend (Seidel) and it is hard for me to sympathize with people who whine about something as inconsequential as being put in jail.

Mead claims that being in or out of jail makes little difference to him. But it's damn important to other people. Four of those subpoenaed are single mothers with children. If they refuse to testify and end up going to jail, they face the possibility of their children being taken away from them because of their "desertion."

One person who was called to testify said that "every time Mead opens his mouth, he hurts someone."

Mead *chose* to engage in illegal activities, so he knew what consequences he was facing. Other people were merely friends of Po's or went to a hearing or answered a telephone call: they did not make a similar choice. And yet they are having to suffer the consequences of someone else's decision. The *arrogance* of the Brigade seems most obvious: they think they know what is needed in America at this point and they intend to involve all the rest of us in their decision. They will "take command" and lead us all to hell.

In addition to the people directly affected by the Brigade through subpoenas, countless others have put in hours in grand jury defense work. Almost all of the lawyers are donating their time or working for pennies. The time the Brigade's actions have taken away from the Left cannot be underestimated, not to mention the emotional strain.

Someone could argue that my criticisms are misplaced; the Brigade did not call the grand jury, they are not the ones putting people in jail, that the legal system is the culprit, and it is good for people to realize how repressive the system is. I am not intending to say that the grand jury system is anything *but* unconstitutional, that the tactics of the

FBI and US Attorney General's Office have been anything but reminiscent of the of the Gestapo. However, the fact remains that all of these repercussions were initiated by the Brigade's choice of terrorism.

III. Terrorist tactics work against the increase of popular support for a revolution

A. Terrorism causes people to fear revolutionaries and identify with the police

When I heard people in stores, hospitals, and buses discussing the Brigade, they did not consider the Brigade class heroes. They did not comment on their newly-gained awareness of the evils of capitalism or the extent of unemployment. The comments indicated a confusion about why anyone would do such a thing, a mild horror about the potential damage and an implicit fear of the Brigade members.

They did not identify with the revolutionaries—but rather with the *police and investigators* who would catch those "crazies." With terrorism the revolutionaries become the enemies and the police friends. Such an emotional bias will obviously not make Americans more open to radical change.

I am not suggesting that people will consistently side with the police over revolutionaries and militant reformers. In some situations that has not occurred, especially during the anti-war movement. However, unless the events and strategy are well-planned, you must expect that result. Anyone with a little foresight can imagine what reaction will come from a bombing at Safeway during store hours.

It is absolutely imperative that the people we are trying to reach not be afraid of us. Naturally we will run up against fear of change, fear of the unknown. But some basis of trust must exist between the revolutionaries and the people. There must be concrete reasons to believe that the revolution would create a society which provides *more* life-quality. Otherwise, people are not going to entertain the risks involved.

More than one person has told me that they would prefer our present government to having the George Jackson Brigade in control. The Brigade members appear as a collection of ruthless souls who have little concern for life—especially their own. And who wants such people in power?

B. Terrorist tactics invite police repression and consequently hurt the Left

Any political group with much sense is not going to take on the State at this point. "The State is always so much stronger than the terrorists, whose only hope for success is to prevent the authorities from using their full powers." (Laqueur)

If the government does not have enough excuses for coming down on Leftists, terrorists give them a license for unlimited attack. Actions such as the Tukwila bank robbery easily enable the government to justify a grand jury investigation. Over and over again the federal prosecutor in the case has made statements to the press that their investigation of such a serious crime must involve *any* and *all* resources. The unconstitutional issues of the grand jury fade in light of the potential danger of the Brigade. Look back to the SLA: the police conducted a *mass slaughter* with little public protest. America watched it on her T.V. screen. People in this country end up believing that we need to suppress such dangerous persons as revolutionaries.

The other more invisible aspect of repression comes from the infiltration of Leftist groups. The FBI should be much more knowledgeable about the Left in Seattle after the grand jury gets through. After the Brigade's actions, it is obvious that more infiltration will occur throughout the Seattle Left community. The long-term negative affects of the Brigade will not be understood for a long time.

Conclusion

When discussing violence, one needs at some point to take the issue out of the abstract and squarely face it. Violence and armed struggle are not just words. They mean increased risks. People being maimed, killed. They mean being prepared to leave everything and go underground at any point. Or to end up in jail, perhaps for the rest of your life.

If a revolutionary movement has large-scale support for its struggle, it is likely to need less violence to achieve control. So to postpone violence until a receptive time may mean significantly fewer deaths and less terror. The revolutionaries also could maintain state power with less resistance, thereby lessening the need for repression.

A humane revolutionary would not increase the level of violence in people's lives without being able to reasonably expect a "greater good" to come from the suffering. In the words of Jill Raymond,[12] a Lesbian feminist jailed for over a year because she refused to talk to a grand jury investigating the Saxe and Power[13] case: "We should only risk lives when it's going to get us somewhere, when we're strong enough."

ON ARMED STRUGGLE:
A CONTINUING DIALOGUE
Michelle Whitnack
Northwest Passage, June 28–July 19, 1976

Dear Roxanne (and other *passage* folks, if appropriate):

I just finished reading your article, "TERRORISM: The Question of Tactics,"[14] and feel a need to make a formal reply to what I consider the most offensive article I've ever read in what's usually a real fine paper. I'll do it point by point, in an attempt to stay reasonably coherent.

I think that your definitions of the terms "revolutionary violence" and "terrorism" were at best wrong—at least in terms of verbalizing the feeling I, or anyone else I know, have for the terms—and at worst, opportunistically contrived to better serve in the weaving and justification of your own political opinion. I'm not going to get into what I would consider more accurate definitions, as I basically agree with what the Left Bank response will have to say to that issue.

You say that you ". . . do not see this country even close to a state of armed struggle." Just who are you talking to? Other lefties? Do you have any contact to speak of with the people locked up in prison anywhere across the country? Do you hear the Black or Native American communities unanimously voting to "postpone violence until a receptive time"? After more than three years in the prison movement, I won't say that my impression is any less one-sided than yours; but I sure as hell will say that there's plenty of people in this country, in and out of the prisons, who wouldn't quite agree with your analysis, and I don't hear you even considering them. What I do hear you saying is that it's all right for poor and oppressed people to fight—just so long as the fighting's not close to home, where it might be a threat to all the folks who've been mouthing left rhetoric for years without realizing that to one hell of a lot of people in this country, every day is next to intolerable, and the concept of revolution is not a romantic, abstract little ego trip.

You point out that ". . . to postpone violence until a receptive time may mean significantly fewer deaths and less terror." If you want to discuss the few days, weeks, or months during which the actual physical overthrow of the government itself occurs, I might agree with you: if everyone in the world but Rockefeller were revolutionaries, I'm sure we could pull off a real bloodless revolution. In that sense, use of violence is an admission of powerlessness. But the fact of the matter is that right now, the other side does have the power—and will continue to have, exactly as long as we allow them to . . . and until we reach that enviable situation where no one is willing to play mercenary to the capitalists, it's going to take violence to stop them. But there is a serious shortcoming to your humane concept of "postponing violence" to lessen deaths and terror: here again, it's real obvious that whoever you're dealing with in your life either feels at least reasonably comfortable with the status quo—or else you're totally insensitive to their suffering. Every day that goes by, the rich and their politicians and police forces and armies are killing, torturing, starving, and imprisoning people. Do these people not count against your toll of "(fewer) deaths and (less) terror"??? Ask Ernest Graham and Eugene Allen (two black prisoners sentenced a few months ago to the gas chamber in California) to explain to you how postponement means "fewer deaths." Ask the scores of prisoners subjected to lobotomies, drug experimentation and other Behavior Modification techniques in Butner, Vacaville, and other American prisons, to argue for patience, in order to make it all easier in the end and create "less terror." Before you purport to speak for the people, Roxanne, I'd suggest you try dealing a little more with the people who are hurting on account of the way things are.

You say, "The arrogance of the Brigade seems most obvious: they think they know what is needed in America at this point and they intend to involve all the rest of us in their decision." I'll be the last to take issue with you about arrogance on the part of the Brigade, and in fact I feel real strongly that the tendency of people doing armed stuff to become arrogant and "heavier than thou" is the greatest danger of that kind of work. What we aboveground can do to cut down this tendency and make the underground more answerable to the aboveground—as well as vice versa—is to offer principled constructive criticism. That doesn't mean self-righteous trashing such as your article offered. I don't think that the George Jackson Brigade has shown itself to be unwilling to accept criticism: for instance, after the unspeakably awful bombing of Safeway during business hours, the Left Bank Collective, of which I was then a member, issued a criticism (which actually was more a condemnation than a constructive criticism), and in fact we issued it to the straight press rather than trying to get it to the Brigade through the "movement" press. This was not even done, in fact (at least on my part), with any expectation that anyone who could do something that wrong was going to be receptive to criticism.

But the fact of the matter is that they did take a long hard look at that action, admitted later that it was wrong, and have since changed their practice in their actions to show the concern for peoples' safety which the Safeway action lacked. As a result, I had to reevaluate my opinion of the Brigade upwards . . . which still doesn't put them among my top ten favorite folks, but I have respect for them as people who are struggling to be revolutionaries—which I think is the most that can be said for any of us, over or underground.

And, Roxanne, I think that everyone who is trying to be part of a revolution in this country—or any country—has an idea of what they think is needed at any given point: you condemn the Brigade for thinking they know and intending to involve all the rest of us in their decision, but can you tell me how exactly you are above the same "accusation"? To advocate inaction is certainly no less telling than to advocate action, once you realize that there's real suffering going on every moment that the status quo continues.

Your statements and analyses of the grand jury situation:

a) "Because of the structure of the grand jury, a person is excused by simply answering that they do not have personal knowledge of the Brigade." I'm sort of assuming that this was a typographical error. If not, please find out the facts before you venture to write next time. This statement is simply, totally false.

b) "So those who refuse to testify end up protecting the Brigade. They also are exercising far more caution and respect for other people than the Brigade has ever done." First, there are a pretty overwhelming number of arguments in favor of refusing to testify even aside from any such concern, whether or not my/our refusal in effect protects the Brigade. For myself, at least, I would refuse to testify even if I thought the only people who could stand to lose by my testimony were the Brigade; but first, that's far from the case, and second, specifics of this case aside, I'm refusing to cooperate at all for the simple reason that I don't talk to the government about my friends, or anyone else. The second part of your statement was, to me, reminiscent of childhood scenes of being held up as an example to other children; pat someone else on the head, Roxanne. I don't want to, and will not, be used by you as a reproach against the George Jackson Brigade.

c) "Mead chose to engage in illegal activities, so he knew what consequences he was facing. Other people were merely friends of Po's, or went to a hearing, or answered a telephone call: they did not make a similar choice. And yet they are having to suffer the consequences of someone else's decisions . . . [T]he fact remains that all of these repercussions were initiated by the Brigade's choice of terrorism." Bullshit. I for one have spent the last several years of my life trying real hard to tromp on the Government's toes any way I could—mostly by doing prison work. Considering that, if I had been really surprised to eventually get a subpoena for my efforts, I'd feel pretty damn sure I either wasn't too bright, or was at least real naïve, and never really had any idea of just what kind of beast it was I'd been fighting against all along. Most of us subpoenaed are leftists, or possibly in some cases, are subpoenaed for living or hanging out with leftists. If we don't want trouble from the government, we don't belong on the Left, we belong in the suburbs. If it wasn't the Brigade, the government would eventually find another excuse. Your willingness to advocate inaction to keep the government off our backs floors me. A revolutionary, if you ever elect to call yourself such, is someone who works to create change. An apologist for the status quo, on the other hand . . .

d) I have real difficulty with your compulsion to cultivate "poor little girlism." I at least was real insulted by your plays for sympathy for us poor vulnerable little girls who are being picked on by the big bad government, which struck me real heavily as the tone of this segment of your article (secondary, of course, to the ever-present trashing of the Brigade). Maybe this brand of sympathy would be in order, were we of the weaker side. But I believe that there is going to be a successful revolution in this country, and I intend to be part of it one way or another; and what this means is that I think the government, whether they know it or not, is ultimately the weaker of the two sides. So I don't go begging for sympathy because I'm getting nipped at a little bit by a frightened animal on the Endangered Species list. Support, yes, by all means: I need it and I welcome it with open arms. But if that brand of sympathy is what you're offering, if you want to feel sorry for me and cater to my weaknesses, keep it. There are people around who understand well enough to offer me the love and support to reinforce my strengths.

In the Struggle,
Michelle Whitnack

"We . . . Support Armed Action . . . Now."
Left Bank Collective
Northwest Passage, July 19–August 8, 1976

The June 7th issue of the *Northwest Passage* contained an article arguing against the need for clandestine urban guerilla activities in the United States such as have been carried out recently in Seattle by the George Jackson Brigade. We believe that the article was rife with confused definitions and analysis, and that it neither reflected any understanding of the historical nature and role of armed struggle, nor an understanding of the unique conditions in the advanced industrial nations at this time. We would like to present another viewpoint, in support of armed actions by revolutionaries now, as an important aspect of the development of the revolutionary movement.

At the outset we feel it is necessary to define armed struggle and terrorism in a radically different way than was suggested in the *NWP*. Armed struggle is *not* of necessity a mass uprising, but rather includes a whole spectrum of militant resistance to the ruling class, including bombings, armed occupations of buildings and land (such as Attica,[15] Wounded Knee[16] and Menominee[17]), prisoner breakouts, armed robbery, kidnapping, assassination, assaults on police and military installations, etc. Armed struggle, as carried out by left revolutionaries, may use the same spectrum of tactics here in Seattle as in Latin America, Europe, Palestine, or Vietnam, with the central proviso that the revolutionary *must always* make concern for the welfare of innocent people a vital part of the planning and execution of actions.

"Terrorism," in its pejorative sense, is armed action which deliberately or callously ignores the welfare of the people, and is not focused on the groups and individuals against which the actor is fighting. It is primarily a right-wing phenomenon, and in addition to the *institutionalized* terrorism of the ruling class and its police forces, it has been carried out again and again by police agents posing as revolutionaries, to discredit the principled actions of guerillas. The state would like people to see all acts of insurgency as "terrorism," but revolutions around the world have consistently made the distinction between revolutionary violence against the ruling class, and the terrorism of random violence employed by the state against the people.

It would be nice if acts of "terrorism" never occurred on the left, but obviously on occasions they have. The G.J.B.'s bombing of Safeway last fall was such an action, coming out of their rage at the death of a guerrilla in Seattle, and the capture of the S.L.A. in California. It was not defensible; but mistakes are made in the development of an armed insurgency; and the fact is that the G.J.B. has publicly criticized themselves for the action, and learned from it. When was the last time you heard a police agency apologize for its acts of terror against the people?

Given this distinction then, it is important to talk about some of the implicit assumptions behind the initiation of armed struggle. It is by now a trite truism of sectarian Marxist-Leninists that they believe that armed struggle will be necessary but *not now!* This particular litany has been repeated over and over again by dogmatists since the successful revolution of 1917 in Russia, in other countries in every stage of technological development, and has been proven wrong repeatedly by armed militants who were not prepared to wait for the "right time."

The rationalizations for this are extensive. In China, after the failure of the Shanghai insurrection of 1927, Mao and a small group of militants went into the countryside without the support of the Chinese Communist Party and against the declared policy of Stalin's Comintern, to begin the armed struggle. Their numbers grew almost continually as the people saw the incredible success which small groups of armed militants could have against the state. In Vietnam, in Laos, in Angola, Mozambique, Algeria, etc., the pattern of guerilla warfare has invariably involved a very small group of fighters, outside the doctrinaire left, growing with their successes to become popular revolutionary movements. Cuba is a classic example: the armed struggle there was begun by 8 fighters, survivors of the Granma expedition, and the Cuban Popular Socialist Party (the main communist party in Cuba) denounced them continually as "adventurists" until it became clear that the guerrillas were going to win.[18]

In other Latin American struggles, the pattern recurs. The legendary Tuparmaros (MLN) of Uruguay, whose numbers were believed to be in the thousands, were begun by a group of no more than 12 people, whose first actions included theft of food trucks and food giveaways, bombing of office buildings, and a gun club robbery. The Movement of the Revolutionary Left (MIR) now considered *the* resistance to Chilean fascism, was rejected by the traditional left during the Popular Unity period because of its "extremism." The People's Revolutionary Army (ERP), which is now waging outright guerilla war against the Argentine junta, began as a small urban "terrorist" organization.

Guerrilla warfare has *always* been initiated by small groups, from whose example other people get the idea and begin to take actions independently. Eventually the groups and individuals begin to link up, and out of growing activity and growing success a movement forms. More people join; the level of activity increases. And for those in the society not engaged in the struggle, the actions produce a change in political climate, a radical challenge to society's assumptions. Actions can be a catalyst for the personal transformation and radicalization of individuals. To fail to see revolutionary warfare as a dialectical process, growing from small to large and continually transforming the material conditions in which it operates, is to ignore the lessons of history.

The argument that the development of armed struggle must wait until some later time when the people are at that stage simply does not hold up under examination. We wonder if folks who have this notion have ever considered how people develop the capability to wage a revolutionary war. People simply do not learn these sorts of skills in the abstract against some later time when they might want to use them. The only time people have the time or the interest in developing such skills is when they are preparing to wage war immediately, or are already engaged in it. Thus preparation and ability to carry out armed struggle begins when people are ready to fight, so that if people *are* ready to fight, there is no "better time" than the present.

The Red Guerrilla Family, an urban guerrilla organization which has been operating in the Bay Area since early last year, summed it up well when they said: "*We have chosen to join the armed struggle now, because there is no reason to wait. Armed struggle is not a substitute for mass struggle, but a necessary part of it. We do not claim to be leaders or followers, but simply the allies of all people who want freedom and socialism. Together, we will win.*"

What Are We Fighting For?

The author of the *NWP* article clearly considers a "revolution" to be consummated by the *transfer of state power* from one ruling group to another. The task of aboveground "organizers" is to sell their particular brand of leadership to the "masses," to gain support and legitimacy for their particular "vanguard" in seizing state power in the name of the people. While that has historically been the outcome of revolutions in the undeveloped nations, that is not what revolution in the advanced industrial nations is about.

In the advanced industrial nations, there has *never* been a successful Communist Party of "Marxist-Leninist" led revolution seize "state power." To the contrary, whenever real revolutionary movements have been underway in advanced nations (such as France and Czechoslovakia in 1968), they have been led by socialists advocating the *abolition* of state power, true worker's democracy, and they have been actively undermined by the traditional left.

If seizing state power is what is conceived of as the goal, then the armed struggle must wait indefinitely for such phenomena as "Building a mass base," "building a revolutionary party to lead the struggle," etc. Such a conception leads also to the posing of inane questions such as whether we prefer to have Gerald Ford or the George Jackson Brigade in control. These are the wrong answers and the wrong questions: we do not seek to have anyone "in control" and the armed struggle cannot wait for the formation of a "vanguard party" under which we have no intention of being subjugated.

In fact, the traditional left has never had much significant appeal to the American people since the '30s, and the reasons for this have to do with some fairly strong anti-authoritarian traditions. People who are literate and live in a technologically sophisticated society do not need a new group to tell them what to do—they aspire to be free, to take control of their own lives! Leftists who are continually drawing elitist distinctions between the "organizers" and the "masses," and who see themselves as distinct from the people, are unlikely to inspire anyone to follow them in an age fundamentally cynical (and rightly so) about leaders.

Furthermore, the sectarian left offers nothing to counteract that cynicism. People are looking for concrete ways to change the conditions of this society, to bring about social control of the means of production and individual liberation. The "leadership" of the sectarian left instead offers the people the chance to join any one of 17 different vanguards, each of which claims to be the true one, and all of which spend most of their energy arguing among themselves over doctrinal disagreements. This is not the place to debate libertarian vs. authoritarian socialism; suffice it to say that there are many people in this society who are looking for ways to drastically change this society, even though they show no inclination to become part of the "mass base" or this or that "Marxist-Leninist" vanguard party.

The Value of the Guerilla Movement

The guerrilla struggle offers one way, although by no means the only way, in which revolutionaries can make militant demands on the system, put cracks in the walls, and break down the capitalist system.

The activities of the New World Liberation Front in California are a striking example. For two years they have been consistently bombing, sabotaging, and disrupting major ruling class institutions such as Pacific Gas and Electric, various landlords, and the San Francisco Police Department, and demanding that the conditions in which poor and working people live be improved at the cost of these agencies. In that period, no known members of the organization have been caught, and no injuries have resulted to innocent bystanders.

In return, they have gotten a startling amount of credibility with people on both sides of the class war. The San Francisco Police Department transferred a policeman who had committed police brutality in Bernal Heights out of the community the same day that a death threat was received from the NWLF. A recent NWLF campaign for a new health facility was supported by massive plugging of parking meters by people in the community, in response to a call from the NWLF. And thus far, two major slumlords in San Francisco have capitulated to NWLF demands that they renovate their buildings at no cost to the tenants, rather than endure sustained attacks. The San Francisco papers are so familiar with the skill and safety of their actions that they even point out the difference between NWLF and right-wing terrorist bombings!

What this proves is that even now, at a time which is not approaching one of mass insurgency, armed militants can both alter the material conditions of our society, and inspire others to begin participating in the armed struggle as well. The traditional left likes to talk about how the SLA didn't accomplish anything, and all ended up dead or in prison. On the contrary, the level of guerilla activity has more than doubled since the SLA blazed its way into our national consciousness with the Hearst kidnapping and food giveaway. The fact of a ruling class reactionary being forced to feed thousands of people may have turned some people off—revolution usually does—but millions of others were really excited about it. And millions of people got a first class demonstration of "due process of law" with the Los Angeles shootout on their evening news.

It is perplexing that many of the quotes used in the *NWP* article were from Walter Zeev Laqueur. Laqueur is a well-known Israeli Zionist journalist, and the main thrust of many of his articles was directed against the PLO. The Palestinian guerillas are an excellent example of an initially small group of activists who, through dramatic media-covered actions, drew worldwide attention to their plight, which eventually translated to growing worldwide support, and isolation of the Zionists. All during this period, the straight media was attacking the "terrorists" and distorting the coverage they provided; yet even so they could not disguise the revolutionary content of the actions. It is a mistake to believe that since the bourgeois media is tremendously biased against revolution, that it can entirely subvert the revolutionary impact of audacious actions on people's consciousness.

The Problem of Fear

One of the underlying elements of the argument against armed struggle is one which is *never* brought out in the open: fear. Undertaking clandestine illegal activities goes against lifetimes of conditioning to accept authority, at the risk of massive retaliation by the state. Facing up to our own fear openly and honestly, and dealing with each other's fear in a loving and comradely manner goes a long way toward overcoming fear. Trying to hide our fears behind mounds of theoretical evasion and a macho front is a sure way to remain trapped in paralyzed inaction or in destructive competitive games.

Lenin once said "A revolutionary is a dead man on furlough." Any kind of activity which genuinely threatens the state and the ruling class will be met with heavy repression, and always has. People need to be able to say: "I'm willing to struggle for revolution, but such and such is just more risk than I can deal with," without shame, and without being put down in a hierarchy of "more revolutionary than thou." In doing so, they both give sanction to comrades who are taking greater risks, and keep themselves out of situations with which they are not prepared to cope. In addition, folks need to realize that there is a wide range of illegal activity which goes into revolution, not all of which is as risky as carrying out a guerrilla operation. Every revolution has an underground, and not all of the people are combatants—there are technicians, writers, printers, forgers, harborers, drivers, suppliers, and a host of others. They are all equally important, and have always been done by ordinary working people, not mythical hero types. But what revolutionaries must begin to confront is that, whatever they are doing, REVOLUTION IS ILLEGAL!

Repression and Resistance

One of the fundamental errors of the article in the *NWP* was in suggesting that the Brigade was responsible for the repression which the state has brought down on the left in Seattle. In fact, the grand jury inquisition and the FBI-ATF-SPD[19] investigation have merely illustrated the fundamentally repressive nature of this state, and have proven that the George Jackson Brigade and other groups like them are among the viable groups on the left.

The events in Seattle are acquainting many white radicals with the nature of police repression which the Black, Chicano, Native American, and Puerto Rican communities have lived under constantly for decades. Although single mothers are certainly entitled to special support and sympathy from the community in the face of this appalling tactic of selecting them for subpoenas, arguments blaming their plight on the Brigade ignore the fact that this repression and abuse are the *status quo* in other communities, and will continue until the state which sponsors these outrages is destroyed, a process from which further repression and abuse can be expected in abundance.

Another point which should be considered is why the state is taking the trouble to send dozens of agents in from across the country to track down a group which they believe numbers about ten people. We believe that the reason is that the ruling class takes the threat which groups like the GJB pose to the continued existence of the state *extremely seriously*. Furthermore, the indications are that such groups are growing, and that the state is nearly powerless to halt their activities. This fact in itself is an indication of a "base of support" in the community, and one which, if not destroyed, may grow into a permanent base of operations for the guerrillas.

One other argument suggested in the *NWP* article is that people become guerrillas because they can't last in the "slow, real work which is needed to turn this country around"; it being "relatively easy to hold up a bank, shoot police, bomb a few buildings." This is ridiculous. People like Bruce Seidel, Ed Mead, and John Sherman came from long backgrounds of doing aboveground organizing, and clearly see their armed work as a natural extension of their past work. Secondly, to assert that robbing banks, shooting police or whatever is "relatively easier" than aboveground work is ludicrous. It just ain't so. At best, the comparison is pointless; for the committed revolutionary aboveground and the fugitive guerilla underground must both constantly contend with the full weight of the state arrayed against their efforts. What is "easiest" is primarily a function of the skills of the individual and not the area of struggle in which the revolutionary is engaged.

Finally, the entire article proceeds on the notion that there is a correct strategy for revolution which can be figured out in detail from this point in time, if we just have the correct theory. Revolution is not an absolute which exists at the end of some length of time: it is, as Marx said, a dialectical process. To assume that it can be anticipated by an enlightened few is to ignore the fact that people make history. The George Jackson Brigade, and the guerrilla movement, are of the people, and they have the right to participate in the process in the way which seems most effective to them. We support them in their decision.

ED MEAD REPLIES
Northwest Passage, August 9–29, 1976

Reading Roxanne (and John [Brockhaus]'s) criticism of the George Jackson Brigade left me with mixed feelings. On the one hand I was put off by the hostile and fearful tone of the *Passage* criticism.[20] At the same time I was please that after more than a year of the Brigade's existence, someone had finally made an attempt to enter into dialogue around the question of armed struggle. Prior efforts in this direction have consisted of little more than verbal abuse masked in the rhetoric of criticism.

The net effect of all this one way "criticism" has been to further the government's basic repressive strategy—to divide. By dividing the aboveground from the underground, the resulting isolation renders the latter more vulnerable to attack. The divisive effect of criticism can be counterbalanced when it is done within the context of general support and is coupled with a self-examination of the writer's political practice.

Criticism is an important tool if used correctly. But when abused it can become destructive. From its inception the George Jackson Brigade has welcomed and responded to legitimate criticisms from the left. Careless use of this weapon, however, by those more interested in rationalizing their own passivity than they are in finding a revolutionary reality, has made it necessary to ask critics of the armed front to counterbalance their hostility with a little love, and to remember that criticism is a two-way street. The *Passage* article did neither.

The following comments are those of an aboveground worker who has had some experience working within the armed front, and do not necessarily reflect the Brigade's position on any matter herein raised. While my heart is with them, circumstances dictate my doing mass work until such time as the rest of me is reunited with the underground.

Definitions

The *Passage* criticism starts its analysis under the caption "armed struggle vs. terrorism" and then proceeds to define the Brigade's work in limited either/or terms—it is either armed struggle or it is terrorism. Then by giving the term 'armed struggle' an overly narrow definition, they leave terrorism as the only valid label to use for those doing armed work. We should first examine their basis for rejecting use of the term armed struggle in connection with the Brigade.

Roxanne argues that the term armed struggle is usually used in situations where an entire population is engaged in or supportive of the military effort, such as in Angola, Viet Nam, etc. While it may be true that we usually hear the term in connection with a highly developed or full scale revolutionary war, this is so because armed struggle is generally not mentioned on the news or in the books until such time as it has reached an advance stage of development.

Like pregnancy, armed struggle grows in stages. An embryonic pregnancy is nonetheless pregnancy, even though we usually think in terms of bulged out bellies in connection with a pregnancy. When Brigade members go out on a bomb run or other dangerous mission [in which] they are armed, they are also engaged in the process of revolutionary struggle. Is it too simplistic to call this an embryonic stage of armed struggle? The seeds of Viet Nam's liberation army did work similarly to Brigade actions, yet Ho Chi Minh did not call them "terrorist units."

For the sake of argument let's assume that armed struggle does not exist until it reaches advanced stages of development. It would then follow that the Brigade is not involved in the process of armed struggle. It would not, however, follow that the Brigade is a terrorist organization.

Roxanne defines terrorism as "the selective use of symbolic violence by a small, clandestine group . . ." This definition is the one used by law enforcement agencies and the pig media. It is wrong. According to the Merriam-Webster Dictionary terror has one distinguishing characteristic: "a state of intense fear." Terrorism is the political use of this fear.

Not all revolutionary violence is terrorist. The various levels of terrorism are weapons of the weak, and are generally employed under conditions of extreme desperation. Terror can be an important tool for raising the consciousness of the masses when the action clearly demonstrates the cause and effect relationship between ruling class violence and revolutionary violence. While revolutionaries cannot match the state in the level of violence, they can slow down some of its more flagrant abuses through the selective use of terror.

The attack mounted by the Brigade against the FBI and BIA in response to FBI and BIA terrorism at Pine Ridge and Rosebud Indian reservations, while not perfect, were good examples of the selective use of limited counter-terror. These two actions are the only time the Brigade has ever used the weapon of terror (the terror resulting from the first

Safeway bombing, where the store ignored the warning, was unintentional and wrong). Every other Brigade action has been in support of some mass struggle (as were the FBI and BIA attacks), be they prisoners, workers or the left, and were accompanied by advanced warning. While terror is one of the weapons in the Brigade's arsenal, it is not a terrorist organization.

There was a political party in pre-revolutionary Russia that elevated terror to a principle.[21] This was incorrect. The use of terror as the principle form of struggle is incompatible with Marxism inasmuch as it cannot be the means for the liberation of the masses. When terror is elevated to the level of principle it becomes, as Lenin said, a form of spontaneism. But Marxism-Leninism rejects no form of struggle, not even terrorism. The use of this weapon, however, should be strictly limited to those rare instances demanding its application.

Where the Brigade Comes From

> The only path to the final defeat of U.S. imperialism and the building of socialism is revolutionary war.
> Revolution is the most powerful resource of the people. To wait, to not prepare people for the fight, is to seriously mislead about what kind of fierce struggle lies ahead.
> Revolutionary will be complicated and protracted. It includes mass struggle and clandestine struggle, peaceful and violent, political and economic, cultural and military, where all forms are developed in harmony with the armed struggle.
> Without mass struggle there can be no revolution.
> Without armed struggle there can be no victory.
> —*Prairie Fire*

What was passing itself off as the non-revisionist left was in reality nothing more than a verbal critique of reformism and revisionism, its practice indistinguishable from that of the left opposition arm of bourgeois politics.[22] What is needed is a practice conforming to such lofty theoretical positions as the one quoted above. A small group of people came together and set themselves to the task of developing the minimum clandestine infrastructure necessary to answer in practice the difficult questions of form, base, coordination with the aboveground movement, and the sustainable level of struggle. They were guided by the teachings of George Jackson:

> In the opening stages of conflict, before a unified left can be es-
> tablished, before most people have accepted the inevitability of war,
> before we are able militarily to organize massive violence, we must
> depend on limited, selective violence tied to exact political purpose.
> —*Blood In My Eye*[23]

The George Jackson Brigade saw such "exact political purposes" as being the armed defense of the aboveground left; the dispensing of revolutionary justice; military support of mass actions; retaliation to extreme manifestations of fascist violence; and armed propaganda. It was also felt that armed actions would help to polarize the left, and that direct action would contribute to the building of revolutionary organization. The Brigade then launched a series of military probes, each of which met one or more of the above purposes, and each of which helped the group to further define itself and test the limits of struggle.

It was not just theoretical considerations that led to the formation of the Brigade, nor was the group's development the simple product of the deepening economic, political and cultural crisis of monopoly capitalism. While revolutionary theory and the growing international retreat of U.S. imperialism were important considerations, the key factor was the collective experience gained from doing years and years of purely mass agitation and organizing. This experience verified that words alone are not enough to achieve even modest reforms. If this means being a "frustrated" radical, then I cannot understand why, given the isolation of the aboveground movement from the masses, more people do not become frustrated with an ineffective practice.

In Response to Criticism
The best place to start is with your [Park's] claim that developing the capacity for revolutionary violence in the present "works against the revolution." You recognize the need for violence at some point, and admit that objective conditions are ripe. But argue that "the subjective conditions . . . are not in any way conducive towards armed struggle at this point." You suggest everyone work at raising people's level of awareness.

I think most people are conscious of the level of oppression and exploitation, or at least there is enough awareness within the advanced sectors to win over the intermediate and neutralize the backwards elements within the progressive communities. What people do not see is a winning way out of the existing situation. This is the task of communists. But so far radicals have focused on raising the awareness of people who want concrete solutions instead of communist rhetoric and marching in circles. What we need is a whole new style of work—one that will demonstrate our determination to make revolution. People are not going to follow anyone who lacks the faith to fight for their convictions.

Let's assume you are correct in saying that what's needed is more of the same old ineffective methods of raising the consciousness of the masses. If raising consciousness is your goal, as you say, then it would seem only natural to accept assistance of the Brigade. They can reach many people with one well-placed and timely bomb. Think what could be accomplished in terms of awareness if the aboveground and underground could only work together.

The reason why it has been difficult to work together is because a lot of people look at things with tunnel vision. They see struggle in narrow either/or terms—it is either mass or armed—without understanding the dialectical interdependence between the two. The Brigade has not tried to pose as an alternative to mass organizing, but as a necessary supplement to it—as another front in the total liberation process. The two are interdependent. The failure to support one is a failure to support the other.

The Black Liberation Army says: "We as a movement will not be able to fight in the future if we do not develop the capacity for revolutionary violence in the present." This is true. The underground isn't going to just pop up one day when we need it—on command. Just as the aboveground movement is not going to become a truly mass movement overnight, the underground will require time to develop its potential. Each take time, energy, risk and sacrifice—trying this, trying that, making mistakes and pushing forward. It's a long hard process, and it is one we all have to do together. What the Brigade is saying is that it is time to start seriously pushing the process forward. The sooner begun the sooner done, as Jonathan Jackson always said.

A group specializing in the armed aspect of struggle is a revolutionary division of labor. It leaves other groups free to do purely mass agitation and organizing. The armed front will not draw energy from the aboveground.[24] The tiny handful who response to "the call to arms" will leave behind them, to do purely mass work, all those who are not yet willing to risk the hardships of life in the underground. Reinforcing our weakest point—the armed front—will strengthen the movement as a whole, it will enable the movement to walk on both legs. Moreover, when the time comes for the next round of Palmer raids, there will be shelter for aboveground workers driven underground.

The Brigade criticism says: "This turning to violence . . . fits so well into the male tradition of needing to prove power." The women in the Brigade might not stoop to responding to such a sexist slur, and as a "male" I do not wish to do so. Instead, I offer you the perceptive insights of my sister and friend, Emily Harris:

> . . . any mass movement can be strong and long-lived, vital and growing only in so far as it builds at its very heart support for the armed struggle. Right now this means a growing consciousness among women of the nature of the enemy and the relationship between the women's movement and the armed actions that complement our struggles. Again, progressive women act as the catalyst in developing this as a priority. A women's movement that is built without finally recognizing the necessity of armed struggle cannot be revolutionary.
>
> Women have a crucial role to play in building and participating in the armed struggle—part of that role is developing right now in the building of the underground as a front capable of surviving and confronting the enemy through armed actions that are responsive to the anti-sexist, anti-racist and anti-classist elements of our communities. The underground presently lacks much of the critical support it deserves because many elements of the aboveground feel that to support armed action will scare people away. This type of thinking denies our progressive role as revolutionary women and men.
>
> —*Dragon*, No. 9[25]

It is next claimed that the Brigade lacks a solid base of support. This is true. But this is not a reason to reject the Brigade; rather it is an indication of the important need to build a strong base of support for the armed front. Combat units can obtain material support from one or more of three sources, each of which has its own special disadvantages. The first is to draw support directly from the people. This is what the Brigade has primarily relied upon for the duration of its existence.[26] The drawback of a base in the urban poor is the sacrifice of security needs. The security needs of a clandestine group dictates that its contact with non-politicized elements be as limited as possible. Also, poverty limits the amount of support poor people can provide, especially when it comes to expensive equipment needs. The second source of support is from the left's aboveground and underground support network. The major disadvantage of left support lies in the chance of betrayal from the rear. As experience has demonstrated, the left tends to abandon instead of support its friends especially during time of stress. The third alternative is direct expropriation and self-sufficiency. The danger of this method of support is of course the possibility of capture or death if the action is incorrectly executed.

The left not only refused to give the Brigade material or even verbal support, it actively petitioned and organized against them, and at one point it actually demanded the group leave town. This criminal failure on the part of advanced sectors within the left forced the Brigade into the third alternative. People then criticized the bank robbery, not because it was incorrectly executed, but because it was an "untimely" and "unnecessary" escalation of the struggle. Herein lies the source of my bitterness toward those who advocate revolutionary violence in their rhetoric, but in practice work against it. Perhaps Carlos Marighella was right when he said ". . . it is impossible for an urban guerrilla to subsist or survive without taking part in the battle of expropriation."[27] I am inclined to think so, at least at this point.

While it is no doubt true that most working people do not yet accept the need for revolutionary violence or the necessity of class war, we need not wait until such time as all those with their motor homes are ready before moving in this direction. Most people were not aware of the real nature of the Viet Nam War, but the left did not put off confrontation politics until a majority saw the light. In fact, it was the new left's militancy that caused them to give the matter some serious thought.

Most people are racist, sexist and anti-communist. Certainly you would not argue from this that racism and sexism are good and the fight for socialism is wrong. Then why use the same twisted logic in your arguments against armed struggle? The "subjective" conditions of which you speak, which is really the basis for your anti-armed struggle line, is rooted in the most backwards aspects of the masses. Most people have been inculcated with bourgeois ideas from birth; it is an error to predicate your non-struggle position on this backwardness. All you have succeeded in demonstrating is the pressing need to combat bourgeois ideological hegemony within the working class. Armed propaganda is one means of achieving this end.

If the left is really interested in raising consciousness they can start by discontinuing the destructive habit of focusing their theoretical energies on attacking the Brigade. If there are not any more Marxist-Leninist fighters, they could at least use their knowledge for the purpose of finding solutions to the left's isolation from the masses.

They might even go so far as to support and explain the need for armed actions (of course this might cost them their legitimacy in the eyes of the ruling class).

Another thing folks could do is to start implementing the lessons of radical therapy. Find the source of oppression responsible for your alienation, become angry instead of internalizing it, and direct this anger against its real source. Organize around your own oppression and fight back. Organize people around their own needs and the struggle for power. People organize to fight. When leaders fail to initiate the conflict, people fall away from these organizations and the remainder bog themselves down in study groups. The answers will not be found in books, but in practice. Theory is a guide to action, not an end in itself. Without a revolutionary practice groups fall into endless debate and internal conflict, they get locked into a cycle of reformism and opportunism. When revolution fails it is the fault of communists, not the people. Leaders who blame the people instead of themselves should be replaced.

As far as the grand jury harassment is concerned, people must come to understand that resistance breeds repression. If some folks want to blame the Brigade for the existence of increased repression, it is their choice to do so. It is only a matter of time before they recognize the real source of this problem. The answer to the problem of repression is not adopting a non-struggle line, as you propose, but in making the advanced sectors of our communities more secure and less available to the eyes of the state. If people followed your reasoning there would never be a revolution as people would never resist.

In any case, the Brigade has been very careful to insure leftists have no information concerning its membership, shape and base. The Brigade knew there would be a grand jury, what surprised them is that it took so long and freaked out so many people when it finally did come. Anyway, the point is that those called before the grand jury know nothing. Anyone not wishing to go to jail need only say they known nothing in order to avoid the possibility of confinement. Those who have stood up have done so out of principle. If they go to jail it will be out of the strength of their convictions, and not because of the Brigade. People who stand up and spit in the face of repression have my love and respect.

Conclusion

Your article has characterized the Brigade as a group of arrogant and suicidal power mongers bent on leading the left to hell. The Brigade members I know are gentle, caring, loving, and kind. They have the same doubts, fears, and uncertainties as their aboveground counterparts, the only essential difference being that the former are perhaps more anxious to close the gap between theory and practice. Above all they are people and deserve the respect due a comrade—even if you happen to disagree with them.

We stand at the threshold of the beginning of the end. Many folks are fearful, and rightly so. Po and Bruce are dead, many more will not survive the uncertain future. This is fascism! Legitimate revolutionary activity will not be tolerated. In the Brigade people deal with their fear by directly confronting it, experiencing it, and then leaving it behind until the next time—which is made a little easier with practice.

Experience is gained from practice, not passive evasion of it. We are human and will make errors. If an error is to be made it should be on the side of action. As Marighella teaches: *It is better to act mistakenly than to do nothing for fear of doing wrong.*[28] This is not 'action in command,' but a simple recognition of the Marxist principle that we learn from our mistakes, and it is practice which enables us to verify the correctness of our theory.

The appetite of the bourgeois has grown larger than its opportunities. In this contradiction lies the source of conflict. The time has never been better for initiating offensive struggle. There exists no unity of governmental will, it is a regime of social crisis. Its massive apparatus of repression is a sign of weakness, not strength. The opportunities to bring about a change in the existing correlation of class forces have never been better. What remains is for the direct interference of the masses. This is the task of communists, to start the process of contending for power; organizing to empower the powerless, for class war.

Discover your proletarian enthusiasm. Reach out. Organize around your own oppression and the immediate needs of poor and working people. Organize above and below, organize to fight. Revolution is aggressive and imaginative, it requires risk, and sacrifice, love and honesty.

Blood in my eye,
Edward Mead

GRAND JURY:
THREE WHO REFUSED TO SPEAK
Interview by Roxanne Park and Emmett Ward
Northwest Passage, June 28–July 19, 1976

What's the scenario when you go into the grand jury room?

Katie: Well, you walk in . . . it's really light and there's all those people sitting there. Something about the atmosphere makes you feel really frightened, really scared. There is no judge, and you don't have a lawyer. There are no friends of yours, and no press. There's nobody but the court reporter, the prosecutor and the jurors. If you want to talk to your lawyer, you have to ask their permission to go out of the room. . . . [T]he prosecutor gives you the distinct impression you are holding up the proceedings as if you want to talk with your lawyer. Everybody gets uptight with you, and you feel like you're not asserting your rights, but you're asking for a privilege . . . to go down the hall every time you talk with your lawyer. And you try to write down the questions, which is hard, because the prosecutor is asking them so fast.

Brenda: One of the things that really bothers me about going in is that from the moment you walk in the door you're on. You don't get a chance to sit down and orient yourself, or look who's there or what the set up is. All the time you're in there, they're asking you questions. I found that really frightening. I felt like I was on totally alien territory. There's just no chance to get a sense of your space.

Katie: It's like you're on stage. The focus is on you from the second you walk in that door.

Brenda: It's strange when you walk in. Everybody else is sitting there really comfortable. The prosecutor knows everybody there, everybody knows everybody else. They know exactly what's going on, they have all this breathing space and you have absolutely none.

I'm getting the idea that it's very difficult to outfox them. I've heard people ask "Why don't you just go to the jury and answer what questions you want—kind of play games with them—because you know what you know and they don't."

Katie: You could answer a question or two, which seemed pretty harmless, like if they ask about some bombing and you say you don't know anything. But somewhere down the line they will ask a question and you say "Hey, they have no business asking this" or you jut don't want to tell them. So you say, "Wait a minute, I'm not going to answer that question," and try to assert your 5th amendment rights. But they say, "Sorry, you can't do that; by talking to begin with, by answering even one question, you have waived your 5th amendment rights." So there you are. You've got no legal ground to stand on.

Have you been told the questions they're interested in asking you?

Brenda: The prosecutor has said that one of the things he wants to know from us is who Po's friends were, because if he knows who was close to him at the time he died, he would then know who would be grieved enough to do the second bombing and thus find the George Jackson Brigade. Which is one of the reasons I don't want to testify. I don't want to talk about who Po's friends were. That's the same kind of reasoning that led them to me and put me in this situation and I have no interest in doing that to somebody else.

What do you think about the government's [claim] that the Brigade is all connected up with Po?

Katie: Even Walter Wright, the reporter from the *Post-Intelligencer*, has come out and said, "Look, the Brigade never claimed Po as a member. Although they've claimed all kinds of other things, they've never claimed him or the bombing he did as one of their actions." After the Brigade bombing at the Safeway store Po's friends issued a statement saying that Po would never have approved of that sort of bombing because it endangered people's lives and he was a gentle person. And Michelle [Whitnack], the other woman subpoenaed, has come out in the press and said that she'd stake her life on the fact that Po wasn't a member of the Brigade.

When I interviewed Ed Mead he said that Po was not a member of the Brigade; he was a comrade trying to achieve the same ends, but not a member.
It sounds like the grand jury subpoenas are a combination of sloppy investigative work and a fishing expedition. Do you have a sense from the government's point of view what they're trying to get from all this?

Brenda: What goes on in their minds is a really good question. I think they don't have a very good understanding of the left community. We went before Magistrate [John] Weinberg on the hearing to get some of our things taken in the search. U.S. Attorney [Peter] Mair justified keeping the things because we showed an interest in dialectical materialism and feminism, because we had radical writings in our house, because we read poetry, because there were the words in someone's diary that said "cozy and comforting"—which is similar to "cozy, cuddly, armed and dangerous," which is in one of the communiques of the Brigade—because we were sorry, grieved that Po died, because we had a criticism of some group which [we put in a form similar to those of the Brigade], since it started out with a quote from a revolutionary: all these things put together showed there was a good chance that we are the George Jackson Brigade. That leads me to believe there must be George Jackson [Brigade] houses all over Capitol Hill, and that many of us who had no idea that we were members, must be.

Katie: I'd like to put another twist on that. From the very beginning . . . when they did this garbage search, the affidavit, and all this business, they've been trying to create this web around us, this fog around us. Prosecutor [Jack] Meyerson came out on the radio and said: "We know that communique was written in that particular house we searched." They're [presenting this in such a way as to make it appear] that we must have something to hide, that we know all these things. What they're doing is trying to make it so that when we go in and try to assert our rights, they can say, "Sure, they're taking the 5th because they have something to hide"—not because we think it's important that people refuse to cooperate with the grand jury.

I'd like to talk about what's happened in your own lives as a result of the subpoenas.

Katie: Two kinds of things have happened. We've gotten a lot of support from some friends, from some people we don't even know at all, although other people, other friends have disappeared into the woodwork.

Do you think that's because they're afraid?

Katie: I don't know. I assume that's why. I get uptight about it occasionally, but on the other hand I've been overwhelmed by the number of other people who have just done incredible things for us, supported us a lot. So that's one side of it. The other side of it is that we are virtually on trial in front of the press for something that we never did. Hell, I've never even been arrested for anything. Nobody's every besmirched my—um, integrity—and suddenly here I am on trial for writing something I never wrote. And yet the government—I mean the FBI, the CIA, there was the Watergate thing—everybody knows that the government lies and cheats and steals and does everything, and yet people are willing to listen to them and believe them. But in our personal lives . . . our landlord got real freaked out about the search of the house and the stuff that's happened, so he's evicting us, we have to be out by the end of the month. That's happening on top of everything else.

Before all this happened, the plans for the immediate future of my life, were to be a gardener, because I like to do that; and I would go to carpentry school in the fall. What's happened is that my garden is overgrown with weeds, I won't get it harvested because I won't be living in this house any more. If I go to jail I won't go to carpentry school. I have a son—I'd like to say before this happened he thought police were wonderful, and in fact when they walked through the door he wasn't upset at all, he was the coolest person here. He thought it was great to have all these cops in his house. But since then I came home one day and there was a sign that he made on the front door that said "no police in here." It's had a big impact on his life and if they send me to jail, it's going to have a *real* big impact because I'm not going to see him for probably a year or more, which means I won't see him til he's 7½.

When you think of your future, do you expect you'll end up in jail?

Katie: I include that as a real strong possibility. I'm superstitious enough to want to say, "Of course I'm not going to jail." But I want to leave the option open in my own mind. I'm making the necessary arrangements.

Brenda: I'm assuming I'm gonna go and the legal advice I get is to make that assumption. I'll be very surprised if I don't and I'm building what's left of my life around this fact. My whole lifestyle has changed and the way I look at everything has changed because of this. Before the police broke into the house, I had always known about police repression and that being a revolutionary, or radical, or whatever it turns out that we are . . . included that occupational hazard. But since this has happened I feel like my life has been totally invaded and there are all kinds of things that are no longer my private things.

The police have gone through my garbage and read things that I threw away, they broke into my house, they ripped off personal letters from my friends, they ripped off diaries, address books, all that kind of stuff is theirs. They could walk around the house and do whatever they wanted. They may be bugging my phone, they might be observing outside. I don't know what is going to happen to me for the next year and a half of my life. I may be spending it totally under other people's control. I am being dragged up in front of the grand jury and being told to say what I know about my friends.

One of the reasons I do not want to testify is that I want them to know that there is a part of me that is *myself*, that they cannot touch, that they cannot have. Since this happened I have had to find myself inside of myself. I have had to find my center really strong inside. I can't use a journal, I can't keep letters to my friends to use as "maps" to my life. It all has to be inside of me, and that is really changing the way I look at the world. It was very hard when I realized they had taken letters from people that I care very much about, and I don't know what it will mean that they had those letters. I don't know what it will mean that they have addresses of my friends. Friends may be subpoenaed because of their association with me. People who have only had personal associations with me can be dragged into this. It has given me a lot to think about. I realize that we need to find ways to take care of ourselves, to protect our friends and to fight back. If we are serious about changing this country, that that's going to have to be part of our lives.

Do you have any specific ideas of what changes that means?

Brenda: I don't want to spread a lot of paranoia around and suggest that everyone is going to get their houses broken into, but I think that people who are radicals ought to think real carefully about what kind of written information is lying around in their house. That people should pick their friends wisely: when people that they know are under attack that they should take that very seriously and support them in every way that they can. That can mean a lot of things, from showing up to demonstrate to making dinner, giving money, coming up to people and just talking to them: letting them know that you are there.

Do you think that your experiences will scare people into retreating?

Katie: Personally I have not been active in the Left for quite awhile. I did not like being in the Left especially, although I carried with me those feelings. I just did not want to do anything. It has not scared me a bit, it turned me into a full-time activist. It was really hard for me for a couple weeks, I went through a personal hell getting myself to give up what I wanted to be doing, and accept the situation that I am now in. And I pretty much have accepted it and I have a whole lot of energy for fighting. This has not scared me, it has made me *real angry*, and really committed to doing everything I can to change it.

Brenda: I am really scared. It is important to let people know that you are scared. If we are serious about what we are doing, then we have to realize that there are going to be times in our lives when we are going to be real, real afraid. What we have to learn to do is keep going in the face of that fear. That's what courage it. When we look at the Vietnamese and we respect them for the courage they had, it is not because they were able to fight in this wonderful situation when they'd had lots of support and help. We respect them because they fought when everything was against them. That is the kind of consciousness people have to develop. We fight to win.

Katie: We run into some people who try to do this super-woman trip on us, because we are not testifying. And we try to say that we are not super, that we are just like everybody else. And that we need people's support to do what we are doing. We need to not feel isolated. It is symbiotic: people care about what is happening to us, therefore we care about people and we keep on refusing to testify.

Does it really make a difference to have people coming down to the demonstrations?

Kathy: Oh yeah! I mean, *that* is putting yourself on the line. That is the strongest form of support. People coming to you privately and saying that they support what you are doing is good energy, but to say that publicly is an act of courage. Particularly to someone who has not gone to demonstrations a lot, it's scary. And that [fear] is important to [work] through.

One of the surprising things to me is how much support I have gotten at Group Health, which is a pretty straight hospital. I am a registered nurse and I work in the emergency room. People have been real supportive, people have given money and have given a lot of personal support and I really appreciate that. My initial response was "*Eeek*! I am going to lose my job." And that has not been the case. Even the people I work with who are real right-wingers have been pretty supportive or have kept their mouths shut; they haven't given me their usual hassle.

How have you gotten across to people, because the whole set up is that you are a dangerous person?

Kathy: They know me, they know me real well. I am open about who I am. The initial response I have gotten from people is "This is ridiculous." Just from knowing me on some fairly intimate level, because we work the night shift and spend lots of time talking to each other. It's like a pajama party, you get to know people pretty well.

The other thing that helps is the response of other friends and the support that takes the form of ordinary day to day activities. Support is if you are crying all night and you can't get to sleep and you call someone at 3:30 in the morning and they come over. Support is cooking dinner, doing daycare. You really need your Mommy at a time like this, you need people to be your Mommies.

The other big effect has been with my son Joshua. It seemed to me that the reasonable way to handle it was to be honest with him to say "I might go to jail," and to try and minimize the change it will make in his life, but it is a big deal for him.

The fact of being a single parent and of facing the possibility of having to leave your child is really heavy. He went through this period of being a clinging two year old, and he is four. He was wetting his bed two or three times a week, which he had totally stopped doing. Those are signs that he is really upset about this. He has also has done some neat things. He made this sign to go to the demonstration which said: "KILL THE DRAGONS. POLICES DON'T PUT KATHY IN JAIL. BREAK THE JAIL DOOR OPEN." He knows what is going on. He plays around with letters on paper and pretends he is making a leaflet. It has its good sides for him. He is real ambivalent about police now, he talks about police all the time. "That's a good police, that's a bad police." He dreamt that "the polices" went into Debray's house and lost his gun there.

And that has been the most painful, the heaviest part for me. Because a year at the age of four is a real big hunk of time.

[to Brenda and Katie] Are you two similarly planning to spend time in jail?

[Katie?]: I feel like I must be ready, whether I go to jail or not is at the whim of the prosecutor . . . it is not anything that is under my control. To the extent that I have said, "I draw the line, there is a line that I will not cross in terms of my integrity." I will not testify about my friends, I will not hurt my friends, or subject them to what I am going through. I will not do that.

Support really helps you to make the stand. I feel that other people's strength really flows through me. When it comes down to it, I am going to be in jail. Any day when you are in jail for civil contempt you just have to call up the D.A. and bingo you're out to testify, you're free. So it's very difficult kind of jail sentence; it's not like you're in jail for a year and you have to wait it out. You have to be strong every minute of every day. I feel like it's real important to go through the emotional work to be ready to do that. And so I don't go? Well, I'll be ready if it ever happens again. The whole muddle is like herpes, you get it once and you're more likely to get it again.

Even if this whole thing is dropped it has changed my life. I feel like I'm more vulnerable, I'm politicized by what has happened. If the federal government thinks that this is a method of repressing political activity, they are mistaken. They are radicalizing me and they are radicalizing all these non-political people who are my friends. It is like this eagle soaring down from the sky and puts its claws on your head. It is really a random feeling.

I had known about Leslie Bacon and I had heard Leslie Bacon speak. So I knew what to do. It made a big difference to me. I was previously educated about grand juries before I was subpoenaed, and had essentially decided three years ago that if I was ever subpoenaed by a grand jury, I was not going to testify. That is very helpful now, because it would be much harder to make that decision now, under pressure, under stress, being pulled different ways. People who I work with, people who are pragmatists, say "Talk and stay out of trouble." To have made that decision in the past gives me strength.

I would encourage people to inform themselves about whether or not they are going to testify. Think about it now, talk about it with their friends now, so they are in a position to get support when it happens. You can be subpoenaed this morning and have to appear this afternoon. So you better be ready to figure out what to do. You certainly better know that you better get a lawyer. The easiest way to do that is to contact the National Lawyers Guild because they have had the most experience with grand juries.

Do you expect there will be other people subpoenaed?

Brenda: I don't think that they will stop with us. They are really trying to get the Brigade. In the meantime, they want to know as much as they can about the Left.

They have not been doing a whole lot of footwork in their investigation, they seem to be relying on the grand jury. Since they won't be getting much from us, I guess they will have to keep going.

I would like to say a commercial. I have been keeping the books for the Committee to End Grand Jury Abuse and we have gotten so many financial contributions, not to mention all the other work people have done. There is now way, as far as I can see, that they Committee can send personal letters to all the people who have contributed. But the appreciation is there real dseep in our hearts.

More Than "Critical Support" for GJB

Papaya
Northwest Passage, February 6–27, 1978, 22

Dear *NWP*,

Debate about the politics and practice of the George Jackson Brigade will be continuing for as long as the GJB exists. My concern in this letter is not which position folks should be taking. I am addressing myself to those who have taken the position of "critical support" for the GJB. I am getting more and more confused about what "critical support" is supposed to mean. So far it seems to mean that the GJB political statement gets discussed in a few study groups, the brigade gets a bit of praise here and a bit of criticism there, and armed struggle comes up as a topic for a few more discussions.

This is certainly more than was happening even one or two years ago, but it's not enough. There are many people who are confused about the armed struggle or don't support the GJB and that's where they're at. But there are also many people who say they do support the GJB. It's time to demonstrate this support. The recent GJB communiques list several things the aboveground can be doing, from letters and phone calls to the jail to sabotage of auto dealers. There seems to be widespread praise for the communiques—why aren't folks acting on them? There are other fronts too. The GJB's Political Statement and the communiques need to be distributed outside of the Left community, to welfare and unemployment offices, laundromats, high schools, etc. It's up to the aboveground to do it. The GJB, as they themselves often state, are isolated and need feedback. They obviously read underground newspapers—where are our letters? I urge anyone who has been *saying* they critically support the GJB to think about what they've been *doing* about it, and choose the actions they can best participate in.

Love and struggle,
Papaya

CAPTURED MEMBERS EXPLAIN THEIR POLITICS
Bill Patz
Northwest Passage, June 13–July 10, 1978, 18–20

In the shadow of the Red Brigade's assassinations and crippling of Italian establishment figures, three members of the Northwest-based George Jackson Brigade come to trial. Therese Coupez and John Sherman will face a judge and jury on June 19th, while Janine Bertram (Jory Uhuru),[29] who recently pled guilty, will be sentenced on July 11th. Meanwhile the regular press has lumped together the bank robberies and property-destroying bombings of the GJB with the kidnappings and shootings of the Red Brigade as the work of "left-wing terrorists."

It may come as a surprise then, that John Sherman is opposed to the kind of campaign the Red Brigade is waging. Although unwilling to comment specifically about the Italian group for lack of in-depth information, he said that "in principle the GJB stand opposed to provoking police repression . . . We feel the masses of working people already know how fucked up things are . . . What they fail to see is the power they have to do something about it . . . Day to day, tedious, long-range organization and education is what's needed, not get-rich-quick schemes."

This, of course, is not the sort of statement that gets into the big daily newspapers. It shows that despite the generous amount of front-page coverage given the GJB, we have not really heard much about their basic thinking. Most reporting so far has aimed at providing a good cops-and-robbers story, or a human interest angle, such as what the group's favorite films are. A few articles, though, have actually made attempts to show Brigade members as serious, intelligent people. These articles brought to light some of their life experiences among prisoners, battered women, prostitutes, and people in mental hospitals. Yet the connection between these experiences and the Brigade's declared commitment to "revolution" and "armed struggle" has generally been left dangling—with almost intended sarcasm. After all, it is implied, who is going to take seriously the Brigade's idea of making a revolution in this country, or challenging the authorities with arms?

My Own Reaction
On several occasions my first reaction to GJB actions has been an inward smile at their having tweaked the noses of the ruling class with seeming impunity. But I also had thoughts similar to those of Del Castle, secretary-treasurer of the Longshoremen's Local 52 and

longtime socialist. In a lunchtime conversation with me he said (speaking for himself and not as a union official), "of course everyone gets a certain feeling of pleasure when they see their enemy dealt a blow. But these more immediate surface reactions are not the kind of thing you want to base a serious political strategy on."

When another three members of the Brigade were arrested and the media heralded the end of the group (though members at large have denied this through communiques),[30] I couldn't help but get caught up in the general curiosity about who these people were. And how could they seriously consider armed work now? The answers were hardly to be found on newsstands or tv, so like others before me, including independent authors who contributed to a *Passage* series on the use of violence two years ago, I started reading and asking questions about the GJB. I interviewed the three now in jail as well as talking to others who have thought about or been affected by the GJB actions. The following article poses some of the questions that arise around the idea of "armed struggle," and sketches the Brigade's basic positions.

What Is Meant By 'Armed Struggle' And Why Practice It Now[?]

Central to the existence of the George Jackson Brigade is the belief that in replacing a capitalist society with a more humane one, force of arms will be needed to some degree. The group's Political Statement, published November 1977, declares that the "main point of unity" in the GJB is to develop this force "here and now." But developing it, in their view, does not mean that everyone should pick up a gun or learn about explosives. Rather, this is a task for small numbers of people. They stress that "armed struggle" is *not* the "axis" around which all other forms of struggle develop." It should, instead, support and follow the lead of the main work which is "mass organizing" of people in their workplaces and communities. But the Brigade does believe that armed work is an "absolutely essential part of the struggle."

Why is it so necessary and why now? Is radical political organizing going on to the extent that it needs to be defended with arms? The Brigade states that "in the end, whatever kinds of progress and reforms are made within the society, the ruling class will resort to violence, even against unarmed movements, to maintain its control." John Sherman supports this argument with the claim that "there are numerous instances throughout US and world history that bear this out . . . To name a few we can look at the response to popular mass actions such as the Ludlow, Colorado-miners' strike around the turn of the century, the Attica, New York prison uprising, the Kent State and Jackson State student demonstrations, the electoral victories of Allende and the Chilean socialists, and so on . . ." He adds that, "it is our position if we don't start to learn the complex processes of armed work, in the end the risk to all of us is greater . . ."

Castle of the Longshoremen's Union, like some who disagree with the Brigade's politics, doesn't reject out of hand the possibility of some-day having to wage armed struggle. But, he believes that "when 'mass struggle' is going on at a level of revolutionary proportions where armed resistance is called for, the workers themselves already possess the skills. There is knowledge of explosives, sabotage, and guns among different sections of workers. So when you really have them on your side you have what forces you will need."

Janine Bertram comments on this position, "We don't think it is so simple . . . It's scary but there is a lot to learn about the military disposition of the state, how the police, army, etc. are deployed . . ."

Brigade members also cite the argument of black revolutionary prisoner George Jackson. Jackson believed that armed groups are needed right now to protect progressive movements for which police harassment and even assassination are realities. In a letter of warning to Angela Davis, contained in his book *Blood In My Eye*, he wrote that "the secret police (CIA, etc.) go to great lengths to murder and consequently silence every effective black person the moment he (or she) attempts to explain to the ghetto that our problems are historically and strategically tied to the problems of all colonial people." Jackson saw many black leaders' fate, from Malcolm X to Martin Luther King, as evidence of this pattern. Shortly before his book was published and his widely publicized trial was to be held, Jackson himself was killed while in prison. Many believe he was assassinated by prison authorities because of his radical views and wide following. It was Jackson's thinking that the ability to carry out acts of violence or sabotage could and should be part of a force to deter the state from going this far in confronting radical groups.

"While we feel defending vulnerable movements in this way is legitimate," says Sherman, it's really beyond the means of armed workers at this point . . . Also, the Brigade is more concerned with developing illegal actions that can be used in 'offensive' ways . . . We see a need to develop long range strategy for confronting the ruling class . . . With this is mind we have acted where we felt we could help advance ongoing struggles [such as worker and prisoner strikes].[31]"

Does Violence Turn People Off?

As one *Passage* collective member said to me, "discussion of armed struggle at this level has a basic flaw: it assumes that sabotage and illegal actions actually benefit particular struggles." "In fact," he contended, "even where there seems to be some justification for its use, in trying to build a mass movement, violence tends to turn more people off than on."

I raised this point with Janine Bertram, who responded, "of course violence is abhorrent to people. In ways it is to us too. But it's important not to lump all kinds of armed political action together and conclude that they are all wrong, or that people are always turned off by violence." She referred to the Brigade's Political Statement which says that while "the bourgeois media calls [the GJB] 'terrorists', in fact we are opposed to terrorism . . . Terror [in the form of killing or threatening people] is an extremely easy tactic to use . . . People employ it to strike fear and confusion into the minds of their enemies [in the hope that they can be scared into changing] . . . It requires no special investigation to shed light on the possible effects of one's actions; it requires no principles to speak of and very little work . . ." While the Brigade makes an exception for "people fighting against extinction, such as the Palestinians," who they say may be justified in using terrorism, they maintain that terror as a tactic "is itself dangerous and should be used very sparingly if at all in this country." Bertram added that in "one instance where we bombed a Safeway store and innocent people were hurt, we received a lot of criticism. We agreed with the response and publicly criticized ourselves . . . It was an experience we learned from."

But how about the terror brought to innocent bank tellers every time the Brigade robs a bank? Sherman's response is that, "we do have to use the threat of violence to rob a bank . . . There are these kinds of contradictions in our work . . . But there is no way that we would ever shoot a teller. We would hopefully surrender or give our own lives before we would shoot a bank teller."

"As far as people being turned on or off by violence," Sherman continued, "we believe that among the working class in this country is an acceptance of armed resistance . . . Historically workers have resorted to arming themselves, to sabotage, and to beating up scabs when they were forced to . . . Worker militancy has been excluded from the history books in the same way as resistance by other oppressed people."

In their Political Statement the GJB also maintains that certain groups in this country inherently understand and accept fighting with force when necessary. "These are the more or less permanently jobless working class people—prisoner, ex-prisoners, old and young people, people trapped into the lowest paid, most temporary shit jobs, people forced on welfare and forced to remain there . . . [It is among] these people, discarded by capitalism . . . that armed struggle . . . has taken root."

How much has it really "taken root" though? Of course we have witnessed spontaneous riots among different poor and Third World communities, and on occasion sabotage and physical resistance by workers, but do these expressions of anger and rebelliousness indicate a deeper willingness to accept, much less support, a program for developing armed resistance?

It is hard to know how to answer this question. The reactions of people I talked with might provide some perspective. Del Castle, whose union has offered strong support to the auto machinists' strike, made these observations about the use of violence. "Historically these acts have generally worked against the interest of workers, bringing police retaliation or loss of public support, and in fact have often been the work of police agents and provocateurs as well . . . The Brigade, if anything, falls into the category of weakening public support for the strike."

In contrast, one auto machinist who has been on the picket line for the duration of the strike said that, "While I don't believe in out and out bombing . . . and I myself wouldn't do what they did . . . it did give us a shot in the arm . . . It's not the kind of thing that will make or break this strike of course."

I also talked to a young white man who works as an orderly at the Children's Hospital, which had to go on generator power as a result of the GJB bombing of the Laurelhurst power substation in support of a City Light workers' strike. (The substation mainly services a wealthy Seattle neighborhood). He said that "people working at the hospital definitely talked about it . . . One thing I noticed was that the people who do the housekeeping and real shitwork there, and who are mostly black women, generally did not seem so offended or freaked out by what the GJB had done. Some even talked about the violence in their lives . . . like trying to raise a family on welfare . . . The nurses and nurses aides (mostly white) were more critical, though, and especially indignant over the inconvenience caused a hospital serving sick and injured children . . . Personally I'm not necessarily turned off by sabotage, but I think the message of what they're trying to do isn't always completely clear."

Then there are people less directly involved, like a middle aged black woman who lives in my apartment building. She spent much of her adult life working as a housekeeper and cook for wealthy Houston families. "I just don't know . . . Yes I remember reading about them in the papers . . . But I really don't like any of this violence . . . People shouldn't be fighting to work out their differences." Or my brother going to medical school in Baltimore, who said, "I think that stuff tends to make people less sympathetic to a cause, but I guess I can see where some things like the coal miners turning over those parked trucks [of a scabbing company during the recent coal miners strike] would help strengthen the spirit of the guys on strike . . . It didn't make me less sympathetic to their demands."

The Brigade feels that the important thing here is the acceptance among those involved in the particular struggle. Their Political Statement says that "following a bombing to protest biased coverage of their strike, Walla Walla prisoners issued a public statement stating support for our action." Bertram mentioned the Laurelhurst substation bombing, "where City Light Workers on strike even set up a picket around it to keeps scabs from repairing it for several days."[32] Therese Coupez was of the opinion that the "numerous [independent] instances of tire slashing [an entire car lot's worth in Bellevue], and broken windows and property damage at new car lots . . ." showed that the Brigade bombings were in harmony with the "striking auto machinists [who] did make sabotage a part of their strike."

"The question here, though," as one *Passage* staff member put it, "is even if there is a surface receptiveness to their actions or similar independent acts by other workers, will workers, prisoners, and others become more aware of the need for fundamental changes in the society because of them? Will the idea of workers controlling their workplaces or prisoners' unity in abolishing prisons be enhanced?"

In reply, Sherman said that it is not the Brigade's main role to do "consciousness raising." "Though it is important to choose to act where there is a real basis for armed work," he explained, "the Brigade does not imagine that it could make much difference in the area of political education. People's political awareness will primarily be affected by above-ground organizing . . . The Brigade's responsibility is to develop armed struggle . . . to learn about it . . . to test out the limits to which it can be successfully carried out . . . and to show people that armed resistance is not something just that state has control over . . . Of course what were doing is real small, but the most important aspect is the learning . . . And in the long haul," he concluded, "to do this, 'practice' is essential."

Who Gives Them The Right!

"The thing that infuriates me," said a labor-journalist friend of mine, "is who gives 'them' the right to decide when it is time for armed actions, and who gives 'them' the authority to bring sabotage into a particular group's struggle?"

The Brigade has said that for armed actions to be successful "those doing it must follow the leadership" of those engaged in political conflicts "aboveground." At the same time they acknowledge that being a small clandestine group poses real obstacles to developing armed work in a democratic way. In fact they see the communications problem as being the main obstacle in their activity. However they categorize this as a "tactical" problem, not one that negates the nature of their work.

Therese Coupez further explains that "obviously because of the illegal nature of armed work we couldn't go to union meetings and ask people what they'd like us to do. Nor could we attend meetings in the left of the community. We took our leadership from people who were already in struggle. We watched labor and community struggles as they developed, learning about them from the alternative and straight media and by talking to people, anonymously, on the picket line. We chose to act in support of struggles that had been going on for a long time, where the people involved had exhausted all 'legal' channels and were still sticking it out against the bosses . . . where we could determine, as far as possible, that the general mood of those involved was not opposed to armed attacks . . ."

"In the case of the auto machinists and City Light workers' strikes," said Bertram, "we spent many hours talking to rank and file workers who were picketing, trying to ascertain their general mood and their feelings about their situation."

The Brigade feels that the alternative and left media could be giving more attention to the issue of armed actions. They see it and the left in general as the key link in their communicating successfully with large numbers of people.

Coupez thought, for example, that "an ideal opportunity to develop dialogue on armed struggle between working people and the left was passed up around the auto machinists' strike. What coverage there has been has ignored the question of armed support [which the Brigade provided]; and very little of the coverage has had much at all about what the workers had to say [about it]. You can be sure they discussed it among themselves."

A Few Reasons Why the Brigade Isn't On The Left's Top Ten Chart
The *Passage* staff has not really reported on the Brigade in great depth, for several reasons. One has simply been resistance to a GJB assumption that left journal necessarily should deal with issues of "armed struggle." Another was some feeling that the highly sensational nature of armed actions diverted attention from less glamorous political issues, despite the Brigade's proclaimed interest in supporting aboveground political activity. Also, though Brigade communiques explained in detail the reasons for their actions, the use at times of phrases like "waging class war" and "sweeping the capitalists into the dust bin of history" seemed both self-serving and romantic. Despite their claim to follow, there was a feeling that the Brigade had indeed placed itself above people working in left movements.

Beyond these reactions have been the basic doubts along the lines of the questions raised in this article. Specifically, some collective members are critical of the entire frame of reference of the discussion of "armed struggle." As one said, "the GJB is part of a small political element tied to the prison movement. All of them were either prisoners or involved in the prison movement. As such they tend to view things with an overly militaristic slant. Violence and repression are certainly very real parts of the lives of people who are in and out of prison. But that doesn't mean that a violent course of action is necessarily a good one. And the Brigade's actions also reflect the societal glorification of violence."

While the Brigade denies their advocacy of militaristic solutions, they have recognized the influence isolation and the societal romanticization of violence have on their activity. "Sometimes we do get caught up in it," Sherman said simply. "For ourselves and others we feel it is important to counter the heroic notions about violence as well as the one that approves only those who use it to preserve the status quo . . ."

The Brigade also recognizes their ties to prison work, but as Coupez says of herself, "my commitment and motivation to armed struggle has come from the sum of my experiences working and living in capitalist society." Sherman said, "I've been doing political work for ten years. I spent 3½ of them doing prison work and serving jail time. The rest was workplace organizing."

A prison activist sympathetic to the Brigade commented that "those who totally discount strategies on the grounds that they have been developed in prison are ignoring the realities of the extent that the state is willing to keep people in line. What happens to prisoners speaks to what may be in store for larger political challenges to the status quo."

The isolation between prisoners and those outside, and between an "underground" group like the Brigade and the rest of us, certainly affects each group's perception of the other. On the question of the GJB's real intent to follow the direction of those working through non-violent political channels, I asked Coupez, "what if the 'aboveground' groups you were in communication with asked you to cool it?" Her response was that "if the groups involved in a particular struggle called for us to 'cool it,' we would engage in discussion (through communiques and media) with them and follow their wishes."

"The thing that is missing from this discussion is the reason many of us have supported the Brigade all along," said one member of the Public Support Committee for the GJB (which is helping with their defense. "We don't necessarily agree with their particular strategies or theory, but neither do we feel that any sure blueprint exist for developing a revolution in a modern industrial society . . . Armed actions may be a part of what's needed . . . Aside from that I, for one, simply tend to respect their courage and the sensitivity they have shown in trying to downplay any notions of themselves as being a vanguard for others."

On Trial In Whose Court[?]

Though cynics will say they have brought it on themselves, it is important to see the Brigade members' upcoming trial in its proper perspective. Janine Bertram, John Sherman, and Therese Coupez will not be tried on whether they have precipitated increased police repression, or detracted from the struggles of community groups, or turned the public off to the potential of socialism. They will be tried for robbing banks and destroying the property of auto dealers or of the state department of corrections. And no doubt the federal prosecutors and the judge will attempt to minimize or entirely silence the Brigade's defense of their actions as building resistance to an oppressive society.

What we can learn from the Brigade's experiences will depend on our abilities to look openly at the issues they raise. Whether or not we agree with their program of carrying on armed struggle at this time, there is clearly an increase in the number of people who do. What is important is to recognize that the violence inherent in a capitalist society is in the end the force that motivates people to fighting back with arms or without.

Part V

PROCESSING

A Collective Interview with George Jackson Brigade Veterans
Bo Brown, Mark Cook, and Ed Mead interviewed by Daniel Burton-Rose

The following interview was conducted October 14, 2005, before a discussion by the former Brigade members at the AK Press warehouse in Oakland, California. Former members Janine Bertram and John Sherman could not be present.

What were your intentions in forming the George Jackson Brigade?

Ed Mead: Global communist revolution! (*chuckles*)

How was the Brigade going to provide a bridge between present realities and global communist revolution?

Mead: We need to build a capacity. It isn't going to fall from the sky when we want it. It is something that has to be built and developed from the ground up.

Everyone involved in the Brigade was doing day-to-day prisoners' rights organizing, which is building and developing a capacity.

Bo Brown: Right, but you have to do more. You can take somebody's kids to prison (to visit them). *So what?!* Anybody can do that, and *should* be doing that.
The state was killing people. When they started shooting down students on campuses they made a qualitative jump in their attack. Other people in the world were putting their lives on the line everyday.

Mead: [George Jackson said] "There is always armed struggle." There is armed struggle today. And as George Jackson said: "If there's going to be funerals, let there be funerals on both sides."

Do you see a difference between building a mass movement for change and providing a check on the state's repressive apparatus?

Mead: Remember a few years ago when some skinheads killed an ARA [Anti-Racist Action] kid in Las Vegas?[1] Where are we? We have no capability for defending ourselves or responding to situations like that.

Some years ago in Chicago somebody drove by the office of the Socialist Workers' Party and threw a brick through the window. The SWP went to the police and then complained in their paper: "The police are so terrible! They won't defend us against these hooligans!" I'm thinking to myself, 'Why aren't you defending yourself? Why are you relying on the enemy state to do it?'

Mark Cook: When I first heard about the George Jackson Brigade, I wasn't the only one—some of the guys down in Walla Walla also heard about it. I was the only one who had an opportunity to explore it. It was Rita [Brown] and Therese [Coupez] who told me about it. It seemed like it was an expansion of the Panther program. But these are white folks. That's my first introduction to 'em, right? Slowly I met some of the final people and some of the earlier people—I seen 'em drivin' around with their explosive in the back of their truck!

I wasn't a part of it, but I contributed to it. I used to give Rita and Therese money to help with the gas to take women [visitors] to [the women's prison in] Purdy. And I knew they were activists and wanted change; that they were revolutionaries. This is what drew me into it. I had to see what was going on. I had to tell the other [Black Panther] Party members what was going on, and I did.

As far as I could see it was good. There was no contradiction with what George Jackson said or what the Panthers said. That was my introduction, but they ran the thing, the principals of the Brigade itself.

They had their problems. I saw it early in the game. And they handled it; to me, they handled it well. It didn't involve no police or anybody else, they handled it by themselves.

How did the character of the Brigade change over time?

Cook: Early on there was a drastic incident and [the people in the collective] said: "This ain't happenin' again!" We all saw what happened at Safeway[2]—it was bad planning—and that again changed the character. They *had* to be more careful about what they were doing.

There was a constant change. To the very end you could see the changes, just reading the communiques. They acknowledged their mistakes.

Brown: Accountability.

The George Jackson Brigade is the only armed group in the United States in the 1960s and '70s which apologized for one of its actions, the first Safeway bombing.

Cook: There was one incident where . . .

Brown: The money was in the purse and we returned the purse to the woman independently and didn't talk about it until after the woman got her purse back. Then *she* called the police and told them: "I got my purse back." All her stuff was in it. We sent her a greeting card and apologized for scaring her.

When the grand jury was terrorizing those single mothers, we drove all the way to Las Vegas and sent a letter with the [torsion arch] bars out of John's mouth to authenticate it. We said in this letter, which we sent to the guy at the *Post-Intelligencer* [Walter Wright], "None of these women were involved. Here's the bar out of his mouth. This is who we are. That's not what we're about. We didn't live there. We think that you're just harassing these people because somebody's girlfriend lived there—*not* one of us." We took responsibility in that way.

What was your code of conduct?

Brown: Human honor. Respectful humanitarian honor: How would you like to be treated? We would try to be responsible for our own actions because we made a decision to do what we did and we were willing to take the weight for that. That's honor: not to throw that off on anyone else. Not to use other people to cover us or protect us. We accepted the choices that we made and we were prepared to deal with the consequences.

Cook: We didn't realize that the government was going to do these [social profiles] of anyone we'd ever related to. They pulled 'em into grand jury investigations, etc. It's one of the things George Jackson, in writing, didn't understand. He understood urban guerilla warfare; he tried to understand it and to give an analysis and strategy as to how to go about it. But these are things that *we* learned while we were in action. Something that wasn't written before. Now it's written.

Slowly, today, there are four people, ex-Panthers, in San Francisco, who are being drawn in to a homicide that happened thirty years ago.[3] In most legal cases they call that "latching"; it's so far in the past it can't be tried. But [the government] is going to call in anybody who can be connected; they've got people in New York they're trying to connect.

Brown: The PATRIOT Act allowed them to open up unsolved cases that were of a political nature or otherwise of interest. The SLA [Symbionese Liberation Army] case here a few years ago may have been a test of that.[4]

The Kathy Soliah prosecution predated 9/11/01 but more people were drawn in afterwards.

Brown: These guys that are in jail are not from here now; they're from all over the country. They might have lived here *then* but they don't live here *now*. They're not well, they're elders with health problems.

Cook: Makes me a little nervous. I came down just when all of this is happening! (*laughs*)

Even before 9/11/01 the statute of limitation on murder never expired. That's what makes the Brigade and the SLA and the BLA cases in San Francisco different: the Brigade never killed anyone, but people were killed in the other cases.

Brown: But those two guys who were accused of killing the Asian-American cop in Berkeley in the 1970s had been investigated before and they were let go.[5] I don't care what kind of case it is, you have to have hard evidence. They *knew* they didn't have a case but they jacked those guys anyway. They kept the black guy in jail for two weeks then they arrested the white guy who was his partner and held him for three or four days, then let them both go, *again*. Maybe next year they'll pick 'em up again. Who knows? They have to justify their existence.

How are you affected by the psychological climate in the United States today, where anything that could be construed as an independent force is aggressively denigrated as "terrorism"?

Brown: It makes me a little more paranoid, it makes me a little more careful. It makes me understand my enemy is still my enemy . . . is *your* enemy, is *his* enemy, is *her* enemy . . .

Cook: It's more sophisticated fascism, that's what it amounts to. It existed back then but they're getting slicker than they ever were before. The Religious Right is able to do things that were unacceptable before. It's getting scary—not for me, but for people I feel for.

One of the distinctive things about the Brigade is that you had all had experiences with the criminal justice system, as very committed organizers and often ex-convicts. Can you talk about the experience of prison work in the formation of the Brigade?

Cook: Before the Brigade was formed we were all involved in prison work. That was the impetus; that's where the strongest movement seemed to be coming from. Both prisoners and prison activists. It moved that way: the SLA and the NWLF did the same thing. They had prison activists that involved prisoners and moved toward armed struggle. I don't know what the phenomena is. It's there, it just happened, and we're just a part of that.

Brown: It was a reflection of the times. There were prison rebellions all over this country—more than we'll ever know, I'm sure. People had been filing lawsuits around conditions and having victories. There was *hope* in the prisons that things could be turned over and changed. Prisoners didn't have anything to lose, they were already in prison. They were trying to better their condition and that moved people on the outside.

Cook: One of the most volatile issues that the Panther paper wrote about was prison issues.

Mead: As prisoners we had a more intimate knowledge of the nature—of the brutality, the viciousness—of the state than our outside counterparts who had never been exposed to that reality. We knew who we were dealing with and we knew what kind of language to speak to them in.

Cook: We get out [of prison] and we don't distinguish between cops and prison guards. It took me *years* to understand that cops and prison guards weren't the same. When you first get out you just see them as guards and it's easy for ex-prisoners to get together and deal with them like we're still in prison.

You saw being outside of prison not as being free, but as being in a minimum-security prison?

Brown: It *is* minimum-security to us.

Mead: Our leash is a little longer.

Brown: Because of the Civil Rights Movement, because of the antiwar movement, there were people who went to jail who brought verbalized classical political theory in with them. There were a lot of cases fought in prisons in the late '60s and early '70s about the First Amendment. Being able to read things, getting literature into prison. That's one thing that's been eroding lately: access to the press, access to . . . *The Little Red Book*, to gay publications. All of those became lawsuits in the late '60s. People had access to more knowledge. When you look at that shit you apply it to where you are, you apply it to your reality. What do you see? You see and you feel the oppressor on your neck. You might have called it something else yesterday, but after you read this you have a broader understanding of the enemy. Prisoners know how to *deal* on a different level, 'cause that's what you have to do to survive.'

Cook: It's not always the political who go in as political prisoners and come out as political prisoners. I was changed while I was in prison. I'd seen the Weather Underground stuff, the Panther stuff, coming into prison; I wanted to be a part of it. The Panther Party issued a ten-point program. I said, "This fits me perfectly." It's the same things I wanted to do. It hit a lot of prisoners in that same way. Each prison would have a little group (to propagate the program). A lot of times when people got out they didn't carry it with them. But if you really believe in those principles, then you *become* principled. When you get out, you look for people (who are doing the same thing). These people [indicating Bo and Ed] came to CONvention. I went to [John] Sherman and Ed when I got out because they were dealing with the prisoners' union, an idea I still had in my head.

We got politicized by a lot of the radical stuff that was going on outside. To me, it was the Panthers, SDS, and the Weathermen. That was the main attraction to me; what started me thinking, what started me reading.

Brown: I was reading George Jackson when he got killed. *I* was in prison.

Mead: The same for me. Outside radicals came in, like Chuck Armsbury, a White Panther.[6] I was reading progressive literature and becoming politically conscious. It was the right wing that was saying: "Lock 'em up, throw away the key. *Yay* to the death penalty. Abolish parole." They were the ones who were for the war; it was the left-wingers who were against the war who broke Timothy Leary out of prison, who were demonstrating in support of prisoners, who were against the death penalty, advocating for quicker and more paroles. It didn't take a rocket scientist to figure out which side you were on.

Brown: In prison there are only so many role models you have about how you walk, how you talk and who you are. Being principled, political, honorable, became a new and better way, one which drew on an earlier tradition of "being a solid con."

Cook: At the time the Brigade was starting up other groups were losing credibility. Weatherpeople lost a whole lot of credibility with some things they did.

Mead: Like not responding to the Panther 21.[7]

Cook: In Seattle they refused to give Leonard Peltier [false] ID when he needed it. Other groups lost credibility. The New World Liberation Front [in San Francisco] was doing slingshot attacks which they called "armed struggle." Even though the Brigade got a lot of criticism from the left, they got a lot of credibility from people who were not even involved in that. One former employee of City Light told me that they used to celebrate the Brigade's attack every year. She just loves us, to this day.

In its political statement the Brigade quoted Amílcar Cabral, the Guinea-Bissau independence leader, on the importance of being sensitive to local conditions in developing a guerrilla campaign. How did the Brigade adapt the guerrilla techniques in play in other countries to the United States?

Brown: Our exposé of the banks and their interlocking directorates with the corporate press, and how that impacted their prison coverage.

Cook: Most of the Brigade's activities were based on struggles that were already in process. The prisoners' struggle, demonstrating that they needed some change; the City Light workers on strike, they weren't getting any action [on their demands]; the United Farm Workers, they were having problems. Everywhere the Brigade gave people a boost. That's my understanding of it.

Mead: When the FBI and the U.S. Marshals invaded Pine Ridge and Rosebud there was a mass march from Seattle to Portland to protest the repression that was taking place on the reservations. The Brigade bombed the FBI headquarters in Tacoma and the Bureau of Indian Affairs office in Everett in support of that march and also to draw heat away from Pine Ridge and Rosebud and onto ourselves.

Cook: It was supporting clear, mass movements that were going on. One of my ideas was that I wanted to bomb Little Black Sambo's restaurants. [Other people in the group] wouldn't do it. It was very offensive to us, but there was no movement going on against it. Not the NAACP, not *anything*.

Brown: They did eventually change their name to "No Place Like Sam's" because of protests.

Mead: Just the fact that we could strike and remain uncaught destroyed the fallacy of the invulnerability of the state. Our continued existence was propaganda.

What was the Brigade's strategy with the media? How did you try to use it without being used by it? How did you communicate directly with the people you wished to reach?

Cook: The Northwest is a slow news day for media up there. It was easy for the Brigade to give 'em some news. They snatched it up. Eventually the FBI got them to give it less coverage.

What do you feel you were able to communicate through the media?

Brown: Seattle had a decent alternative press. We had the *Northwest Passage* and *Open Road*, an anarchist paper that came out of Vancouver, B.C. It contained *a lot* of good information. Then we hooked up with a guy at the *Post-Intelligencer* and he became our guy. Eventually he was moved out of town [by the company].[8]

Mead: Ho Chi Minh started the National Liberation Front in Vietnam with nine armed propaganda officers. There's hope that you can build a successful movement with that kind of work.

The revolutionary movements of the 1950s and '60s had a very strong belief and will, that you could make things happen, regardless of odds.

Mead: It's *always* the will, but you can push things forward all you want, and if its not the right moment in history you're just beating your head against the wall. At other times, when the moment is right, when there are mass movements in the streets, you can accomplish a great deal.

Cook: The Vietnam War brought out a lot of different issues. When the war wound down the issues were still there. Some people stopped the movement, but other people said: "Something *has* to be done." That's why there were groups like the Brigade, that were so small, here and there. There was no longer a mass movement, but the issues were still there.

Brown: There were thousands of things happening. We weren't the only ones. We weren't in isolation. We were in the Northwest but there was something happening everywhere.

Mead: As the mass movement was winding down we were trying to pump new life into it. We were trying to substitute violence for the absence of a mass struggle.

Brown: We weren't conscious of that. Maybe that's what was happening everywhere.
As far as media, there were more things published from other places in the world that gave insight into various levels of struggle. The Tupamaros [in Uruguay], things that were going on in Africa . . . We had access to more things to make you think.

Cook: The Native movements were really strong.

Mead: We didn't play to the media.

Cook: Right, we didn't do it just because they had a slow day, but it was easier to get in because there was a slow day.

You're a hot story for a few minutes then you're old news. You can't build through the press.

Brown: Because the Brigade was different—who was involved, the class issues, the diversity of it, that it had more women—you didn't have to deal with the ego question to the same extent. That white male gigantic ego: "Oh my god, I get to be the superhero today!" We analyze things a whole lot differently and people in the collective were not afraid to say: "No, we're not gonna do that. That's wrong."

Cook: We were more grassroots than Weatherman. They came out of SDS: they were *all* intellectuals. The government created them by whuppin' on 'em, by letting them know that they can get beat up too.

Most people in SDS would say that those who became Weathermen were very definitely not intellectuals, that their inability to think critically caused them to divide thought and action and become all action, no thought, at least up until the townhouse disaster forced a reconsideration.
Because so many of the Brigade's activities were violent and destructive it can be difficult for people to discern what the group was for. What are your ideals, what is your utopian vision.

Cook: I'm a communist, a Maoist, based on the principles of the Party. It's utopian, it's not going to happen, but it gives direction.

Mead: We were probably all fighting for a different vision. The vision I had is a communist society, a stateless society, in which classes no longer existed. There was an administrative mechanism for the distribution of goods and services, but no government as such. No apparatus of repression and things were done for people's needs, not for private profit. In the society I envisioned the distinction between art, work and play was eliminated. It was a communist utopia. (*chuckles*)

Brown: We were all prison abolitionists, though we didn't call ourselves that. That doesn't mean you open the door and let everybody out. This society has created a lot of sickness.

I don't know if I ever thought about utopia. What would I like to be? I'd like to not have to go to work today and I'd like to be able to eat. I'd like to be in a world in which we don't have rape, we don't have child abuse, we don't have hunger, we don't have oppression or genocide, or discrimination based on color or whatever. These are basic grassroots issues.

Every time I walked down the streets of Seattle and people realized I was a dyke, I was getting knocked down, I was getting tripped. There was that kind of oppression in my life that was daily.

I think we're making a stew that's going to feed the world and change the world and we're putting a whole lot of different ingredients into it based on all these movements and all these needs.

Mead: In terms of the transition, Men Against Sexism dealt with gay oppression on the inside, rapists on the inside, we dealt with the rapists themselves. *Everybody*—irrespective of the bourgeois Constitution—has a right to life, liberty and the pursuit of happiness. During this transition period there are people or groups of people who won't have access to liberty because the existing culture has so fouled them. But they will have the right to the pursuit of happiness.

Cook: Their needs will be met.

Mead: It won't be anything like prisons today. The interaction between communities and incarcerated people would be richer. On a political level rapists, for example, at the very least, would be able to thoroughly verbalize, if not internalize, women's issues and understand the harm on a gut level before they would go to the next step [of supervision]. They would not be locked up in a 6' by 8' cage with a stranger.

Brown: It's about *healing*. Take drug addicts: There's a process you have to go through to [purge the poison]. Or abuse: people who are abused become the abuser. It's a cycle that takes years to break. You can't eliminate it by saying: "It's over." It's a process. This government that we endure is an abuser. It doesn't get better in a minute or a day or a week.

Cook: Our communist future could move along. After that we wouldn't need prisons, you'd stop sending people to prison. If they can't find a job, the community is going to give 'em a job. It's gonna be a livable job. Giving everyone a job at a livable wage is not a difficult thing to do. Capitalism makes billions of dollars in profits. Instead we've got to force them. What I wanted to do when I was a Panther—what the Panthers tried to do—is to respect ourselves and know that we cannot be pushed around. Just because you're lower class doesn't mean the government or the people running big business can push you around. "You fire me, I'll blow up your transformers!" (*laughs*) "I do good work. I may criticize you, but don't you fire me." That's what unions are about. The weaker unions get, the stronger capitalism becomes. The only real voice we have is labor. Labor should look out for people who do *not* have jobs, and they're not doing that.

There have been movements in the United States in the last twenty years which have tried to strike a balance between above ground and underground work, primarily animal rights and environmental activists. What's your take on these groups?

Cook: I don't think they're clear enough. People see the fires and they don't see the message. They've got to do it another way.

Mead: Anything anybody does to develop the underground is a good thing. Earth First! and the Earth Liberation Front are essential elements of our movement.

Cook: They are necessary.

Brown: Anything that people do to explore the necessity of the aboveground-underground [divide] is of value. I understand, in theory, about animal liberation and *definitely* about environmentalism. I grew up in Oregon, which is a conservationist state.

What's your perspective on the impact of the Brigade.

Cook: I got to do the same thing with the Panthers. It politicized a lot of people. The Brigade did the same thing: The government isn't strong as they think they are. They can't push us around. The Panthers said, "When something needs to be done, do it." When someone needs to be fed, go to your refrigerator or beg food but feed kids. You need a free clinic? We can do it. The Brigade, or other people in the underground, can come up with money to support things like that. The lower class can get itself out of this hole which capitalism has dug us into. What we did wasn't in vain. We didn't want to go to prison, but when we *did* go, we knew that what we'd done was important. We remained principled from then 'til now.

It was a process of trial and error. We learned the hard way. The Panthers tried to politicize street gangs. We couldn't cure 'em: They knew the drug scene and everyone liked to have fun. You couldn't wash that out of them while we were trying to get Panther work done.

The Brigade misjudged the momentum. Not only the Brigade, but all of us in all groups did. We looked too much to the Vietnamese Revolution, to the Chinese Revolution, to the Cuban Revolution. There was momentum: build, build, and build. It started that way. We saw that, but we misjudged [the way in which] capitalism in the United States is different than anywhere else in the world. They keep their eye on the people, and when the people rise up they'll do everything they can to keep us down.

Mead: We thought that the forces of progress were on our side, that we were in tune with the march of history. We knew that right was on our side. We didn't see Ronald Reagan right around the corner.

Brown: One of the most important things we did was to bring the prison struggle closer to the forefront of regular people's minds by talking about what was going on in Walla Walla. What was happening in Walla Walla was so extreme and so intense. We exposed that. That consciousness remains, to some extent in the Northwest: that was *the bomb.*

Mead: The struggle around Walla Walla was the pinnacle of the Brigade. I can't think of a better application of the complimentary work between the armed front and the mass front. That was outstanding.

Brown: Tactically, we shouldn't have moved so fast in some areas and been quite so braggadocious. It's important to claim your victories, but perhaps we should have stayed further under longer.

We didn't know they had doubled their FBI force. What was that in the Northwest, four instead of two? We didn't know that they had quadrupled it. We didn't know that they had a special GJB shoot-'em-up team. We listened to the police all the time, but we didn't have the FBI's frequencies, and we were never going to get them. If we had that information, we would have weighed it into our defenses.

Mead: A brigade has an intelligence unit, a supply unit and a combat unit. All we had was a combat unit.

Brown: We were trying to be all free. We maintained communication with people above ground, through our communiqués and their criticisms, but it wasn't enough.

Mead: The tide of history had turned. A lot of groups which were doing armed actions just folded up their tents and stopped. That's probably what the Brigade should have done.

Brown: We were trying to move in that direction, but we never got far enough down the road. It was too hot, and we were trying to do another bigger thing. It was time for another time out.

Cook: There are people in Seattle who criticize the Brigade, but there are also people who want the image of the Brigade. I don't know if you know how many guys in jail actually claimed they were Brigade members and the police thought they were.

Mead: People would come up to me in prison and say: "You were in the Brigade, then you must know so and so, he was a member of the Brigade"!

Brown: I know there was a lot of fear in the women's community when we split town.

Cook: People were very supportive of the Brigade. They helped case a joint or do a drive away. It was a very strange but impressive movement. I'd support anything that came up and started again. I don't have that much, but I'd give that much to support 'em again.

Notes

Preface

1   For discussion, see Ward Churchill with Mike Ryan, *Pacifism as Pathology: Reflections on the Role of Armed Struggle in North America*, 2nd ed. (Oakland: AK Press, 2007); Peter Gelderloos, *How Nonviolence Protects the State* (Cambridge, MA: South End Press, 2007).

2   Excellent overviews and analyses of the Panthers will be found in Charles E. Jones, ed., *The Black Panther Party [Reconsidered]* (Baltimore: Black Classic Press, 1998); Kathleen Cleaver and George Katsiaficas, eds., *Liberation, Imagination, and the Black Panther Party* (New York: Routledge, 2001). On the WUO, see Jeremy Varon, *Bringing the War Home: The Weather Underground, the Red Army Faction, and Revolutionary Violence in the Sixties and Seventies* (Berkeley: University of California Press, 2004); Dan Berger, *Outlaws of America: The Weather Underground and the Politics of Solidarity* (Oakland: AK Press, 2006). Unfortunately, the only good collection of Panther documents remains G. Louis Heath's now very rare *Off the Pigs! The Literature and History of the Black Panther Party* (Metuchen, NJ: Scarecrow Press, 1976). For Weather documents, see Bernardine Dohrn, Bill Ayers, and Jeff Jones, eds., *Sing a Battle Song: The Revolutionary Poetry, Statements, and Communiqués of the Weather Underground, 1970–1974* (New York: Seven Stories Press, 2006).

3   These data do not include the hundred of incendiary bombings carried out during the period's many ghetto rebellions. Nor do they reflect bombings perpetrated by the Ku Klux Klan, Secret Army Organization (SAO), and other such white supremacist groups of the extreme Right.

4   Berger, *Outlaws of America*, 116–17; Varon, *Bringing the War Home*, 117–18.

5   Berger, *Outlaws of America*, 245. Although the group is discussed to varying extents in studies of other organizations, no comprehensive overview or analysis of the FALN has been published. A useful collection of communiqués during the period 1974–1978 was released under the title *Toward People's War for Independence and Socialism in Puerto Rico: In Defense of Armed Struggle* by the Movimiento de Liberación Nacional, Chicago, circa 1979, but it is now even more rare than *Off the Pigs!*.

6   Again, although it is mentioned—and usually disparaged—in studies of other organizations, nothing resembling a thorough overview/analysis of the SLA has been published. The best material presently available will be found in a pair of more or less contemporaneous books, both of which should be approached with obvious caution. See John Bryan, *This Soldier Still at War* (New York: Harcourt Brace Jovanovich, 1975); Vin McLellan and Paul Avery, *The Voices of Guns: The Definitive and Dramatic Story of the Twenty-Two-Month Career of the Symbionese Liberation Army, One of the Most Bizarre Chapters in the History of the American Left* (New York: G.P. Putnam's Sons, 1977).

7   On Tongyai, see Robert Justin Goldstein, *Political Repression in Modern America: From 1870 to 1976*, 2nd ed. (Urbana: University of Illinois Press, 2001), 474–75. On Perry, see Ward Churchill, "'To Disrupt, Discredit and Destroy': The FBI's Secret War Against the Black Panther Party," in Cleaver and Katsiaficas, *Liberation, Imagination, and the Black Panther Party*, 93–95.

8   There is little material on either the RNA or RAM, per se. Although I usually refrain from referring readers to memoirs, in this instance I recommend RNA leader Imari Abubukari Obadele's *Free the Land!* (Washington, D.C.: House of Songhay, 1984); and RAM leader Muhammad Ahmad's *We Will Return in the Whirlwind: Black Radical Organizations, 1960–1975* (Chicago: Charles Kerr, 2007) as the best available sources. Plainly, much additional work needs to be done on both organizations.

9   See generally, Timothy B. Tyson, *Radio Free Dixie: Robert F. Williams and the Roots of Black Power* (Chapel Hill: University of North Carolina Press, 1999).

10   See, generally, Lance Hill, *The Deacons for Defense: Armed Resistance and the Civil Rights Movement* (Chapel Hill: University of North Carolina Press, 2004).

11   See, generally, Hassan Kwame Jeffries, *Bloody Lowndes: Civil Rights in Alabama's Black Belt* (New York: New York University Press, 2009). See also Stokely Carmichael with Ekwueme Michael Thelwell, *Ready for the Revolution: The Life and Struggles of Stokely Carmichael {Kwame Ture}*, (New York: Scribner, 2003), 457–83.

12   Unlike most of the organizations mentioned herein, the very nature of the actions the BLA was designed to undertake precludes anything along the lines of full disclosure of its personnel and/or operational history. For an excellent disquisition on those aspects of the organization which *are* open to discussion, see Akinyele Omowale Umoja, "Repression Breeds Resistance: The Black Liberation Army and the Radical Legacy of the Black Panther Party," in Cleaver and Katsiaficas, *Liberation, Imagination, and the Black Panther Party*, 3–19. A smattering of analyses and reflections by self-identified members of the BLA have also been published. Apart from the relevant portions of Assata Shakur's 1987 autobiography, see, as examples, Dhoruba Bin Wahad, "War Within: Prison Interview" and "Toward Rethinking Self-Defense in a Racist Culture: Black Survival in a United States in Transition," both in Jim Fletcher, Tanaquil Jones, and Sylvère Lotringer, eds., *Still Black, Still Strong: Survivors of the War Against Back Revolutionaries* (Brooklyn: Semiotext(e), 1993), 59–77; Kuwasi Balagoon, *A Soldier's Story: Writings by a Revolutionary New African Anarchist* (Montréal: Solidarity, 2001); Jalil Muntaquin, *We Are Our Own Liberators: Selected Prison Writings* (Montréal/Toronto/Paterson, NJ: Abraham Guillen Press/Arm the Spirit/Anarchist Black Cross Federation, 2002); Nuh Washington, *All Power to the People* (Toronto/Montréal: Arm the Spirit/Solidarity, 2002); Russell "Maroon" Shoats, "Black Fighting

Formations: Their Strengths, Weaknesses, and Potentialities," in Cleaver and Katsiaficas, *Liberation, Imagination, and the Black Panther Party*, 128–38. See also Safiya Bukhari, *The War Before: The True Life Story of Becoming a Black Panther, Keeping the Faith in Prison, and Fighting for Those Left Behind* (New York: Feminist Press, 2010).

13 Aside from occasional mentions in texts devoted to other organizations/topics, the only material available on the group is Ronald Fernandez's *Los Macheteros: The Wells Fargo Robbery and the Violent Struggle for Puerto Rican Independence* (New York: Prentice Hall, 1987).

14 See Jane Alpert, "A Profile of Sam Melville," and John Cohen, "Introduction," in Samuel Melville, *Letters from Attica* (New York: William Morrow, 1972), 3–43, 47–80.

15 Alpert's repulsively self-serving memoir was published under the title *Growing Up Underground* (New York: William Morrow, 1982).

16 The group carried out a series of bombings in and around Madison, Wisconsin, most spectacularly that of a military research center on August 23, 1970. While there is a substantial book on the "New Year's Gang," its actions, and the outcomes, wherein much useful information is contained, readers are advised that its author offers often superficial—i.e., liberal—political analyses and frequently indulges in pop psychology as an "explanatory" mechanism. See Tom Bates, *Rads: The 1970 Bombing of the Army Math Research Center at the University of Wisconsin and Its Aftermath* (New York: HarperCollins, 1992).

17 Originating in Maine, the Melville/Jackson Unit, reorganized as the UFF in 1982, was formed in 1974. Functioning throughout its existence on a clandestine mixed-race basis, the collective is credited with several bank expropriations and at least nineteen bombings of such targets as the U.S. Capitol Building, the South African consulate, and various corporate facilities. See Ward Churchill and Jim Vander Wall, *The COINTELPRO Papers: Documents from the FBI's Secret War against Dissent in the United States*, Classics ed. (Cambridge, MA: South End Press, 2003), 315–19. Also see the portion of UFF member Ray Luc Levasseur's presentencing statement excerpted under the title "On Trial" in Joy James, ed., *Imprisoned Intellectuals: America's Political Prisoners Write on Life, Liberation, and Rebellion* (Lanham, MD: Rowman & Littlefield, 2003), 231–47.

18 The RATF is often—and, in my view, somewhat erroneously—depicted as being simply an element of the BLA. While the group drew personnel from the ranks of BLA veterans, some were from other black liberation organizations (notably the RNA). Additionally, several whites—mostly former members of the Weather Underground—were active participants. The RATF was thus discernibly different from any of the organizations from which it emerged. See Churchill and Vander Wall, *COINTELPRO Papers*, 309–12; Akinyele Omowale Umoja, "Set Our Warriors Free: The Legacy of the Black Panther Party and Political Prisoners," in Jones, *Black Panther Party*

[Reconsidered], 429–31. For participant analyses, see Balagoon, *A Soldier's Story*; Marilyn Buck, David Gilbert, and Laura Whitehorn, *Enemies of the State: A Frank Discussion of Past Political Movements, Their Victories and Errors, and the Current Climate for Revolutionary Struggle in the USA* (Montréal/Toronto: Abraham Guillen Press/Arm the Spirit, 2002).

19 On the Armed Resistance Unit/Red Guerrilla Resistance, see Churchill and Vander Wall, *COINTELPRO Papers*, 312–15. It should be noted that the ARU/RGR is often conflated with the May 19th Communist Organization, from which it arose and of which it *may* have been a component. The hundred-member May 19th organization was *not* a clandestine entity, however. That most of the dozen or so participants in the ARU/RGR were—or had been—members of May 19th does not render the two entities interchangeable.

20 The best material I've been able to locate on the organization is a 1977 summary of its actions up to that point is Celine Hagbard, "NWLF: good hit, no pitch," *Open Road* (Vancouver, BC), no.3, Summer 1977, 8, available at http://radicalarchives.org/2010/02/06/nwlf-1977.

21 Actually, a bit *is* known about the Melville/Jackson Unit (see note 17). Much remains cloudy about its composition and relations/interactions with similar entities, including the NWLF. On March 12, 1975, for example, one of the unit's founders, Ray Luc Levasseur, together with Cameron David Bishop, was arrested on weapons and conspiracy charges. Bishop, a former SDS member at Colorado State University, was at the time one of the FBI's "Most Wanted" fugitives, credited with the January 1969 bombings of several towers in the Denver area power grid, but is unlinked to a particular clandestine group. After his arrest, Bishop was prosecuted for sabotage and sentenced to 20 years, but the case was dismissed on appeal. See Kirkpatrick Sale, *SDS* (New York: Random House, 1973), 513; Churchill and Vander Wall, *COINTELPRO Papers*, p. 416n70; *U.S. v. Cameron David Bishop* (555 F.2d 771 (10th Cir., May 5, 1977)).

22 Yippie! (or Youth International Party) is mentioned in virtually every history of the period, as well as many of studies focusing on particular organizations or events. Virtually nothing of a serious nature has been done to describe/analyze the nature/actions of this most renowned "anti-organization" of the late 1960s/early 1970s, however. Beyond the early screeds of Abbie Hoffman, Jerry Rubin, and a couple of others among the original participants—as well as several autobiographies/biographies of Hoffman—there is mostly a vacuum. As concerns the Motherfuckers, the *only* thing available is Osha Neumann's recent *Up Against the Wall Motherf**ker: A Memoir of the '60s, With Notes for the Next Time* (New York: Seven Stories, 2008).

23 The Young Lords, a Puerto Rican street gang in the Lincoln Park area of Chicago, was transformed into a political organization along the lines of the Black Panther Party by its leader, José "Cha Cha" Jimenez. The YLO, along with the Rising Up Angry collective (an SDS splinter group) and the Young

Patriots (a politicized gang of displaced Appalachian whites on the near North Side), then functioned within the original Rainbow Coalition engineered by Chicago Panther leader Fred Hampton in early 1969 (yes, it was later ripped off and neutered by Jesse Jackson). Rather astonishingly, the entire context remains virgin territory, neither chronicled nor documented. It should be noted that there *is* a recent book about New York's Young Lords *Party*, which was organized after, and on the basis of, the YLO. See Miguel "Mickey" Melendez, *We Took the Streets: Fighting for Latino Rights with the Young Lords* (New York: St. Martin's Press, 2003).

24 White Panther founder John Sinclair's *Guitar Army: Street Writings/ Prison Writings* (Detroit: Rainbow Books, 1972) retains a certain utility in explaining the group's perspective, as does accused Ann Arbor CIA office-bomber Pun Plamondon's recent memoir, *Lost from the Ottawa: The History of the Journey Back* (Cloverdale, MI: Plamondon, Inc., 2004). Neither book discusses the spread of White Panther collectives throughout the Midwest in 1969–1970, however. Less still do they discuss/analyze the effectiveness of the group's various armed actions, its mode(s) of organization, communication, and the like.

25 Mostly mentioned in connection with a disastrous 1972 action in which it freed a prisoner being transported to court from the California penal facility at Chico and/or the fact that most of the SLA's cadre strength split off from it, the Venceremos Organization clearly had a broader—and virtually unknown—operational existence. On the 1972 action, see Eric Cummins, *The Rise and Fall of California's Radical Prison Movement* (Stanford: Stanford University Press, 1994). The broader scope is alluded to in Jo Durden-Smith, *Who Killed George Jackson? Fantasies, Paranoia and the Revolution* (New York: Alfred A. Knopf, 1976), 109–10, 110n.3, 159–61, and *passim*. For an original framing of the organization's purpose, by one of its founders, see Bruce Franklin, *From the Movement Toward Revolution* (New York: Van Nostrand Reinhold, 1971), 128–29, 141–43.

26 Jackson, who was serving an "indeterminate"—one-year-to-life— sentence for an armed robbery committed in 1960, when he was still a teenager, became politicized in prison. In 1966, he was instrumental in forming the Black Guerrilla Family (BGF), a "Marxist/Maoist/Leninist revolutionary organization with the stated goals to eradicate racism . . . maintain dignity in prison, and overthrow the U.S. government." In June 1970 he was accused, along with two other BGF members, Fleeta Drumgo and John Cluchette, of killing a Soledad prison guard in retaliation for the murder of three black prisoners in January the same year. The "Soledad Brothers" case quickly became a *cause célèbre* on the left, in part because Jackson, already serving a life term, faced the death penalty, partly because of his gifts as a writer, and partly because of his highly-developed political consciousness. This combination of factors led to his appointment as a Panther field marshal, the station from which

he began to organize the People's Army, employing select BGF members to fill key positions as they were released from prison. Although Jackson himself was assassinated in San Quentin on August 21, 1971, the BGF still exists. See, generally, George Jackson, *Soledad Brother: The Prison Letters of George Jackson*, 2nd ed. (Chicago: Lawrence Hill Books, 1994); Gregory Armstrong, *The Dragon Has Come* (New York: Harper & Row, 1974); Paul Libertore, *The Road to Hell: The True Story of George Jackson, Stephen Bingham, and the San Quentin Massacre* (New York: Atlantic Monthly Press, 1996), esp. 19, 93–94, 199, 264.

27 As with the BLA, the nature of the operations for which the People's Army was designed precludes anything approaching full disclosure and discussion. Still, there are undoubtedly aspects of its organizational existence which might be revealed without compromising the safety of former members and from which lessons might be usefully drawn by a new generation. As things stand, while Jackson's conception of applying the *foco* method of guerrilla warfare to the U.S. context is set forth in his posthumously published *Blood in My Eye* (New York: Random House, 1972), the only reasonably coherent sketch of its implementation will be found in Durden-Smith, *Who Killed George Jackson?*, 102–03, 158–61, 243.

28 Daniel Burton-Rose, *Guerrilla USA: The George Jackson Brigade and the Anticapitalist Underground of the 1970s* (Berkeley: University of California Press, 2010).

29 "Philosophers have only *interpreted* the world in various ways; the point is to *change* it." Karl Marx, "Theses on Feuerbach (11)," in *Karl Marx and Frederick Engels: Collected Works, Vol. 5; Marx and Engels, 1845–47* (New York: International, 1976), 5.

30 Jackson, *Blood in My Eye*, 54.

Introduction

1 George Jackson, *Soledad Brother* (New York: Bantam, 1970), 164.

2 Jackson, *Soledad Brother*, 238.

3 The background information on the George Jackson Brigade in this introduction is a cursory overview of material covered in detail in my *Guerrilla USA: The George Jackson Brigade and the Anticapitalist Underground of the 1970s* (Berkeley: University of California Press, 2010). That work is the result of more than ten years of interviews with former members and their acquaintances, as well as immersion in primary sources of the sort gathered in this collection.

4 The most extensive source on Mead is his unpublished "Autobiography." The copy in the author's collection is dated January 2009.

5 For an overview of the rhetoric and practice of antiestablishment violence on the radical Left in the fifteen years preceding the advent of the George Jackson Brigade, see Burton-Rose, *Guerrilla USA*, 1–38.

6   The standard reference on the first wave of domestic bombings is Scanlan's *Suppressed Issue*, 1971. On the short-lived *Scanlan's* see the brief account in cocditor Warren Hinckle's autobiography, *If You Have a Lemon, Make Lemonade* (New York: Putnam, 1990 [first published 1974]), 362–63. The source material for the publication—accounts from various urban newspapers around the country—is badly in need of revisiting and extending beyond the cut off date of *Scanlan's* own publication.

Although couched in a defeatist narrative, Eric Cummins, *The Rise and Fall of California's Radical Prison Movement* (Palo Alto: Stanford University Press, 1994) remains the best source on the late 1960s and early 1970s prison movement.

7   This group, responsible for the kidnapping of Patricia Hearst and her subsequent superficial conversion to gun-totting, Stockholm Syndrome-suffering revolutionary, was greeted by a hail of books directly after its first emergence, but absolutely no substantive reappraisal in the thirty-five plus years since its first emergence. The one ostensible exception, William Graebner, *Patty's Got a Gun: Patricia Hearst in 1970s America* (Chicago: University of Chicago Press, 2008) is remarkable for the extent to which it presents no new information. Robert Pearsall, ed., *The Symbionese Liberation Army: Documents and Communications* (Amsterdam: Rodopi, 1974) collects useful primary documents, but was published before the organization petered out, so is not comprehensive. Kenneth Reeves and Paul Avery, eds., *The Trial of Patty Hearst* (San Francisco: Great Fidelity Press, 1976) assembles trial transcripts in the Hearst case; the transcripts of other SLA members, particularly Joe Remiro and Russ Little, the first to be arrested, would also make for interesting reading. Although sensationalist true crime narratives, Leslie Payne and Timothy Findley, with Carolyn Craven, *The Life and Death of the SLA* (New York: Ballantine Books, 1976) and Vin McLellan and Paul Avery, *The Voices of Guns: The Definitive and Dramatic Story of the Twenty-Two-Month Career of the Symbionese Liberation Army* (New York: Putnam, 1977) contain much intriguing—if ultimately unreliable—information.

Hearst is the only former member to do an autobiography, though she was not capable of writing it herself: Patricia Hearst and Alvin Moscow, *Every Secret Thing* (Garden City, NY: Doubleday, 1982). A handful of other former members received biographies, some post-mortem: John Bryan, *This Soldier Still at War* (New York: Harcourt, Brace, Jovanovich, 1975) on Joe Ramirez; Jean Brown Kinney, *An American Journey: The Short Life of Willy Wolfe* (New York: Simon and Schuster, 1979) (Willy Wolfe); Fred Soltysik, *In Search of a Sister* (New York: Bantam Books, 1976) (Patricia Soltysik); and Sharon Darby Hendry, *Soliah: The Sara Jane Olson Story* (Bloomington, MN: Cable Publishing, 2002) (Kathy Soliah). Even Hearst's cuckolded ex-fiancé, an opportunist journalist who broke elements of the story of Hearst's kidnapping, and the Federal Marshall who guarded her got their two cents in: Steven Weed with Scott

Swanton, *My Search for Patty Hearst* (New York: Crown Publishers, 1976); Marilyn Baker, *Exclusive! The Inside Story of Patricia Hearst and the SLA* (New York: Macmillan, 1974); and Janey Jimenez, *My Prisoner* (Kansas City: Sheed Andrews and McMeel, 1977). This later is interesting in regards to the gender and racial integration of the law enforcement apparatus in the early 1970s, itself the ambivalent fruit of the preceding decades' social movements.

This list does not exhaust the books on the subject, but does contain the ones I consider to be worth reading.

8   Despite their remarkable productivity and endurance there is no detailed secondary literature on this organization. Ideally they would be the subject of a documentary history volume along the lines of the present volume and that of J. Smith and André Moncourt, eds., *The Red Army Faction: A Documentary History. Volume 1, Projectiles for the People* (Oakland: PM Press, 2009). Yet to a certain degree the advent of these volumes and other recent works of "guerrillaology" such as Jeremy Varon, *Bringing the War Home: The Weather Underground, the Red Army Faction, and Revolutionary Violence in the Sixties and Seventies* (Berkeley: University of California Press, 2004), and Dan Berger, *Outlaws of America: The Weather Underground and the Politics of Solidarity* (Oakland: AK Press, 2006), were contingent on contact with veterans of the organizations under scrutiny. In the case of the NWLF, whose members were never caught, this is not possible.

The NWLF's communiqués fill the pages of *Dragon*, a Berkeley clearing-house for missives from the underground commencing in 1975 and tapering off a few years later, and *TUG* (*The Urban Guerrilla*), which the NWLF produced with their own underground printing press. *Dragon* is archived in the University of Michigan's Underground Press microfilm collection; copies of both publications are held by the Freedom Archives in San Francisco (http://www.freedomarchives.org).

9   See Burton-Rose, *Guerrilla USA*, 46–65.

10   "Capitol Hill Safeway, September 18, 1975" in Part II.

11   For this first Safeway bombing and reactions to it, see Burton-Rose, *Guerrilla USA*, 141–44.

12   Ford's girlfriend Brenda Carter produced a memorial collection of his writings and drawings entitled "none of us is greater than all of us." It is not publicly available.

13   "New Year, 1976," in Part II.

14   The Weather Underground's "New Morning" communiqué, criticizing itself for the "military error," was explicitly not tied to "a bombing for a specific action." (Bernardine Dohrn, Bill Ayers, and Jeff Jones, eds., *Sing a Battle Song: The Revolutionary Poetry, Statements, and Communiqués of the Weather Underground, 1970–1974* [New York: Seven Stories Press, 2006], 162). It was, of course, prompted by the inadvertent detonation of an explosive device in the home of their Manhattan collective, killing three members: Ted Gold,

Terry Robbins, and Diana Oughton. Had the antipersonnel device reached its intended destination, a dance of noncommissioned officers and their dates at nearby Ft. Dix, the results might well have been even more catastrophic. Varon elaborates what the possible outcomes could have been:

> The bombing might have inspired some small number of Weathermen and others to commit similar acts. The government, which often disregarded civil liberties in pursuing dissidents, and two months later at Kent State would again break the taboo against killing white demonstrators, might have abandoned all restraint in its efforts to destroy Weatherman. Mass arrests or even murders of suspects might have been followed, in turn, by movement reprisals, conceivably kidnappings or assassinations. In short, had Fort Dix been attacked, it is possible that Americans would now speak of the 1970s as a "decade of terrorism," as do people in countries like Germany and Italy, where "Red Armies" clashed with their governments in grim cycles of lethal violence. By the same token, those responsible for the murderous plan might have been denounced and marginalized by other Weathermen, effectively stopping the escalation of the group's violence (*Bringing the War Home*, 174–75).

15 For a grim survey, see Mike Davis, *Buda's Wagon: A Brief History of the Car Bomb* (London: Verso, 2007).

16 John Brockhaus and Roxanne Park, "Ed Mead Speaks from Prison," in Part IV.

17 "New Year, 1976," in Part II.

18 In particular see Part IV: Roxanne Park, "Terrorism and the George Jackson Brigade," and the indignant stream of retorts it elicited.

19 As far as I have been able to determine, no copies of this publication survive.

20 See Smith and Moncourt, *The Red Army Faction*, 510–20.

21 "Our Losses are Heavy . . ." in Part II.

22 "We're Not All White and We're Not All Men," in Part II.

23 For al-Qaeda's self-presentation, see Robert O. Marlin IV, ed., *What Does al-Qaeda Want? Unedited Communiques* (Berkeley: North Atlantic Books, 2004) and Bruce Lawrence, *Messages to the World: The Statements of Osama bin Laden* (New York: Verso, 2005).

24 Again, the *Scanlan's* "Suppressed Issue."

25 On these later groups, see, for example, *Build a Revolutionary Resistance Movement! Communiqués from the North American Armed Clandestine Movement, 1982–1985* (New York: Committee to Fight Repression, no date [mid-1980s]).

26 George Jackson, *Blood In My Eye* (New York: Bantam, 1972), 67.

27 Smith and Moncourt, eds., *The Red Army Faction*, 96.

28 *Orca* no.2, Winter 1977–1978, is housed at www.gjbip.org.

Part I

1   Explicitly vanguardist organizations flourished in the late 1960s and early 1970s. Of those which chose armed struggle, Weatherman and Madison, Wisconsin's "Vanguard of the Revolution"—more commonly known as the "New Year's Gang," an appellation it did not choose for itself—were large blotches on the FBI's radar screen five years before the Brigade even began. Indeed, the FBI was so hot to get the "Vanguard of the Revolution" that it expanded its "Ten Most Wanted" list to fourteen to accommodate the suspects. See Tom Bates, *Rads: The 1970 Bombing of the Army Math Research Center at the University of Wisconsin and its Aftermath* (New York: HarperCollins Publishers, 1992).

A whole range of vanguardist sects which did not choose armed action existed as well; for an account of their rising and declining fortunes see Max Elbaum, *Revolution in the Air: Sixties Radicals Turn to Lenin, Mao and Che* (New York: Verso, 2002). Brigade member John Sherman had belonged to one of these groups, the Revolutionary Union, but left as it became the Revolutionary Communist Party. Sherman's dissatisfaction stemmed in part, from the disavowal of the organization's leadership of immediate armed struggle.

2   Federal Bureau of Investigation, "George Jackson Brigade," http://foia.fbi.gov/foiaindex/georgejacksonbrigade.htm.

3   A disclosure made public in Phil Campbell, "Day of the Panther," *The Stranger*, October 14, 1999, 11.

4   For my own comprehensive summary, which differs from each of these, see the table and accompanying maps in *Guerrilla USA*, xv–xviii.

5   This was clearly not a Brigade action and no press account ever implied that it was. The SPDID seems to have been inclined towards attributing unsolved bombings to the Brigade; at this late date in the underground organization's trajectory, there was little justification for doing so, beyond the institutional imperative to clear the books.

6   This, too, was clearly not a Brigade action; the Brigade Safeway bombing on the 18th was in response to it.

7   This was not a Brigade action.

8   The arrest of Rita Brown and subsequent raid on the deserted Brigade safehouse at 13746 Roosevelt Way North.

9   Censored in original.

10   Censored in original.

11   The person the author was referring to was Janine Bertram.

12   I was not able to ascertain who these support people were, but I speculate that there was some overlap between them and those who composed the "Our Losses Are Heavy . . ." statement reproduced on page 140.

13   The report is confused here: Ford died on September 15; the Brigade responded on September 18.

14   This bombing attempt, also listed in the Seattle Police Department

Intelligence Division Report (See Part I), was not committed by the Brigade.

15 The *Seattle Times* ran a similar profile. Authored by Lee Moriwaki and John Arthur Wilson, "The Psychological Anatomy of a Revolutionary," published April 1, 1976, is also based on interviews with Mead and covers similar ground. I have selected the *Post-Intelligencer* piece due to its detail.

16 Mark Cook was convicted of this shooting.

17 On New Year's Eve, 1976, the Brigade bombed a transformer belonging to City Light, Seattle's public utility. The action was in support of striking City Light workers. It caused a power outage throughout the affluent Laurelhurst neighborhood. See Burton-Rose, *Guerrilla USA*, 157–64.

18 The Washington State Reformatory in Monroe.

19 The cases were severed later in April at Cook's request. See John Arthur Wilson, "New Trial Date Set For Suspect in Tukwila Bank Robbery," *Seattle Times*, April 29, 1976.

20 This insertion is Seidel's emendation of Jackson's gender-biased language.

21 This organization was by no means racially exclusive, although, as with the Washington State prison population, it was predominantly white.

22 "Bill" and "Rachel" were John Sherman and Therese Coupez. See Burton-Rose, *Guerrilla USA*, 229.

23 St. James founded the original COYOTE chapter in San Francisco in 1973. She remains active in prostitutes' rights work.

24 Florynce Kennedy (1916–2000) was a lifetime civil rights and feminist activist in legal, legislative, and cultural battlefields. The mid-1970s were perhaps the height of her acclaim and notoriety. Her autobiography, *Color Me Flo: My Hard Life and Good Times* (Englewood Cliffs, NJ: Prentice-Hall, 1976), was published shortly before this letter.

25 One of the jurors was a Safeway employee. Cook wrote, in his post-trial letter, "It is very hard to conceive that he was or is unaware of Safeway stores having been bombed four times, allegedly by the George Jackson Brigade. And that he could objectively have rendered a verdict of exclusive of critical emotions when Meyerson flaunted the name of the Brigade before the jury in his closing arguments. That misconduct carried too much potential of inflaming that one juror whose subsequent personal deliberations may have tainted the whole jury." (footnote in original article.)

26 The periods of her life described here are covered in Burton-Rose, *Guerrilla USA*, 89–126.

Part II

1 Dick Clever, "'Brigade' Takes Credit for Blast at State Office," *Post-Intelligencer*, June 2, 1975, 1; back page.

2 The SS Mayaguez was seized by the Khmer Rouge May 12, 1975. The United States reclaimed it three days later.

3   The SLA took issue with Foster's proposal to implement identification cards for students and integrate school security with that of the police.
See their "Communique #1" in Pearsall ed., *The Symbionese Liberation Army*,
34–39, and in Payne and Findley, *The Life and Death of the SLA*, 339–44.

4   The Resident Government Council was the prisoner self-governing
body at the Washington State Penitentiary.

5   Ralph "Po" Ford, a member of the Left Bank Collective and a United
Farm Workers supporter, was killed on September 15, 1975, when a bomb
he was planting behind the Safeway at 14th and East John exploded in his
hands.

6   Bill and Emily Harris, Patricia Hearst—all three survivors of the
May 17, 1974, "Compton Massacre" of six other SLA members—and Wendy
Yoshimura, an antiwar fugitive who was living with Hearst, were arrested on
the morning of May 18 in San Francisco.

7   Ted Gold, Diana Oughton, and Terry Robbins died on March 6, 1970,
when a bomb they were producing accidentally detonated.

8   Sandra Pratt ("Nsondi ji Jaga")—the wife of Vietnam veteran and
Black Liberation Army organizer Geronimo Pratt—was killed in 1971.

9   Shakur died on May 3, 1973, in the New Jersey Turnpike shootout
which left a police officer dead and Assata Shakur (Joanne Chesimard) and
Sundiata Acoli (Clark Squire) in custody.

10   Meyers was ambushed by a joint FBI-NYPD force in the Bronx
on November 14, 1973. After he was gunned down, New York Police
Commissioner Donald Cawley crowed that his men had "broken the back"
of the BLA (Akinyele Omowale Umoja, "Repression Breeds Resistance: The
Black Liberation Army and the Radical Legacy of the Black Panther Party," in
Kathleen Cleaver and George Katsiaficas, eds., *Liberation, Imagination, and the
Black Panther Party* [New York: Routledge, 2001], 13). In the original Brigade
communiqué, Meyers's name was given incorrectly as "Twymon Myers."

11   The preceding six names are *noms de guerre* and nicknames of the SLA
members killed in Compton: Nancy Ling Parry, Donald DeFreeze, Patricia
Soltysik, Camilla Hall ("Gabi"), William Wolfe ("Cujo"), and Angela Atwood,
respectively.

12   This is an allusion to the title of a popular anthology on political prisoners, which addressed Magee's case: Angela Y. Davis, ed., *If They Come in the
Morning: Voices of Resistance* (New York: Third Press, 1971).

13   In the early hours of Monday, September 15.

14   City Light is Seattle's public utility. At the time of the bombing workers had been on strike since October 17, 1975.

15   A parenthetical insert by the Brigade.

16   Assata Shakur was a member of the New York chapter of the Black
Panther Party who became active with the Black Liberation Army. On May
2, 1973, she survived a shootout with New Jersey State Troopers in which

she sustained two bullet wounds, and her comrade Zayd Malik Shakur and trooper Werner Foerester were killed. After six and a half years in prison, she was freed from the Clinton Correctional Facility for women and given asylum in Cuba in 1984. The United States and New Jersey governments continue to press for her extradition, with the FBI placing a million-dollar price on her head on May 2, 2005. See www.assatashakur.org for updates, and Assata Shakur, *Assata: An Autobiography* (Westport, CT: L. Hill, 1987).

17 Amílcar Cabral (1921–1973) was a creative revolutionary theoretician who led the independence struggle against the Portuguese in Guinea-Bissou. His writings available in English include: Amilcar Cabral, *Unity and Struggle*, trans. Michael Wolfers (New York: Monthly Review Press, 1979); *National Liberation and Culture*, trans. Maureen Webster (Syracuse, NY: Syracuse University, 1970); *Return to the Source: Selected Speeches* (New York: Monthly Review Press, 1973); and *Revolution in Guinea: Selected Texts*, trans. Richard Handyside, (New York: Monthly Review Press, 1972 [first published in 1969]). See also Patrick Chabal, *Amílcar Cabral: Revolutionary Leadership and People's War* (Cambridge: Cambridge University Press, 1983), and John Fobanjong and Thomas K. Ranuga. *The Life, Thought, and Legacy of Cape Verde's Freedom Fighter Amilcar Cabral (1924–1973): Essays on his Liberation Philosophy* (Lewiston, NY: Edwin Mellen Press, 2006).

For an idea of how Brigade members may have read Cabral, see the discussion of his significance as an anticolonial thinker in Butch Lee and Red Rover, *Night-Vision: Illuminating War and Class on the Neo-Colonial Terrain* (New York: Vagabond Press, 1993), 61–66. They write: "Cabral was perhaps the most extraordinary revolutionary leader of his generation," "a political-military genius" whose "uniqueness doesn't fully come through in print because his writings are only a shadow of the concepts he brought alive in practice" (61–62). Former Brigade member Brown provided a promotional quote for the jacket of this book, asserting that it "should be read by anyone who give a damn about a non-racist, non-sexist, non-homophobic future."

18 This epigraph is from Jackson, *Soledad Brother*

19 "Politics in Command," signed by "Celia Sojourn" and Billy Ayers, was printed on the Weather Underground's own printing press in 1975. The seven-page document is not anthologized, but is preserved in the Tamiment Library of New York University in the "Weather Underground" file (copy in author's possession). The second communiqué referred to appears as "The Symbionese Liberation Army: Patty Hearst Kidnapping," in Jonah Raskin, ed., *The Weather Eye: Communiqués from the Weather Underground, May 1970–May 1974* (San Francisco: Union Square Press, 1974), 96. Although *The Weather Eye* is reproduced in Dohrn, Ayers, and Jones, eds., *Sing a Battle Song*, 131–227, this communiqué has been dropped without comment, presumably in order to avoid embarrassment to the editors. This omission highlights the desirability of documentary collections by independent parties.

20 Sostre (1923–) was a black liberationist who was politicized as a
Black Muslim in the course of a twelve-year sentence for drug charges. After
his release from the New York State Penitentiary in Attica in 1964 he left the
Nation of Islam and began the Afro-Asian Bookstore in Buffalo, which became
a consciousness-raising center for black youth. On July 14, 1967, only days
after a major black uprising in Buffalo, police raided the bookstore and, his
supporters claimed, planted heroin on Sostre. In a politically charged atmosphere, Sostre was portrayed in the press and before a United States Senate
committee as an instigator of the riot, an arsonist, and a high-rolling drug
peddler. He was convicted of the only charges brought against him—those
relating to drugs—and sentenced to thirty to forty-one years. He spent much
of his first year in prison in solitary, writing legal briefs, and correspond-
ing with supporters. See *Letters from Prison: A Compilation of Martin Sostre's
Correspondence from Erie County Jail, Buffalo, New York; and Green Haven
Prison, Stormville, New York* (Buffalo, NY: n.p., 1969), and Vincent Copeland,
The Crime of Martin Sostre (New York: McGraw-Hill, 1970).

21 Names omitted in the original.

22 The fugitives, according to Ed Mead, were Leonard Peltier and a companion, before events on the Pine Ridge Oglala Sioux reservation in South
Dakota made Peltier this country's most prominent political prisoner.

23 "Capitol Hill Safeway" communiqué; See Part II in this volume.

24 In an extensive review of local media coverage of this action I have
not encountered these quotes.

25 Le Duan (1907–1986), a Vietnamese communist leader who was a
driving force behind the war with the United States. In 1969 he replaced Ho
Chi Minh and led a unified Vietnam from 1975 until his death in 1986.

26 On July 27, 1973, prisoners took over the Oklahoma State
Penitentiary in McAlester. They held the prison—and, at one time, twenty-
one hostages—for several days. There were frequent instances of inmate on
inmate violence, resulting in three prisoner deaths. In terms of damage to the
prison itself, the OSP rebellion may have been the most costly in American
history, estimated between twenty to thirty million dollars. The prisoners'
clearly articulated demands and declaration "It's a revolution!" remind that
the prisoners' rights movement of the late 1960s and early 1970s affected the
entire country, not just the East and West coasts.

27 I.e., the killing of George Jackson and repression of his comrades on
August 21, 1971.

28 "All other units" was Mark Cook. Rita Brown was waiting at a switch
car away from the bank.

29 Again, "comrade."

30 Susan Saxe was a lesbian antiwar activist who joined forces with three
male ex-convicts and her Brandeis college roommate Katherine Power to steal
documents from a National Guard Armory and rob banks to fund further

activities. In the course of one of the robberies one of the ex-convicts killed a police officer. Saxe and Power hid out on women's land, stumping the FBI, who couldn't infiltrate lesbian communities for lack of appropriate personnel. To compensate for this "failure of intelligence," the FBI launched grand juries in women's communities where Saxe and Power were believed to have visited. These grand juries, which polarized political and apolitical elements in the gay community, were denounced as "witch hunts." Seven of those subpoenaed were jailed for refusing to participate.

31 Assata Shakur; see note 16.

32 George Jackson.

33 Jill Raymond resisted the Lexington grand jury inquisition seeking information on Susan Saxe and Kathrine Power. Jill's sister Laurie was partners with Michelle Whitnack, who was jailed for resisting the Seattle grand jury investigating the George Jackson Brigade.

34 Martin Sostre; see note 20.

35 Charles Manson and his "family." Brown would later serve time with Lynette "Squeaky" Fromme at the Administrative Segregation Unit in Davis Hall, Federal Correctional Institute, Alderson, West Virginia. Despite overtures Brown and her comrade Assata Shakur reviled the Manson follower as a white supremacist and kook.

36 This is a reference to both the "dykes niggers cons" line in the "International Women's Day" communiqué and to Ed Mead's claiming of two bombings investigators had had no previous confirmation that the Brigade committed, on which see Walter Wright, "Jailed Comrade Speaks: 'Brigade Bombed FBI,'" *Post-Intelligencer*, March 30, 1976, A1.

37 John Arthur Wilson had covered the Brigade periodically since the 1975 New Year's Eve bombings: e.g., John Wilson, "Residents Still Face Total Outages," *Seattle Times*, January 2, 1976. His consistent coverage of the Brigade prompted the defense in Ed Mead's first-degree assault trial to call him as an expert witness regarding prejudicial press coverage on the Brigade: "Times Reporter is Subpoenaed," *Seattle Times*, April 6, 1976, A15. Wilson testified that the Brigade had received significant media attention.

38 John Arthur Wilson, "Bombs: Jackson Brigade speaks out again," *Seattle Times*, May 13, 1977, A20.

39 Paul Henderson, "State-prison aide defended," *Seattle Times*, May 5, 1977, D2. Henderson reported on Walla Walla for the rest of the week: "Prison Lockup: Tension Mounts Under Enforced Calm," *Seattle Times*, May 7, 1977, A1; "Guards Fear Reform Will Mean 'Replay' of Prison Violence," *Seattle Times*, May 7, 1977, A4; "Changes Pledged at Prison," *Seattle Times*, May 8, 1977, A1; "Guards Back Changes at Prison," *Seattle Times*, May 9, 1977, D1.

40 John Arthur Wilson, "Prison Inmates to be Let Out of Cells Tomorrow; Guards Wary," *Seattle Times*, May 23, 1977, A1.

41 Marshall Wilson, "Lockup Still in Effect; Prison Guards Walk Out,"

ST, May 24, 1977, A1. The same afternoon representatives of the guards' union, the Washington Federation of State Employees, sought an injunction in Thurston County Superior Court to prevent the reopening. The motion was denied and the next morning, after last minute negotiations with the administration regarding safety precautions, the staff's "indefinite" walkout was called off and the cell doors opened. See Dean Katz, "Guard's Motion Denied: Bid to Block Prisoner Release Fails," *Seattle Times*, May 25, 1977, A14; Paul Henderson, "Doors Unlocked: Inmates Enjoy First Day of 'Freedom,'" *Seattle Times*, May 26, 1977, A14.

42 When I asked Mead what percentage of Walla Walla Brothers communications he authored, he replied: "I would say all of it" (Interview with author, February 2, 2006). For other public communications by the Walla Walla Brothers, see "In the Hole at Walla Walla," *Northwest Passage*, August 9–29, 1976, 4, 23; "Letters from Walla Walla," *Northwest Passage*, November 8–21, 1976, 12–13, 22. Both issues contain separate letters signed by Mead in his own name: "Ed Mead," *Northwest Passage*, August 9–29, 1976, 22–23; "No Medical Aid for the Beaten," *Northwest Passage*, November 8–21, 1976, 1.

43 John Arthur Wilson, "Officials Unfair, Says Prison Letter," *Seattle Times*, May 24, 1977, C1.

44 Paul Henderson, "46 Days in Lockup; 'Your mind starts playing tricks on you,'" *Seattle Times*, May 27, 1977, A1.

45 Dean Katz, "Probe Set at Penitentiary," *Seattle Times*, May 26, 1977.

46 "Rainier" is misspelled "Ranier" in the original, as it is in the political statement.

47 The Department of Social Health Services oversaw mental health and penal institutions.

48 Shelton was the site of a newer, lower-security prison.

49 Smith and Moncourt write:

> With the group of RAF fighters who seized the West German embassy in Stockholm on April 24, 1975, "the focus of the revolutionary struggle" had changed. During the 1970–1972 period, the RAF had been preoccupied with things like radical subjectivity, workers' alienation, the exploitation of the Third World, police violence, a left wing out of touch with rebel youth, and a "new fascism" exemplified by social democratic corporatism and general repression . . .
>
> The initial openness now gave way to a single-minded focus on a "new fascism" defined as attacks on the prisoners and their legal team, and hardly anything else.
>
> Clearly, the prisoners' struggle was not only guiding the RAF, drawing in almost all of its new recruits; it was now defining its very politics.

Elsewhere they reiterate: "The guerilla became locked in on the prisoners to the exclusion of all other social contradictions." Smith and Moncourt, eds., *The Red Army Faction*, 336–37, 452.

50 This quote, originally prose, was converted into a stanza by the Brigade.

51 On the press blackout, see "GJB gets silent treatment," *Open Road* (Vancouver, BC), Fall 1977.

52 Berger, *Outlaws of America*, 201–202.

53 John Brown Book Club, "introduction," *The Split of the Weather Underground Organization: Struggling against White and Male Supremacy* (Seattle: John Brown Book Club, 1977), held by the Tamiment Library (copy in author's possession). On this publication see Berger, *Outlaws of America*, 232, 234.

54 On these last desperate gasps of Weather see the partisan account in Mark Rudd, *Underground: My Life with the SDS and the Weathermen* (New York: William Morrow, 2009), 276–80.

55 John Brown Book Club, *The Split*, 40.

56 This last issue is also taken up in "Open Letter to the Revolutionary Committed from Native American Warriors," dated Jan. 1977 and included on pages 41–42 of *The Split*, as well as, corrected, on page 44.

57 I.e., Bruce Seidel.

58 While the murder thesis is far from universally accepted, I agree with Smith and Moncourt that due to systematic misconduct the burden of proof is on the German government. The following observation is on point: "Without a shadow of a doubt, the decline of the murder thesis is a direct consequence of the decline of the RAF and its support scene. It is a chilling example of how, once a revolutionary tendency disappears, the state's version simply wins the contest by acclamation, no actual facts required." Smith and Moncourt eds., *The Red Army Faction*, 394.

59 Smith and Moncourt eds., *The Red Army Faction*, 381–432.

60 On the Stammheim deaths see Smith and Moncourt eds., *The Red Army Faction*, 510–20. The Stammheim death occurred against the background of the kidnapping and eventual murder of German industrialist Hanns-Martin Schleyer by the RAF and the skyjacking of a Lufthansa jet by a Palestinian militant group, in order to reinforce the demands of Schleyer's kidnappers. See Smith and Moncourt eds., *The Red Army Faction*, 477–509.

61 Smith and Moncourt eds., *The Red Army Faction*, 521–24.

62 This was misspelled as Hans Martin Schleyer in the original.

63 The collective's internal name for John Sherman.

64 The collective's internal name for Therese Coupez.

65 This is referring to a plan to kidnap a state official or high corporate officer. See "Brigade tells of fantastic scheme to kidnap McNutt," *Tacoma News Tribune*, May 2, 1978, and Burton-Rose, *Guerrilla USA*, 248–49.

66 "TUG" is an acronym for "The Urban Guerrilla." It gained currency in militant circles in part due to a Bay Area publication of the same name.

67 Jori Uhuru, *nom de guerre* of Janine Bertram, Brown's abruptly *ex-*

girlfriend at the time of writing. Although in later documents Bertram spelled her pseudonym Jory with an 'i,' here it appears in the original communiqué with a 'y.'

Part III

1   "Excerpts From Political Statement of the George Jackson Brigade," *Northwest Passage*, December 21, 1977–January 9, 1978, 15.

2   Bruce Seidel and Ed Mead put out the first two issues of this publications; Ed did the third one while incarcerated in the Washington State Penitentiary. To the best of my knowledge, none are extant.

3   Bruce Seidel, Rita Brown, Ed Mead, and John Sherman.

4   At this time, only Janine Bertram and Therese Coupez.

5   Seventy-five percent at the time this was written: Janine Bertram, Rita Brown, and Therese Coupez, with John Sherman being the only male.

6   One lesbian and two bisexuals.

7   For Seidel's denunciation see, "Communique Fragment" in Part II. It is not clear which of Mead's prolific statements is being referred to. The Brigade also authored one collectively: "Open Letter to the John Brown Bookclub," in Part II.

8   *Prairie Fire: The Politics of Revolutionary Anti-imperialism Political Statement of the Weather Underground* is the major manifesto of the Weather Underground Organization. It was distributed anonymously in 1974 and reprinted at least once. It is reproduced in Dohrn, Ayers, and Jones, eds., *Sing a Battle Song*, 231–378, minus a long list of political prisoners which appears in the original.

9   It appears that the Brigade was never able to solve the security problems and make this a viable means of communication.

10   In the "Chronology of Brigade Actions" that follows, the Brigade claims actions that had not been previously linked to them in the press.

11   Included in Part II.

12   The Bay Area Radical Collective, publishers of the urban guerrilla communiqué clearinghouse *Dragon*.

13   A Maoist guerrilla cell active in the San Francisco Bay Area. Practically nothing has been written on them beyond the prolific primary sources in the *San Francisco Chronicle*, *Dragon*, *TUG*, *Berkeley Barb*, and other regional publications.

14   A publication begun in Detroit as an underground tabloid in 1965. In 1975, it took on an anti-authoritarian position, which it continues today: http://www.fifthestate.org.

15   A survivor of the Attica prison revolt whom prison activists who later joined the Brigade brought to Seattle to speak in the early 1970s.

16   A prisoner support publication affiliated with the National Lawyers Guild.

17 The *Fuerzas Armadas de Liberación Nacional*, a Puerto Rican independence organization, claimed responsibility for dozens of bombings in the 1970s.

18 Emily and Bill Harris were a married couple who joined the SLA and inadvertently survived the 1974 Compton massacre with Patricia Hearst by running an errand just before the police encirclement began. They were arrested in San Francisco September 18, 1975, provoking the Brigade's first attack on Safeway.

19 Remiro and Little were SLA members convicted of the assassination of popular African American school superintendent Marcus Foster. In 1981 Little was retried for the Foster murder and acquitted. Remiro remains incarcerated. On the early events surrounding their case and biographical background see Bryan, *This Soldier Still at War*.

20 A prisoner support publication in Massachusetts with ties to the National Lawyers Guild.

21 Bishop was an independent antiwar radical tried for bombing power lines leading to a defense plant in Colorado in 1968.

22 In the original the surname is incorrectly given as "Powers."

23 *Euskadi Ta Askatasuna*, Basque for "Basque Homeland and Freedom."

24 *Brigate Rosse*.

25 The most readily available source on this group in English, which is not particularly recommended, is William Farrell, *Blood and Rage: The Story of the Japanese Red Army* (Lexington, MA: Lexington Books, 1990). There is also Aileen Gallagher, *The Japanese Red Army* (New York: Rosen Publishing Group, 2003). This title appears in the series Inside the World's Most Infamous Terrorist Organizations which, bizarrely, are introductory children's books on armed nonstate actors the world over.

26 Written by Janine Bertram and Rita Brown.

27 This is the title of a pamphlet of Ralph "Po" Ford's writings collated by his girlfriend, who was also a Left Bank Collective member, after his death.

28 To the best of my knowledge there is no comprehensive collection of SLA communiqués; Pearsall, *The Symbionese Liberation Army*, is the closest contender, but is limited by having gone to press before the Compton massacre. While the continued pariah status of the SLA among activists is understandable and to a certain degree welcome, that scholars would ignore such a significant phenomenon is objectionable. Some communiqués are reprinted in Payne and Findley, *The Life and Death of the SLA*, 329–69, and McLellan and Avery, *Voices of Guns*, 499–523.

29 Authored by Therese Coupez and John Sherman.

30 This document appears to be no longer extant.

31 This refers to Leroy "Bud" Welcome, owner of the J. J. Welcome Company. See Lee Moriwaki, "Tyree Scott: 'We don't retaliate,'" *Seattle Times*,

October 3, 1975, A6.

32 The bomb was placed late on the night of May 31. It detonated at 1:22 a.m. on the morning of June 1. See Dick Clever, "'Brigade' Takes Credit for Blast At State Office," *Seattle Post-Intelligencer*, June 2, 1975, 1, back page, and John Wilson, "'Brigade' says it set off explosion," *Seattle Times*, June 2, 1975.

33 The takeover occurred on December 31, 1974.

34 Ed Mead first claimed these actions on behalf of the Brigade in a jailhouse interview. See Lee Moriwaki and John Arthur Wilson, "'Brigade Bombed FBI': Jailed Comrade Speaks," *Seattle Times*, April 1, 1976, C5.

35 Ralph "Po" Ford.

36 Bill and Emily Harris, Patricia Hearst, and her roommate non-SLA member Wendy Yoshimura.

37 Mark Cook. See Michelle Celarier, "Does the State Conspire? The Conviction of Mark Cook," in Part I.

38 As in the original communiqué, this word is misspelled "Ranier" throughout.

39 After the Rainier National bank bombings the Washington Bankers Association announced a reward of $25,000 for information leading to the arrest of John William Sherman and Rita Darlene Brown; the only two publicly confirmed, indicted Brigade members at the time. See "Bankers Offer $2,500 Reward," *Seattle Post-Intelligencer*, June 18, 1977, A12 and "Bankers' group offers reward for 2 fugitives," *Seattle Times*, June 19, 1977.

40 Center for Research on Criminal Justice, *The Iron Fist and the Velvet Glove: An Analysis of the U.S. Police* (Berkeley, CA: Center for Research on Criminal Justice, 1975). Editions followed in 1977 and 1982. Center for Research on Criminal Justice was a radical sociology institute associated with the University of California, Berkeley, and the publishers of *Crime and Social Justice* (1974–1987), currently published as *Social Justice*.

Part IV

1 Eileen Kirkpatrick, "Staff Comments," *Northwest Passage*, July 19–August 8, 1976, 2.

2 "Letters from the GJB—'Tell No Lies,'" *Northwest Passage*, August 1–21, 1977, 3; "Jackson Brigade Supports," *Northwest Passage*, October 24–November 7, 1977, 2; "Excerpts From Political Statement of the George Jackson Brigade," *Northwest Passage*, December 21, 1977–January 9, 1978, 15.

3 In a May 11 phone call to Walter Wright of the *Post-Intelligencer*, Sherman claimed the signature as his own. Over a month later the U.S. Attorney directing the grand jury reluctantly conceded this match. See "Brigade Communique Finding," *Seattle Post-Intelligencer*, June 19, 1976, A3.

4 Ho Chi Minh (1890–1969).

5   Walter Wright, "FBI Fumes Over Threats By Radicals," *Seattle Post-Intelligencer*, March 29, 1976, A4.

6   Though he was not out at the time, Mead was bisexual and would be sexually active with men in prison. He also participated in conjugal visitation programs in Arizona and Washington.

7   In the original Brockhaus and Park insert the note: "The next part of the interview in which Mead described the time he spent in prison from the age of 19 to his thirties, was lost to the clanging of doors and a fuzzy phone connection." They paraphrase: "While he was in prison he became renowned as a 'Jailhouse Lawyer,' picking up on his own enough law to help other prisoners. Mead also talked about his early efforts at prison organizing strikes and reform work." Mead's self-narration is similar to that given in Walter Wright, "Ed Mead: Two Faces of a Dangerous Man," reproduced in Part I.

8   A collective which provided lodging to people journeying to visit prisoners on McNeil Island, a short ferry ride across Puget Sound.

9   Jill Kray, Mead's girlfriend before he went underground and the first person subpoenaed to the Brigade grand jury. To Mead's chagrin, she testified.

10   In composing this piece Park acknowledged "much help from John Brockhaus and members of my study group."

11   It was a two-part series. The first, Walter Wright's "Pages in the Life of Bruce Seidel," appears in Part II of this collection; "Communiqué Fragment" in Part II reproduces most of the second.

12   See Part II.

13   Incorrectly given as "Powers" in the original. On their case see Part II, note 30.

14   "Terrorism and the George Jackson Brigade," the preceding article in this collection.

15   September 9–13, 1975.

16   A siege lasting from February 27–May 5, 1975.

17   On New Year's Day of 1975, the Menominee Warrior Society occupied an unused abbey in Gresham, Wisconsin, intending to turn it into a health center. The occupiers were immediately besieged by several hundred law enforcement officers, who, in turn, were supplemented by armed white vigilantes. After an exchange of gunfire, the National Guard was dispatched under strict orders from the governor to enforce a ceasefire.

18   There were actually eighty-two men on the Granma, which sailed from Mexico to Cuba to launch the Cuban Revolution. Jon Lee Anderson, *Che Guevara: A Revolutionary Life* (New York: Grove Press, 1997), 207.

19   Bureau of Alcohol, Tobacco, and Firearms, and the Seattle Police Department.

20   Here *Passage* editors objected to the characterization of Park's criticisms as their own by inserting "*sic*"; they had repeatedly stressed that she did

not speak for the editorial collective as a whole.

21 *V-Narodnik* ("To the People"), a group of aristocratic youth who went to the countryside to raise the consciousness of peasants. Frustrated with the pace of change, they turned to assassinations of nobles, most notably Czar Nicholas II, after which they were crushed.

22 I.e., the Democratic Party.

23 George Jackson, *Blood In My Eye* (New York: Bantam, 1972), 27–28.

24 This is not a convincing argument, considering the grand jury probe that struck Seattle's progressive community in direct response to the Brigade.

25 "Dear Comrade," a letter from Emily Harris dated May 22, 1976, appeared in the June 1976 issue of *Dragon*, 11–18.

26 The Brigade primarily relied on the resources—legitimately earned or stolen—of its own members.

27 For Marighella on expropriation, see "The Bank Assault as Popular Model," *Mini-Manual of the Urban Guerrilla* (Montreal, Quebec: Abraham Guillen Press, 2002). The first English-language edition was published as the "Mini-Manual of Urban Guerrilla Warfare" by the San Francisco–based Red Guerrilla Family in 1969, the same year it was first published in Spanish in the Cuban journal *Tricontinental*.

28 The relevant passage reads: "It is better to err acting than to do nothing for fear of making a mistake." Marighella, *Mini-Manual of the Urban Guerilla*, 5.

29 "Jori" rather than "Jory."

30 Communiqué, singular: see "Our Losses Are Heavy . . ." in Part II.

31 Brackets in this article are those of Patz.

32 "Bomb Damage Repair: Strikers Refuse to Help, City Says," *Seattle Post-Intelligencer*, January 3, 1976, A1.

Part V

1 On the weekend of July 4, 1998, Lynn "Spit" Newborn and Daniel Shersty, both active with the Las Vegas chapter of Anti-Racist Action, were found dead in the desert. Shersty was beaten then executed with a single bullet; Newborn's body was riddled with bullets, possibly as a result of attempting to escape. Both had had recent run-ins with neo-Nazis, who are considered responsible for their deaths. "Anti-Racist Youth Murdered in Las Vegas," *Revolutionary Worker*, August 16, 1998.

2 The September 18, 1975, bombing.

3 Cook is referring to the case that came to be called the San Francisco 8, in which eight former Panthers, two already in custody, were charged with the 1971 killing of Sgt. John Young at the Ingleside police station. In 2009, the two previously incarcerated Panther and Black Liberation Army veterans, Herman Bell and Jalil Muntaqim, pled guilty to voluntary manslaughter, and

no contest to commit voluntary manslaughter, respectively. See http://www.freethesf8.org.

4   I.e., the reincarcerations of Kathy Soliah (Sara Jane Olson) and Bill and Emily Harris.

5   Ronald Tsukamoto became Berkeley's first Japanese-American police officer in 1969 and then, on August 20, 1970, its first officer killed in the line of duty. Berkeley police headquarters bear his name. On May 24, 2004, Alameda County law enforcement officers arrested Don Juan Graphenreed for the crime, then abruptly released him. Karl Fischer, "Arrest, but no charges in 1970 killing of officer," *Berkeley Voice*, May 28, 2004, A1, A11.

6   Armsbury was actually a member of the Patriots Party, who, like the White Panthers, saw themselves as a white, working class adjunct to the community serve, anti–law enforcement positions of the Black Panthers. On the White Panthers, see Jeff A. Hale, "Total Assault on the Culture," in Peter Braunstein and Michael William Dayle, eds., *Imagine Nation: The American Counterculture of the 1960s and '70s* (New York: Routledge, 2001), 125–156. On the meeting of Mead and Armsbury in McNeil Island federal penitentiary in 1970, see Burton-Rose, *Guerrilla USA*, 56–58. Armsbury is currently an organizer with the November Coalition against the punitive policies of the Drug War: see http:// www.november.org.

7   On Weather's conundrum on whether or not to reply to a collective letter from the jailed leadership of the New York chapter of the Black Panther Party, urging that they not abandon armed action, see Varon, *Bringing the War Home*, 185–86.

8   Walter Wright, author of the profiles of Mead and Seidel in Part I. For a list of his articles on the Brigade, see the Selected Newspaper Articles on the George Jackson Brigade, 1975–1978, below.

Selected Newspaper Articles on the George Jackson Brigade, 1975–1978

Abbreviations
DJA   *Daily Journal American*
EH   *Everett Herald*
NYT   *New York Times*
PO   *Portland Oregonian*
SP-I   *Seattle Post-Intelligencer*
SS   *Seattle Sun*
ST   *Seattle Times*
TNT   *Tacoma News Tribune*

(Editor's Note: I do not have page numbers for each article but have opted to provide those I do have.)

"Man Killed by Bomb Identified," *ST*, September 16, 1975.
"Supermart Blast Victim Identified," *SP-I*, September 17, 1975.
"Several Hurt in Safeway . . ." *ST*, September 19, 1975.
"Bomb Threats Sweep the Seattle Area," *SP-I*, September 20, 1975, A1.
"Bombing Shows Need for Strong Safeguards," *SP-I*, September 21, 1975, B2.
"Guards Conducting Searches at Bombed Capitol Hill Safeway," *ST*, September 26, 1975.
"Fire Explosion Jolts City Lights Substation," *SP-I*, January 1, 1976, A1.
"Laurelhurst Residents Asked to Curb Power Use," *ST*, January 1, 1976.
"Weather Underground Behind Bombings?" *ST*, January 2, 1976.
"57 Bombings Here since 1969," *ST*, January 3, 1976.
"Bomb Damage Repair: Strikers Refuse to Help, City Says," *SP-I*, January 3, 1976, A1.
"No Pickets at Power Site," *ST*, January 4, 1976.
"Editor, the *Times*," *ST*, January 6, 1976.
"None Need Help from Bomb Brigade," *SP-I*, January 7, 1976, A8.
"Inquest Jury to Weigh Bank Shoot-Out Evidence," *SP-I*, February 18, 1976, A4.
"Bank Robbery Probe Halts for a Week," *SP-I*, March 5, 1976, B4.
"Radical Wounds Officer to Help Inmate Escape," *SP-I*, March 11,

1976, A1.

"City Light Substation Rebuilt," *ST*, March 20, 1976.

"Law Agencies on Brigade's Trail," *SP-I*, March 27, 1976, A11.

"'Brigade is a Challenge,'" *SP-I*, March 30, 1976, A12.

"Text of Brigade Communique," *SP-I*, March 31, 1976, F6.

"Grand Jury Calls Attorney in Tukwila Case," *SP-I*, April 4, 1976, A4.

"Times Reporter is Subpoenaed," *ST*, April 6, 1976, A15.

"U.S. 'Intimidation' Charged in Bank Case," *SP-I*, April 10, 1976, A3.

"Mead Trial Delayed to Give Him Time to Prepare Case," *SP-I*, April 13, 1976, A6.

"Bar Group Backs Lawyer in Dispute," *ST*, May 2, 1976.

"Government Accused of 'Fishing,'" *ST*, May 5, 1976.

"Review Ordered of Material Seized in House," *ST*, May 7, 1976.

"Another Woman Subpoenaed in Grand Jury Bomb Probe," *SP-I*, May 9, 1976, A11.

"Four Denied Meeting Sherman," *SP-I*, May 13, 1976, A4.

"Sleuths on the Write Track?" *ST*, May 18, 1976.

"Brigade Communique Finding," *SP-I*, June 19, 1976, A3.

"Bank Robbery Defendant Refuses Psychiatric Test," *SP-I*, June 20, 1976, H5.

"Judge Refuses to to [Sic] Hold Contempt Hearing for Grand-Jury Witness," *ST*, June 29, 1976.

"Policemen Reviewed for Mead 'Macing,'" *SP-I*, July 7, 1976, A7.

"A Poor Way for them to be Noticed," *ST*, July 17, 1976.

"Officials Want Woman in Bombing-Case Line Up," *ST*, July 24, 1976.

"Jackson Brigade's Mead, Cook Get 30 Years," *SP-I*, August 7, 1976, A9.

"Jackson Brigade Member Draws 40-Year Minimum," *ST*, November 3, 1976.

"Fugitive Phones *PI* Fifth Time," *SP-I*, November 9, 1976, A13.

"Wilsonville, Eastgate Bank Branches Robbed," *PO*, February 8, 1977, A9.

"Two More Automobile Dealers Hit," *ST*, May 25, 1977.

"Bankers Offer $2,500 Reward," *SP-I*, June 18, 1977, A12.

"Bankers' Group Offers Reward for 2 Fugitives," *ST*, June 19, 1977.

"Brigade: We Did It," *SP-I*, June 23, 1977, A5.

"Bomb Defused in Olympia Power Station," *ST*, July 5, 1977.

"Investigators Seeking Clues to Bomb Planting," *TNT*, July 5, 1977.

"George Jackson Brigade Bombers May Get Nastier," *TNT*, July 7, 1977.

"Jackson Brigade Suspect in Eastside Robbery," *ST*, September 9, 1977.

"Bank Heist a 'Brigade' Hit?" *SP-I*, September 20, 1977, D12.

"Jackson Brigade Note Left in Bank Robbery," *ST*, September 20, 1977.

"Edward Mead Loses Plea," *SP-I*, September 24, 1977, A3.

"Gasoline Bomb found at Seattle Auto Dealership," *ST*, October 8, 1977.

"Bomb Probe Stepped Up," *ST*, October 18, 1977, A3.

"Striking Auto Mechanics File Slander Suit Against Dealers," *ST*, October 27, 1977.

"The Brigade again," *SP-I*, November 3, 1977.

"Jackson Brigade: Bombing Suspect Seized Here," *SP-I*, November 5, 1977, A1.

"FBI Pursues Jackson Brigade Man, Friend," *SP-I*, November 6, 1977.

"Brigade-Suspect Search Fruitless," *TNT*, November 7, 1977.

"Alleged Brigade Chief's Pal Sought," *TNT*, November 8, 1977.

"Sherman Friend Subpoenaed?" *SP-I*, November 8, 1977, A3.

"Ray Among Brigade Targets?" *SP-I*, November 22, 1977.

"Paper Studying F.B.I. Request for Letter," *ST*, December 4, 1977.

"Bomb Explodes at Renton Substation," *SP-I*, December 24, 1977, A14.

"Small Bomb Set Off at Renton Power Station," *ST*, December 24, 1977.

"Kent Bombing Follows Brigade Call," *ST*, December 25,. 1977.

"Investigation Continues into Local Bombings," *ST*, December 26, 1977.

"Brigade Bombs in Renton and Kent," *SS*, December 28, 1977.

"FBI Ties Holdups to Jackson Bunch," *TNT*, January 11, 1978.

"Brigade Makes Explosive Appearance, Fizzles on Arrest," *TNT*, March 23, 1978.

"Sherman Preparing to Rob a Bank?" *TNT*, March 25, 1978.

"Brigade Tells of Fantastic Scheme to Kidnap McNutt," *TNT*, May 2, 1978.

Alters, Diane. "Bomb Explodes at Car Dealership After Jackson Brigade Call." *ST*, November 2, 1977.

Anderson, Ross. "Ruling on Radicals: Police Justified in Entering Apartment." *ST*, August 25, 1976.

_____. "Grand Jury may See Evidence, Judge Rules." *ST*, September 11, 1976.

Associated Press. "Drop Charges, Bank Suspect Asks." *TNT*, April 1, 1976, C12.
_____. "'Comrade' on Trial in Seattle." *TNT*, April 5, 1976.
_____. "Judge Denies Dismissal of Mead Assault Charges." *TNT*, April 6, 1976.
_____. "Tukwila Police Tell of Holdup." *TNT*, April 7, 1976, B6.
_____. "Trial 'Hears' Escapee." *TNT*, April 9, 1976.
_____. "Mead Trial Continued One Week." *TNT*, April 13, 1976.
_____. "Agents Will Seek to Link Brigade." *ST*, May 3, 1976, A14.
_____. "New Raid made in 'Brigade Case.'" *TNT*, May 3, 1976.
_____. "Agents Went Beyond Limits." *TNT*, May 18, 1976.
_____. "Radical Will Plead Insanity." *TNT*, June 20, 1976.
_____. "Mead Trial Opens in Bank Robbery." *TNT*, July 6, 1976.
_____. "Brigade Member Guilty of Bank Job." *TNT*, July 8, 1976.
_____. "Bank-Robbing Radical Gets 40-Year Term." *TNT*, November 4, 1976.
_____. "Leftist Group Defends Jackson Brigade's Latest Bombings." *TNT*, May 19, 1977, B11.
_____. "Brigade Takes Credit for Bellevue Holdups." June 24, 1977, A5.
_____. "FBI Terrorist Hunt." *TNT*, June 27, 1977.
_____. "Brigade Robber Hits Bank." *TNT*, September 9, 1977.
_____. "FBI Says 'Brigade' Letter Real." *TNT*, October 19, 1977.
_____. "Brigade Says Bombing Backed Terrorists." *TNT*, November 2, 1977, B8.
_____. "FBI Still Seeking George Jackson Pair." *TNT*, November 6, 1977.
_____. "Bomb Explodes at Renton Power Station." *EH*, December 24, 1977.
_____. "Ineffectual Bomb Linked to Brigade." *DJA*, December 24, 1977.
_____. "Bomb was Retaliation for Capitalist Activity." *TNT*, December 25, 1977.
_____. "2 Bombings have Police on Alert." *DJA*, December 26, 1977.
_____. "Jackson Bunch Claims Bombs." *TNT*, December 26, 1977.
_____. "Radicals Say they Set Off 2 Bombs." *EH*, December 26, 1977.
_____. "FBI Arrests Fugitive Radicals." *PO*, March 22, 1978, A1.
_____. "Radical Held on $1 Million Bail." *DJA*, March 22, 1978, A1.
_____. "FBI Hunt Clues to Radical Suspect's Past." *PO*, March 23, 1978, A14.

_____. "Letter Claims Radicals 'Fight on.'" *PO*, March 23, 1978, Metro, back page.

Associated Press and *SP-I* Staff. "A Second Bomb Blast." *SP-I*, December 25, 1977, A1, A19.

_____. "Law 'Alert' for More Bombings." *SP-I*, December 26, 1977.

Associated Press, United Press International, and *SP-I* Staff. "State Capital Bomb Plot Foiled." *SP-I*, July 5, 1977, A1.

Birkland, David. "Store Bomb Meant to Kill, Say Police." *ST*, September 19, 1975, A1.

_____. "Man in 40s Listed as Bombing Suspect." *ST*, September 23, 1975.

_____. "Burglary Suspects' Release Hurt Bomb Case, Says Chief." *ST*, October 4, 1975, A3.

_____. "Unexploded Bomb Found at Car Agency." *ST*, October 7, 1977.

Boyd, Paul. "Bomb Planter Believed Killed in Safeway Blast." *SP-I*, September 16, 1975.

Brack, Fred. "A Lot of 'Bits and Pieces': Store Bombing Clues Sifted." *SP-I*, September 25, 1975, A3.

Brown, Larry. "Officers' Files Ruled 'Off Limits.'" *ST*, April 1, 1976.

Chadwick, Susan. "The Grand Jury: Why Are Those People Refusing [to] Testify." *SS*, May 12, 1976, 8.

Clever, Dick. "'Brigade' Takes Credit for Blast at State Office." *SP-I*, June 2, 1975, 1, back page.

Collins, Tony. "George Jackson Brigade Probe Leads to Subpoena of Two Women." *UW Daily*, May 5, 1976, 4.

Foster, George. "City Police Fear More Bombings." *SP-I*, January 2, 1976, A1.

Gillie, John. "Brigade Bomb Disarmed in Olympia." *TNT*, July 4, 1977.

Gough, William. "Security Rules Cancel Medical Appointment." *ST*, April 4, 1976, B5.

Hannula, Don. "Police Fear 'Bombing Increase.'" *ST*, September 20, 1975.

_____. "Support Denounced." *ST*, January 2, 1976.

Henderson, Paul. "Hoax: But Versions of What Happened are Vastly Different." *ST*, May 1, 1976.

_____. "Pipe Bombs Damage 5 Cars." *ST*, October 17, 1977.

Hopkins, Jack. "Jury Given 2 'Pictures' of Brigade Pair." *SP-I*, June 24, 1978.

Ledbetter, Les. "Coast Bombing Expected to Go on Despite Arrests." *NYT*, March 24, 1978, A7.

McCarten, Larry and Fred Brack. "Bomb Victim was Activist." *SP-I*, September 20, 1975, A14.

McCarten, Laurie. "Revolutionary Hideout Sought: Hoax Calls Triggers Police Raid on a Peaceful Couple." *SP-I*, April 30, 1976, A10.

Miletich, Steve. "Juanita Bank Hit, Brigade Claims Credit." *DJA*, September 9, 1977.

_____. "Bombs Explode in Bellevue Car Lot." *DJA*, November 2, 1977.

Modie, Neil. "Seattle Women Defy Jury in Bombing Probe." *SP-I*, June 23, 1976, A10.

_____. "Brigade Leader Captured: Sherman, 2 Women Seized by FBI at Tacoma Drive-in." *SP-I*, March 22, 1978, A1, A20.

Moriwaki, Lee. "Man Killed by Safeway Bomb 'Gentle, Polite . . . Concerned.'" *ST*, September 20, 1975.

_____. "Local Leftists Condemn Bombing of Safeway as 'Irresponsible.'" *SP-I*, October 3, 1975, A8.

_____. "No Network seen in Safeway Bombings." *ST*, December 30, 1975.

_____. "Bomb Threat may be on Police Tape." *ST*, January 2, 1976.

Moriwaki, Lee and John Arthur Wilson. "Of Life and Death in Radical Circles." *ST*, March 30, 1976.

_____. "The Psychological Anatomy of a Revolutionary." *ST*, April 1, 1976.

Morris, Maribeth. "U.S. Offices Guarded: Bomb Alert in Seattle." *SP-I*, September 16, 1975, A1, A16.

Nadler, Eric. "SLA Reprisal?: Bomb in Seattle Store Hurts Five." *SP-I*, September 19, 1975, A1.

O'Connor, Paul. "Brigade is Back with a Bang." *SP-I*, May 13, 1977.

Pyle, Jack. "FBI Warns People on 'Kidnap List.'" *TNT*, November 22, 1977.

Rinearson, Peter. "North End Home Yields Jackson Brigade Clues." *ST*, November 6, 1977.

_____. "Few Clues found in Car Linked to Brigade." *ST*, November 7, 1977.

Roberts, Larry. "The New Year's Bombers: Who and Why?" *SS*, January 14, 1976, 6.

_____. "Police Raid Hill Apartment." *SS*, April 28, 1976, 1, 4.

_____. "Police Department Changes Story on Apartment Raid." *SS*, May 5, 1976.

Sanger, S. L. "Redmond Bank Bombed; Bellevue Bomb Diffused." *SP-I*, May 13, 1977, A1.

United Press International. "Kelly Cites Brigade." *SP-I*, February 12, 1976, A2.

_____. "Member of Revolutionary Group Arrested by the F.B.I. in Seattle." *NYT*, November 6, 1977.

_____. "FBI Nabs Leader of George Jackson Brigade." *EH*, March 22, 1978.

Webster, Kerry. "Indictments Due in Brigade Bust." *TNT*, March 27, 1978.

Wilson, John Arthur. "'Brigade' Says it Set Off Explosion." *ST*, June 2, 1975.

_____. "Laurelhurst 'Getting by.'" *ST*, January 2, 1976.

_____. "Residents Still Face Total Outages." *ST*, January 2, 1976.

_____. "Terrorist Unit Says it Shot Officer." *ST*, March 28, 1976.

_____. "Affidavit Pushes for Testimony by Lawyer." *ST*, April 2, 1976, A8.

_____. "Jury Selected in Mead Assault Trial." April 6, 1976, A15.

_____. "Mead Says Police Fired First." *ST*, April 8, 1976.

_____. "Mead Convicted of Assault; Faces Federal Charges." *ST*, April 9, 1976, A10.

_____. "Mead Granted Trial Delay." *ST*, April 12, 1976.

_____. "Dead Radical's Roommate Sought." *ST*, April 21, 1976.

_____. "Radical Gets 2 Life Terms for Shooting in Robbery Try." *ST*, April 22, 1976.

_____. "Federal Bank-Robbery Trial of Edward Mead Delayed." *ST*, April 23, 1976.

_____. "Federal Agents Raid House." *ST*, May 2, 1976.

_____. "Possible Residence of Radicals is Searched." May 3, 1976.

_____. "Agents Seize Typewriters, Wire." *ST*, May 5, 1976.

_____. "Seized Items . . ." *ST*, May 8, 1976, C8.

_____. "More Items Taken from House Sought." *ST*, May 11, 1976.

_____. "Federal Grand Jury Under Fire again." *ST*, May 18, 1976, A10.

_____. "Shot Officer Testifies about Escape Attempt from Hospital." *ST*, June 17, 1976.

_____. "Mead Sticks to Insanity Plea." *ST*, June 19, 1976.

_____. "Search Nets Guns, Radical Literature." *ST*, June 21, 1976.

_____. "Radical, Seized Items Subpoenaed." *ST*, June 22, 1976.

_____. "Radicals Charge Illegal Search." *ST*, June 24, 1976.

_____. "Jury Chosen, 'Brigade' Member's Trial Begins." *ST*, July 6, 1976.

_____. "Judge Refuses to Allow Mead to Plead Insanity." July 7, 1976.

_____. "Mead Convicted of Bank Robbery." *ST*, July 7, 1976.

_____. "George Jackson Brigade may be Dead, Says Mead." *ST*, July 8, 1976.

_____. "Lists Seized in Raid on Radicals' Home." *ST*, July 13, 1976.

_____. "Woman Appears in Line-Up in Bombing of Substation." *ST*, July 26, 1976.

_____. "Woman Picked from Line-Up in Bombing Case." *ST*, July 28, 1976.

_____. "Radical Fears 'Frame-Up' in Bombing." *ST*, August 4, 1976, E14.

_____. "Brigade Member Tied to Oregon Bank Robberies?" *ST*, October 1, 1976, B3.

_____. "Government Still Probing Activist, Unsolved Bombings." *ST*, December 22, 1976.

_____. "Seized Weapons Returned to Activists," *ST*, April 21, 1977.

_____. "Bombs: Jackson Brigade Speaks Out Again." *ST*, May 13, 1977, A20.

_____. "Radicals Blame Bombing on Abuse of Inmates." *ST*, May 13, 1977, A1.

_____. "Bank-Robbery Charge: Brigade Fugitive Indicted." *ST*, May 14, 1977, A1.

_____. "F.B.I. Steps Up the Hunt for Brigade Members." *ST*, June 25, 1977.

_____. "F.B.I. Studying Defused Bombs." *ST*, July 6, 1977.

_____. "Fugitive's Thumbprint on Letter, Says F.B.I." *ST*, October 19, 1977, D7.

_____. "Jackson Brigade Suspect Arrested here." *ST*, November 5, 1977.

_____. "Rita Brown Ordered to Stand Trial." *ST*, November 14, 1977.

_____. "Suspected Brigade List Names Local Officials." *ST*, November 22, 1977.

_____. "Jackson Brigaders Relate Flight from N. End House." *ST*, December 1, 1977.

_____. "Long Hunt for Remnant of Elusive Brigade Ends Quietly."

ST, March 22, 1978, A1.

_____. "Brigade Suspect was Devoted, Says Family." *ST*, March 23, 1978, A14.

_____. "F.B.I. Expected Letter from 'Rest of Brigade.'" *ST*, March 31, 1978.

_____. "Sherman had Lived 'Next Door.'" *ST*, April 4, 1978.

_____. "Support for Auto Strike: Sherman Admits Fire-Bombings." *ST*, April 27, 1978.

_____. "Sherman Tells of Joining Brigade." *ST*, July 6, 1978.

Wilson, John Arthur and Lee Moriwaki. "Brigade Deserves Respect, Say Leftists." *ST*, March 31, 1976.

_____. "Sent to Newspaper; Tests Fail to show Bullet was Fired in Attempted Bank Robbery." *ST*, n.d., A6.

Works, Martin. "A Former Convict Tells Why the Prisoners at Monroe Want a Union." *SP-I*, October 22, 1973, A1.

_____. "Bomb Fragments to be Analyzed." *SP-I*, January 3, 1976, back page.

_____. "Brigade Linked to Bombings." *SP-I*, October 19, 1977, A1.

_____. "Sherman's Car found Near Bus Depot." *SP-I*, November 7, 1977, A9.

Works, Martin and Walter Wright, "Escape Case Hunt Intense." *SP-I*, March 12, 1976, A1.

_____. "A Quiet Arrest . . . the Tukwila Bank Robbery Case Develops." *SP-I*, March 13, 1976, A11.

Wright, Walter. "Jury Clears Tukwila Policemen in Fatal Shooting," *SP-I*, February 20, 1976, A4.

_____. "Grand Jury Defied by Two Witnesses." *SP-I*, March 24, 1976, A6.

_____. "New Twist in Tukwila Bank Case." *SP-I*, March 25, 1976, A6.

_____. "Destruction, Bloodshed, Threatened by Radicals." *SP-I*, March 28, 1976, A1.

_____. "FBI Fumes Over Threats by Radicals." *SP-I*, March 29, 1976, A4.

_____. "'Brigade Bombed FBI': Jailed Comrade Speaks." *SP-I*, March 30, 1976, A1, A12.

_____. "Jailed Comrade Speaks: 'Brigade Bombed FBI.'" *SP-I*, March 30, 1976, A1.

_____. "Brigade's Promised Proof; Station Gets Dental Evidence." *SP-I*, March 31, 1976.

_____. "Security Tight as New Trial Starts." *SP-I*, April 6, 1976, A10.

_____. "Officers Tell of Gun Battle." *SP-I*, April 7, 1976, A5.

_____. "Accounts of Gun Battle Differ Widely." *SP-I*, April 8, 1976, A5.

_____. "Jury Convicts Mead in Bank Robbery Case." *SP-I*, April 9, 1976.

_____. "Ed Mead: 2 Faces of a Dangerous Man." *SP-I*, April 11, 1976, A6.

_____. "Slain Man's Document: Self-Implication in Three Bombings." *SP-I*, April 21, 1976.

_____. "Mead Says He'll Plead Not Guilty Due to 'Insanity.'" *SP-I*, April 22, 1976, A4.

_____. "Mead Gets Prison Sentence." *SP-I*, April 23, 1976, A7.

_____. "3 Deny Link to Brigade." *SP-I*, May 4, 1976, A5.

_____. "Capitol Hill Home Search Defended." *SP-I*, May 7, 1976, A7.

_____. "Search Items, A Review." *SP-I*, May 8, 1976, A11.

_____. "Revolutionary Phones *PI*: Mystery Call from a Fugitive." *SP-I*, May 11, 1976, A1.

_____. "No Telltale Fingerprints." *SP-I*, May 12, 1976, A1.

_____. "Grand Jury Hands Out New 'Brigade' Charges." *SP-I*, May 19, 1976, A11.

_____. "Brigade Probe Twist: Woman Sues U.S." *SP-I*, May 20, 1976, A8.

_____. "U.S. Wants Sherman's Handwriting." *SP-I*, June 14, 1976.

_____. "Leftist Called in Bomb Probe After Accidental Raid." June 22, 1976, C14.

_____. "Sherman Calls to Say He'll 'Clear Others.'" *SP-I*, June 25, 1976, A6.

_____. "Jury Finds Mead Guilty of Armed Robbery Try." *SP-I*, July 8, 1976, A12.

_____. "Sherman Hunt: FBI in Oregon." *SP-I*, July 27, 1976.

_____. "'Revolutionary' May Be 60 After Prison." *SP-I*, August 8, 1976, F6.

_____. "Fugitive Sherman Denies Oregon Robbery Link." *SP-I*, October 12, 1976, B4.

Selected Bibliography

Build a Revolutionary Resistance Movement! Communiqués from the North American Armed Clandestine Movement, 1982-1985, New York: Committee to Fight Repression. n.d. (mid-1980s).

Anderson, Jon Lee. *Che Guevara: A Revolutionary Life*. New York: Grove Press, 1997.

Baker, Marilyn. *Exclusive! The Inside Story of Patricia Hearst and the SLA*. New York: Macmillan, 1974.

Bates, Tom. *Rads: The 1970 Bombing of the Army Math Research Center at the University of Wisconsin and its Aftermath*. New York: HarperCollins, 1992.

Berger, Dan. *Outlaws of America: The Weather Underground and the Politics of Solidarity*. Oakland: AK Press, 2006.

Bryan, John. *This Soldier Still at War*. New York: Harcourt, Brace, Jovanovich, 1975.

Burton-Rose, Daniel. *Guerrilla USA: The George Jackson Brigade and the Anticapitalist Underground of the 1970s*. Berkeley: University of California Press, 2010.

Cabral, Amílcar. *National Liberation and Culture*. Trans. Maureen Webster. Syracuse, NY: Syracuse University, 1970.

_____. *Revolution in Guinea: Selected Texts*. Trans. Richard Handyside. New York: Monthly Review Press, 1972 (first published in 1969).

_____. *Return to the Source: Selected Speeches*. New York: Monthly Review Press, 1973.

_____. *Unity and Struggle*. Trans. Michael Wolfers. New York: Monthly Review Press, 1979.

Center for Research on Criminal Justice. *The Iron Fist and the Velvet Glove: An Analysis of the U.S. Police*. Berkeley: Center for Research on Criminal Justice, 1975.

Chabal, Patrick. *Amílcar Cabral: Revolutionary Leadership and People's War*. Cambridge: Cambridge University Press, 1983.

Copeland, Vincent. *The Crime of Martin Sostre*. New York: McGraw-Hill, 1970.

Cummins, Eric. *The Rise and Fall of California's Radical Prison Movement*. Palo Alto: Stanford University Press, 1994.

Davis, Angela Y., ed. *If They Come in the Morning: Voices of Resistance*. New York: Third Press, 1971.

Davis, Mike. *Buda's Wagon: A Brief History of the Car Bomb*. London:

Verso, 2007.

Dohrn, Bernardine, Bill Ayers, and Jeff Jones, eds. *Sing a Battle Song: The Revolutionary Poetry, Statements, and Communiqués of the Weather Underground, 1970–1974*. New York: Seven Stories Press, 2006.

Elbaum, Max. *Revolution in the Air: Sixties Radicals Turn to Lenin, Mao and Che*. New York: Verso, 2002.

Farrell, William. *Blood and Rage: The Story of the Japanese Red Army*. Lexington, MA: Lexington Books, 1990.

Fobanjong, John, and Thomas K. Ranuga. *The Life, Thought, and Legacy of Cape Verde's Freedom Fighter Amílcar Cabral (1924–1973): Essays on his Liberation Philosophy*. Lewiston, NY: Edwin Mellen Press, 2006.

Gallagher, Aileen. *The Japanese Red Army*. New York: Rosen Publishing Group, 2003.

Graebner, William. *Patty's Got a Gun: Patricia Hearst in 1970s America*. Chicago: University of Chicago Press, 2008.

Hearst, Patricia, and Alvin Moscow. *Every Secret Thing*. Garden City, NY: Doubleday, 1982.

Hendry, Sharon Darby. *Soliah: The Sara Jane Olson Story*. Bloomington, MN: Cable Publishing, 2002.

Jackson, George. *Soledad Brother*. New York: Bantam, 1970.

———. *Blood In My Eye*. New York: Bantam, 1972.

Jimenez, Janey. *My Prisoner*. Kansas City: Sheed Andrews and McMeel, 1977.

John Brown Book Club. *The Split of the Weather Underground Organization: Struggling Against White and Male Supremacy*. Seattle: John Brown Book Club, 1977.

Kinney, Jean Brown. *An American Journey: The Short Life of Willy Wolfe*. New York: Simon and Schuster, 1979.

Lawrence, Bruce. *Messages to the World: The Statements of Osama bin Laden*. New York: Verso, 2005.

Lee, Butch, and Red Rover. *Night-Vision: Illuminating War and Class on the Neo-Colonial Terrain*. New York: Vagabond Press, 1993.

Marighella, Carlos. *Mini-Manual of the Urban Guerrilla*. Montreal, Quebec: Abraham Guillen Press, 2002 (first published in 1969).

Marlin IV, Robert O., ed. *What Does al-Qaeda Want? Unedited Communiques*. Berkeley: North Atlantic Books, 2004.

McLellan, Vin, and Paul Avery. *The Voices of Guns: The Definitive and Dramatic Story of the Twenty-two-month Career of the Symbionese*

Liberation Army. New York: Putnam, 1977.

Payne, Leslie, Timothy Findley, and Carolyn Craven. *The Life and Death of the SLA*. New York: Ballantine Books, 1976.

Pearsall, Robert, ed. *The Symbionese Liberation Army: Documents and Communications*. Amsterdam: Rodopi, 1974.

Raskin, Jonah, ed. *The Weather Eye: Communiqués from the Weather Underground, May 1970–May 1974*. San Francisco: Union Square Press, 1974.

Reeves, Kenneth, and Paul Avery, eds. *The Trial of Patty Hearst*. San Francisco: Great Fidelity Press, 1976.

Rudd, Mark. *Underground: My Life with the SDS and the Weathermen*. New York: William Morrow, 2009.

Shakur, Assata. *Assata: An Autobiography*. Westport, CT: Lawrence Hill, 1987.

Smith, J., and André Moncourt eds. *The Red Army Faction: A Documentary History. Volume 1, Projectiles for the People.* Oakland: PM Press, 2009.

Soltysik, Fred. *In Search of a Sister*. New York: Bantam Books, 1976.

Sostre, Martin. *Letters from Prison: A Compilation of Martin Sostre's Correspondence from Erie Country Jail, Buffalo, New York; and Green Haven Prison, Stormville, New York*. Buffalo: n.p., 1969.

Steinhoff, Patricia G. "Hijackers, Bombers, and Bank Robbers: Managerial Style in the Japanese Red Army." *The Journal of Asian Studies* 48, no. 4 (1989): 724–40.

Umoja, Akinyele Omowale. "Repression breeds resistance: The Black Liberation Army and the Radical Legacy of the Black Panther Party." In Kathleen Cleaver and George Katsiaficas eds. *Liberation, Imagination, and the Black Panther Party.* New York: Routledge, 2001.

Varon, Jeremy. *Bringing the War Home: The Weather Underground, the Red Army Faction, and Revolutionary Violence in the Sixties and Seventies*. Berkeley: University of California Press, 2004.

Weed, Steven, and Scott Swanton. *My Search for Patty Hearst*. New York: Crown Publishers, 1976.

Index

*Let Freedom Ring: A Collection of
Documents from the Movements to
Free U.S. Political Prisoners*
Edited by Matt Meyer
978-1-60486-035-1
$37.95

Let Freedom Ring presents a two-decade
sweep of essays, analyses, histories, interviews, resolutions, People's Tribunal ver-
dicts, and poems by and about the scores
of U.S. political prisoners and the cam-
paigns to safeguard their rights and secure
their freedom. In addition to an extensive
section on the campaign to free death-row
journalist Mumia Abu-Jamal, represented
here are the radical movements that have
most challenged the U.S. empire from
within: Black Panthers and other Black liberation fighters, Puerto Rican in-
dependentistas, Indigenous sovereignty activists, white anti-imperialists, environmental and animal rights militants, Arab and Muslim activists, Iraq war
resisters, and others. Contributors in and out of prison detail the repressive
methods—from long-term isolation to sensory deprivation to politically inspired parole denial--used to attack these freedom fighters, some still caged
after 30+ years. This invaluable resource guide offers inspiring stories of the
creative, and sometimes winning, strategies to bring them home.

Contributors include: Mumia Abu-Jamal, Dan Berger, Dhoruba Bin-Wahad,
Bob Lederer, Terry Bisson, Laura Whitehorn, Safiya Bukhari, The San Fran-
cisco 8, Angela Davis, Bo Brown, Bill Dunne, Jalil Muntaqim, Susie Day,
Luis Nieves Falcón, Ninotchka Rosca, Meg Starr, Assata Shakur, Jill Soffiyah
Elijah, Jan Susler, Chrystos, Jose Lopez, Leonard Peltier, Marilyn Buck, Os-
car López Rivera, Sundiata Acoli, Ramona Africa, Linda Thurston, Desmond
Tutu, Mairead Corrigan Maguire, and many more.

Reviews:
"Within every society there are people who, at great personal risk and sacrifice, stand up and fight for the most marginalized among us. We call these
people of courage, spirit and love, our heroes and heroines. This book is the
story of the ones in our midst. It is the story of the best we are."
    —asha bandele, poet and author of *The Prisoner's Wife*

The Angry Brigade: A History of Britain's First Urban Guerilla Group
Gordon Carr
978-1-60486-049-8
$24.95

"You can't reform profit capitalism and inhumanity. Just kick it till it breaks."
— Angry Brigade, communiqué.

Between 1970 and 1972, the Angry Brigade used guns and bombs in a series of symbolic attacks against property. A series of communiqués accompanied the actions, explaining the choice of targets and the Angry Brigade philosophy: autonomous organization and attacks on property alongside other forms of militant working class action. Targets included the embassies of repressive regimes, police stations and army barracks, boutiques and factories, government departments and the homes of Cabinet ministers, the Attorney General and the Commissioner of the Metropolitan Police. These attacks on the homes of senior political figures increased the pressure for results and brought an avalanche of police raids. From the start the police were faced with the difficulty of getting to grips with a section of society they found totally alien. And were they facing an organization—or an idea?

This book covers the roots of the Angry Brigade in the revolutionary ferment of the 1960s, and follows their campaign and the police investigation to its culmination in the "Stoke Newington 8" conspiracy trial at the Old Bailey—the longest criminal trial in British legal history. Written after extensive research—among both the libertarian opposition and the police—it remains the essential study of Britain's first urban guerilla group.

This expanded edition contains a comprehensive chronology of the "Angry Decade," extra illustrations, and a police view of the Angry Brigade. Introductions by Stuart Christie and John Barker (two of the "Stoke Newington 8" defendants) discuss the Angry Brigade in the political and social context of its times—and its longer-term significance.

Reviews:
"Even after all this time, Carr's book remains the best introduction to the culture and movement that gave birth to The Angry Brigade. Until all the participant's documents and voices are gathered in one place, this will remain THE gripping, readable and reliable account of those days. It is essential reading and PM Press are to be congratulated for making it available to us."
—Barry Pateman, Associate Editor, The Emma Goldman Papers, University of California at Berkeley

The Red Army Faction,
A Documentary History
Volume 1: Projectiles For the People
Edited by J. Smith & André Moncourt
978-1-60486-029-0
$34.95

The first in a two-volume series, this is by far the most in-depth political history of the Red Army Faction ever made available in English.

Projectiles for the People starts its story in the days following World War II, showing how American imperialism worked hand in glove with the old pro-Nazi ruling class, shaping West Germany into an authoritarian anti-communist bulwark and launching pad for its aggression against Third World nations. The volume also recounts the opposition that emerged from intellectuals, communists, independent leftists, and then—explosively—the radical student movement and countercultural revolt of the 1960s.

It was from this revolt that the Red Army Faction emerged, an underground organization devoted to carrying out armed attacks within the Federal Republic of Germany, in the view of establishing a tradition of illegal, guerilla resistance to imperialism and state repression. Through its bombs and manifestos the RAF confronted the state with opposition at a level many activists today might find difficult to imagine.

For the first time ever in English, this volume presents all of the manifestos and communiqués issued by the RAF between 1970 and 1977, from Andreas Baader's prison break, through the 1972 May Offensive and the 1975 hostage-taking in Stockholm, to the desperate, and tragic, events of the "German Autumn" of 1977. The RAF's three main manifestos—The Urban Guerilla Concept, Serve the People, and Black September—are included, as are important interviews with *Spiegel* and *le Monde Diplomatique*, and a number of communiqués and court statements explaining their actions.

Providing the background information that readers will require to understand the context in which these events occurred, separate thematic sections deal with the 1976 murder of Ulrike Meinhof in prison, the 1977 Stammheim murders, the extensive use of psychological operations and false-flag attacks to discredit the guerilla, the state's use of sensory deprivation torture and isolation wings, and the prisoners' resistance to this, through which they inspired their own supporters and others on the left to take the plunge into revolutionary action.

FRIENDS OF

These are indisputably momentous times—the financial system is melting down globally and the Empire is stumbling. Now more than ever there is a vital need for radical ideas.

In the three years since its founding—and on a mere shoestring—PM Press has risen to the formidable challenge of publishing and distributing knowledge and entertainment for the struggles ahead. With over 100 releases to date, we have published an impressive and stimulating array of literature, art, music, politics, and culture. Using every available medium, we've succeeded in connecting those hungry for ideas and information to those putting them into practice.

Friends of PM allows you to directly help impact, amplify, and revitalize the discourse and actions of radical writers, filmmakers, and artists. It provides us with a stable foundation from which we can build upon our early successes and provides a much-needed subsidy for the materials that can't necessarily pay their own way. You can help make that happen – and receive every new title automatically delivered to your door once a month – by joining as a Friend of PM Press. And, we'll throw in a free T-shirt when you sign up.

Here are your options:

- $25 a month: Get all books and pamphlets plus 50% discount on all webstore purchases.
- $25 a month: Get all CDs and DVDs plus 50% discount on all webstore purchases.
- $40 a month: Get all PM Press releases plus 50% discount on all webstore purchases
- $100 a month: Sustainer. - Everything plus PM merchandise, free downloads, and 50% discount on all webstore purchases.

For those who can't afford $25 or more a month, we're introducing Sustainer Rates at $15, $10 and $5. Sustainers get a free PM Press t-shirt and a 50% discount on all purchases from our website.

Just go to **WWW.PMPRESS.ORG** to sign up. Your Visa or Mastercard will be billed once a month, until you tell us to stop. Or until our efforts succeed in bringing the revolution around. Or the financial meltdown of Capital makes plastic redundant. Whichever comes first.

 PM PRESS was founded at the end of 2007 by a small collection of folks with decades of publishing, media, and organizing experience. PM Press co-conspirators have published and distributed hundreds of books, pamphlets, CDs, and DVDs. Members of PM have founded enduring book fairs, spearheaded victorious tenant organizing campaigns, and worked closely with bookstores, academic conferences, and even rock bands to deliver political and challenging ideas to all walks of life. We're old enough to know what we're doing and young enough to know what's at stake.

We seek to create radical and stimulating fiction and non-fiction books, pamphlets, t-shirts, visual and audio materials to entertain, educate and inspire you. We aim to distribute these through every available channel with every available technology - whether that means you are seeing anarchist classics at our bookfair stalls; reading our latest vegan cookbook at the café; downloading geeky fiction e-books; or digging new music and timely videos from our website.

PM Press is always on the lookout for talented and skilled volunteers, artists, activists and writers to work with. If you have a great idea for a project or can contribute in some way, please get in touch.

PM PRESS
PO Box 23912
Oakland CA 94623
510-658-3906
www.pmpress.org